W9-CON-774

DATE DUE

SEP 1 0			

WEALTH BUILDING

Also by the author:

Tax-Smart Investing

Rosentreter's Rules:
100 Financial Strategies to Reach High Net Worth

WEALTH BUILDING

KURT ROSENTRETER, CA

INSOMNIAC PRESS

Library and Archives Canada Cataloguing in Publication

Rosentreter, Kurt
  Wealthbuilding / Kurt Rosentreter.

Includes index.
ISBN 1-894663-85-3

  1. Finance, Personal--Canada. 2. Wealth--Canada. I. Title.

HG179.R683 2005   332.024'01   C2005-900247-6

The publisher gratefully acknowledges the support of the Canada Council, the Ontario Arts Council and the Department of Canadian Heritage through the Book Publishing Industry Development Program.

Disclaimer: This publication contains opinions of the writer and may not reflect the opinions of Berkshire Securities Inc.* The information contained herein was obtained from sources believed to be reliable, but no representation, or warranty, express or implied, is made by the writer or Berkshire Securities Inc. or any other person as to its accuracy, completeness or correctness. This publication is not an offer to sell or a solicitation of an offer to buy any of the securities. The securities discussed in this publication many not be eligible for sale in some jurisdictions. If you are not a Canadian resident, this report should not have been delivered to you. This publication is not meant to provide legal or account advice. As each situation is different, you should consult you own professional advisors for advice based on your specific circumstances.

Printed and bound in Canada

Insomniac Press
192 Spadina Avenue, Suite 403
Toronto, Ontario, Canada, M5T 2C2
www.insomniacpress.com

THE CANADA COUNCIL LE CONSEIL DES ARTS
FOR THE ARTS DU CANADA
SINCE 1957 DEPUIS 1957

ONTARIO ARTS COUNCIL
CONSEIL DES ARTS DE L'ONTARIO

* member CIPF

To Mom and Dad, Allan and Donna, Jack and Heather, Rieva and Andy, Kelly, Katie, Jim and Mae, Trevor and Deb, Meghan and Brianna, and my girls Chloe and Kira.

It only takes a moment together with all of you to realize that real wealth has nothing to do with money.

Table of Contents

Introduction

Wealthbuilding is a book for all Canadians. Proper financial management has nothing to do with how much money you have. There are opportunities and threats to the financial peace of mind of all Canadians, and we can all benefit from the advice of experts at one time or another.

If you have little wealth today, planning is important to get you on track towards financial success. If you have a lot of wealth today, there are more threats against and opportunities for your wealth than ever before, so you need to be extra savvy to protect and grow your wealth.

Wealthbuilding is a book about evolution. This book will cover the evolution of your personal finances over the course of your life. The way you manage your finances when you are young should be different than the way you manage your finances when you are older.

This book will address how you should manage the various components of your personal finances as your wealth development progresses during the course of your life. We will explore how you should change your approach to your taxes, your investments, your retirement, your debt, your advisors, even your attitude, and much more as you age and progress through your own wealthbuilding process.

Wealthbuilding should motivate you to take action. I hope this book will be an eye-opener for you. I think we all need a collective "shake" when it comes to our finances, as I find in my travels that far too many Canadians are poorly informed about the state of their finances or rely on poorly trained financial advisors. It is always a good idea to get a second opinion on the state of your financial picture, and the more you delegate control to your advisor, the more you need a second opinion on what he or she is telling you to do or buy. Wealthbuilding will teach you how to effectively control your finances, hire professionals to help you, and describe how to change your solutions over time.

Wealthbuilding is a state of mind and a commitment to process, not product. It will require you to challenge your status quo. So much of Canadian personal finance is transaction-oriented. For example, some key transactions each year include the RRSP contribution deadline at the end of February, filing a tax return by the end of April, watching financial TV shows focused on hot and cold stocks, and signing up for group insurance through an employer. These events are all transactions. They rarely focus on the big picture of setting your goals and developing a logical plan to meet those goals.

Wealthbuilding is a process. A logical framework of goal setting, developing strategies to meet those goals, updating and measuring progress annually, and buying products as tools to reach those goals. This process of wealthbuilding changes over time, as you will see in this book. Thinking of your finances in a transaction-oriented way is shallow, incomplete, and is no way to gain peace of mind. Want proof? When was the last time you heard a financial guru on TV pause and say that the stocks you buy should be part of a plan that reflects your short-term and long-term goals? You rarely hear this, yet don't we all want to meet our goals?

Wealthbuilding may require you to change. By the end of this book, I hope you will begin to develop a proper financial plan based on your wealth level today, and leave the transactional approach to your finances behind. However, it won't be easy as many of your trusted financial advisors, brokers, bankers, accountants, and insurance agents cannot or choose not to follow a wealthbuilding approach. Sometimes it is easier or more profitable for them to sell a product and ignore the creation of a proper goal-based plan first.

Wealthbuilding requires commitment. This book is about a logical framework to manage finances effectively. It is not a fad and it has no place for emotion or attitude. In fact, this process is designed to operate by using a disciplined approach, keeping emotions at bay, for financial decision making.

Proper wealthbuilding requires an objective point of view. We will address the importance of objective professional advisors and disclosed visible compensation to these advisors as key parts of your wealthbuilding process.

As hard as it may be personally, changing your advisors may be required in order to get you on track toward wealthbuilding. If you aren't sure, get a second opinion. Your financial peace of mind is too important to gamble with.

Kurt Rosentreter, CA, CFP, CIMA, TEP, FMA

Senior Financial Advisor, Berkshire Securities Inc.* (*Member CIPF)
Insurance Representative, Berkshire Insurance Services Inc.
Chartered Accountant, Kurt Rosentreter & Associates Inc.
1-866-ASK-KURT, www.kurtismycfo.com

Explaining Financial Evolution

The financial strategies that you implement, the financial products that you buy, and the financial advisors you engage when you only have $5,000 in an RRSP, may not be appropriate for you when you have $600,000 in your savings, own three pieces of real estate, put the children through private school, and are approaching retirement. While these are extreme examples, it demonstrates that your finances will change over time and that your financial planning should change with it.

Wealthbuilding deals with life changes by adapting financial plans according to your evolving situation. Life changes can happen gradually or suddenly. Either way, the approach to your finances should change to reflect the new realities of your life. You may need to revise your goals, change your strategies, change your products (e.g. investments and insurance), and change your advisors to those more specialized.

In this book, I will show you how the many faces of your personal finances should evolve over time. We will cover the evolution of:

Your goals.
The fees that you pay.
Taxes and tax planning.
How and why you invest.
Future retirement plans.
Living in retirement today.
Death and what matters to you.
Your parents.
Your children, your spouse, and your grandchildren.
Debt.
Risk.
Charity.
Insurance: How much and what kind.
Financial advisors: How many and what kind.
Income and expenses.
Your career(s).
Real estate.
Your attitude.

You may think that all of this sounds like common sense. But remarkably, to many Canadians it is not. So many of us fail to evolve our financial planning to reflect our evolving lives. Effectively, many of us are stuck in yesterday's solutions. Here are a few examples of failing to evolve and failing to follow a wealthbuilding approach:

- A fifty-eight-year-old dentist with $1.5 million of retirement savings is still buying rear load mutual funds (DSC) and paying an annual RRSP trustee fee of $137.50. A portfolio of this size is entitled to lower fees, tax deductible fees, and no RRSP trustee fee.
- A sixty-year-old retired executive owns eight term life insurance policies even though they ceased to be necessary after his children moved away from home.
- A forty-year-old professional prepares her own tax return, overlooking five major tax-planning opportunities that could save her $20,000 a year in taxes on her $200,000 salary.
- The estate of an elderly man whose handwritten Will failed to include a testamentary trust to hold his estate assets, costing his family an additional $75,000 of income tax.
- A fifty-five-year-old construction worker is forced into early retirement and now has to live off one-third of his income because he never examined whether he had enough retirement savings.
- A thirty-six-year-old widow and mother of two has to move in with her parents because her deceased husband failed to buy life insurance before they had their two children.

All of these situations can be avoided by following a disciplined wealthbuilding process to managing your finances.

The Categories of Wealthbuilding

Wealthbuilding evolves through four stages:

1. Emerging Wealth
2. Wealth Creation
3. Wealth Management and Preservation
4. Wealth Transfer

Emerging Wealth: This is the period in life where there is little money and a lot of debt. Making RRSP contributions is only a pipedream and making financial goals seems far off. However, this is the first stage of wealthbuilding where your first steps towards pru-

WEALTHBUILDING IN A PICTURE

Four phases of Wealthbuilding over the course of your life

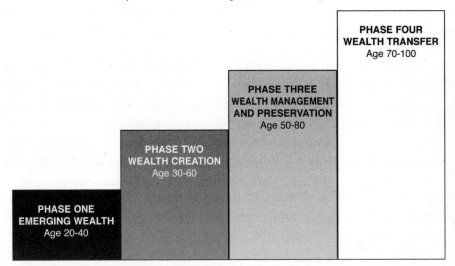

PHASE FOUR
WEALTH TRANSFER
Age 70-100

PHASE THREE
WEALTH MANAGEMENT
AND PRESERVATION
Age 50-80

PHASE TWO
WEALTH CREATION
Age 30-60

PHASE ONE
EMERGING WEALTH
Age 20-40

How you manage your finances in each phase is different. Many Canadians don't realize this and fail to evolve their financial approach over time. Wealthbuilding will show you how to change your financial strategies as you age and build wealth.

dent financial planning set the stage for future success.

Wealth Creation: This phase is characterized by a higher income and a more established career. Annual bonuses, company stock or stock options, a mortgage, maximizing RRSP contributions, and spending more money on a lifestyle and children are all common traits of this phase.

Wealth Management and Preservation: This phase is characterized by stability—a solid career (possibly senior level), realizing wealth, converting stock options, and generating significant savings in an RRSP. Typically, there is no debt and children's university educations are paid for. Cash flow is ample and spending money is easy. Retirement is in sight and well in hand. Emphasis on savings shifts from growth to preservation.

Wealth Transfer: The last stage of wealthbuilding usually encompasses the elder years and concerns shift to inter-generational wealth planning. Gifting money to children and grandchildren becomes a regular occurrence and estate planning becomes more important. One spouse will eventually pass away first, leaving the other with an entirely different financial situation. Health care can become a priority. Death ends the lifelong wealthbuilding process, with the estate either passing to heirs or to charity.

How This Book Works

The four stages of wealthbuilding will be repeated in every chapter of this book, as I relate different personal finance topics to each phase. This framework will help you understand how to evolve your finances as your life progresses.

I Don't Fit into Your Model, Kurt

Yes, you do. Whether you are a business owner, a fifty-year-old bachelor, a thirty-eight-year-old widow, unemployed, in jail, or in school, you too will evolve over time and can look at your financial situation with the same logic that is covered throughout this book. No, you may not have all of the characteristics of every stage, but, frankly, no one will. In a book like this I try to cover all possible realities—it is up to you to complete the fine tuning.

Wealthbuilding is Not Linked to Certain Ages

It is very tempting to attach ages to the various stages of wealthbuilding. For example, it is easy to assume that the first stage of emerging wealth sounds like someone who is approximately twenty-five years old. While this may be the case, I don't believe that age should be linked to wealthbuilding. I have met fifty-year-old students and twenty-five-year-old millionaires. Age is not relevant for wealthbuilding and I believe it is more important to assess your financial wealth alone than to assess which stage you are in. There is nothing wrong with setting financial goals by certain ages (e.g. be debt free by fifty), but I encourage you to distinguish goal setting from wealthbuilding. The bottom line is that the process of wealthbuilding is not age specific, it is wealth specific.

What is Wealth?

Wealth is your financial net worth. Summarize your assets and deduct your liabilities. The difference is your wealth.

For example, here is a calculation of wealth:

Cash	$11,000
RRSP	$230,000
Investments	$60,000
House Value	$200,000
Antiques	$20,000
Total Assets	$521,000

Mortgage	$100,000
Car loan	$20,000
Credit card	$1,000
Total Debt	$121,000

Net Worth or "Wealth" $521,000 - $121,000 equals $400,000.

By definition, wealthbuilding is the growth of your assets and the elimination of debt, leading to the largest possible net worth or total wealth.

Take a moment and calculate your net worth. This should be an annual exercise whereby you compare your net worth over time to see your progression towards wealthbuilding. If you have a financial advisor, this is their job. If they have not been doing this, you may want to consider a new financial advisor who is committed to wealthbuilding and helping to define your goals.

Wealthbuilding is About Evolution...Should Everything Evolve?

Some aspects of your finances should not evolve as your finances change.

Progress measurement: You need to consistently measure progress, check results, and adjust your plan. No matter how much money you may end up with, it is still very important to judge results against your evolving goals.

Accountability: If you manage your own finances, or if you engage brokers, insurance agents, accountants, lawyers, etc., you need to maintain a consistent level of accountability in holding you or them responsible for your plan. This is particularly true if you are paying for advice. Further, you need to judge the experts against the results you expect. And, if there is consistent underperformance or lack of value, you should be prepared to fire your advisors, including firing yourself if you cannot effectively manage your own finances.

Value measures: It is important that you know what you pay for your professional services and products. You should compare this cost to the value that you receive and regularly assess this value. There should be good value for whatever you pay. Many advisors are well worth their high cost. But it is your job to track and measure this value.

Goal setting: No matter what your wealth level, you will always have goals. Some goals will be for the financial security of your family, and others will be tax minimization or saving for a new car. Regardless of the type of goal, it is important to regularly quantify them and assess progress towards them. Your goals will change with time, but the importance of setting them and tracking them should not.

Remember, wealthbuilding is about evolving your financial goals, strategies, products, and advisors as your life and finances progress. But, at the same time, your control over your finances, as measured by value, accountability, and progress evaluation, should be consistently applied to ensure you progress properly through the wealthbuilding stages.

Take the Wealthbuilding Test

Answer the following questions about your own personal finances and judge if you are properly wealthbuilding or if you failed to evolve.

1. Are your financial goals written down?
2. Have your financial goals been updated from five years ago?
3. Do you have a financial plan or do you just "buy various investment products without a real plan?"
4. Could you fire your financial advisor or have you lost your objectivity because you "like them?"
5. What is the total amount of fees that you paid to your lawyer, accountant, insurance agent, or broker last year and is this amount appropriate for your wealth level?
6. Have you had a tax-planning review in the last three years by someone other than the person who prepares your personal tax returns?
7. If you are working for a living, do you know what you need to save each year to reach your desired retirement income?
8. Do you know when you should stop buying mutual funds?
9. Do you know when you should stop buying stocks?
10. Does your financial advisor specialize in clients at a certain wealthbuilding stage or does he/she try to be everything to everyone?
11. Are you generally buying the same investment products and insurance policies for the same cost as you were five years ago?
12. Is your Will up to date? (Has it been updated in the last five years?)
13. Are you doing an annual net worth calculation to judge progress of your wealthbuilding?
14. Do you know whether you should hire a bank, a trust company, an investment counselor, a broker, a financial planner, a portfolio manager, a wealth specialist, a private wealth consultant, or an insurance financial consultant to assist you with your finances?
15. Are you completely confident that you are doing everything possible to minimize tax on your income? Tax on your investments? Tax on your estate? Tax on your real estate? And tax on your family's income?
16. If you are retired, did your approach to tax planning change after your RRSP was converted to an RRIF? It should!
17. Have you used an RESP, in-trust account, or a formal trust to save money for your children? The right answer depends on your and their wealth level!
18. Do your employer benefits match your needs now that you are earn-

ing more and have been promoted?

19. If you save money outside of an RRSP or RRIF, do you use a different investing approach with a greater sensitivity to income tax given this money is taxable each year? (An RRSP or RRIF is not.) Do you use different investment products and avoid duplication of the same products in multiple accounts?

20. Do you feel in control of your financial future and confident that you are doing what you should be at this stage of your wealthbuilding?

How Did You Do in This Quiz?

If you had five or more negative answers, following a wealthbuilding approach to your finances should enhance your peace of mind about money matters.

WEALTHBUILDING
Evolving Your Approach to Financial Management
Over a Lifetime

Chapter One
Goal Setting Within the Wealthbuilding Process

As you progress through the wealthbuilding process, you will have many financial and non-financial goals.

GOAL SETTING DURING THE WEALTHBUILDING PROCESS

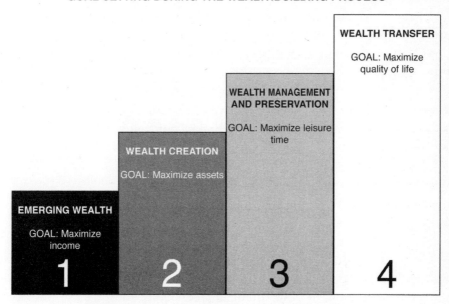

You should start planning for goals 3 and 4 while still at phase 1.

Set Goals

Here are some examples of financial goals for a middle-aged couple with teenage children who are in the "wealth creation" phase of wealthbuilding:

- Save for an enjoyable retirement
- Pay off the mortgage on their house
- Buy a new car
- Retire early
- Fund the children's university costs

We all have dreams and objectives—some more far-fetched than others—so goal setting is something that comes naturally to most of us.

Write Them Down

However, it is less natural to formalize goals in writing. It is also less natural to share your goals with a financial advisor and have them help you build a financial plan to reach those goals. But if you do both, you will increase the likelihood of reaching your goals. Writing down your goals brings them into focus and makes you and your financial advisor more accountable for achieving them.

Clearly Defining Your Goals

Listing and sharing your goals is only the first step. You should also attach time deadlines to accomplish your goals, along with the cost. See how the goals listed above become more clearly defined when we do this:

• Save $1 million for retirement in twelve years
• Double your mortgage payments to pay it off within three years
• Spend $40,000 on a new car next year
• Retire five years early
• Save $20,000 per child per school year of university

Prioritize Your Goals According to Importance

Prioritize your goals so that the most important can be met:

Essential: Retirement planning and saving for your children's future schooling. Essential goals are your most important goals where planning for them is essential to your financial well-being.

Non-essential: Paying the mortgage off early would be nice, but is not essential. You could likely drive that car a few more years and skip early retirement if you had to. Non-essential goals are goals that may not "make or break" your financial future and can be delayed or skipped entirely if compromises must be made.

Prioritize Your Goals According to Time

You have goals that you need to accomplish in a week, in a year, and in twenty years. Part of the planning for your goals includes dividing them up according to time. You may want to save for the car you need this year, then focus on children's university savings before building your own retirement savings. Be careful here: if you exclusively focus on one goal after another, you may not leave yourself enough time to reach all of the essential goals. This is where an advisor can help you with integrated planning to consider all of your goals, both short term and long term. If some goals must be compromised for the sake of others, the objective opinion of a professional advisor can help you make the best decision.

Goal Setting and the Four Phases of Wealthbuilding

Phase One: Emerging Wealth

For people in this phase, it is often hard to see beyond the next pay-cheque or the next year. Long-term planning for retirement is hard to comprehend, and, often, short-term goals, like debt repayment, first home purchases, and getting a desirable career, dominate thinking. But having the discipline to set a wide range of goals is important. Goal planning at this phase sets the groundwork for future progress and success. No matter what your wealth level, there are dreams that should be put on paper and revisited annually. Only with this early target setting can you progress into the next phase of wealthbuilding.

Phase Two: Wealth Creation

As you start to create wealth, your personal income rises and the number and type of goals that you set increases. More cash flow means more desires. Enjoying your cash flow is pleasant, but must be done within reason. Many people in the wealth creation phase are guilty of excessive upscaling. If they get a raise, they buy a more expensive car, super-size the house, buy a cottage, or move the children to private school. I have often seen many high-income Canadians spend every-thing they make, rather than taking a balanced approach to wealthbuild-ing. I recently met with an architect who earns $400,000 a year and is fifty-five years old. He wants to retire in three years, but his retirement savings are only $350,000. Even at his very high income level he failed to plan properly, choosing instead to spend excessively. Now, as retirement approaches, his ability to save is limited. He will likely have to work until seventy while saving aggressively in order to accumulate enough savings to provide for the rest of his family's life.

The challenge in phase two is to balance spending on short-term goals with long-term goals. Getting an early start on your retirement, for example, is critical to the ultimate success of saving enough money.

Phase Three: Wealth Management and Preservation

You're over the hump now and you have made it financially. Goal set-ting in this phase changes from accumulating wealth to preserving it. Phase three of the wealthbuilding process is almost the opposite of phase two. You have spent the last several years creating wealth, working hard, and striving to meet your goals. Many of your original goals are achieved and a new set of goals arise—tax minimization, estate preservation, helping children and grandchildren, and enjoying life become more important. In this phase, you must rethink your approach to your finances—all strategies, products, and targets—as your life is much different. Many Canadians fail to see this huge change and often carry on with their old approach.

Many people are tempted to link the start of this phase with the start of retirement. That is not correct. It is possible to reach phase three well before retirement or sometimes well into retirement. Once again, reaching this phase is more a function of the goals you set, rather than reaching a milestone like retirement. In fact, many people get a rude awakening when they retire, because they didn't goal set and build a proper retirement plan.

Phase Four: Wealth Transfer

Wealth transfer is about passing your wealth to your heirs upon death. But phase four starts long before death. It starts when a person feels elderly. This can be triggered by a health breakdown or by the death of a spouse. Advanced age can cause people to think differently about their finances. Will planning becomes important. People start giving major chunks of their wealth to their children, often inappropriately. Phase four of wealthbuilding is another phase where getting the advice of a professional is critical—someone who can look objectively at your situation to help you to make the right decisions. Your children cannot do this and neither can you.

Why I Wrote So Much About Goal Setting

You may be wondering why I gave so much coverage to setting goals. After all, it is common sense right?

Based on my experiences interviewing hundreds of Canadians, we all have goals, but very rarely are our financial plans built to address these goals. Many Canadians blindly pay tax, buy insurance or mutual funds, or contribute to an RRSP without giving much consideration to building a proper plan. Fundamentally, setting your goals, writing them down, and tracking progress is probably the most important thing you can do.

Goal Setting Tools for You

Here is a list of goals shared by many people. Please identify your goals according to the time frame you have in mind to achieve them. Add any other goals that may be relevant to you. Give this chart to your financial advisor and ask him or her to build a plan to address your goals.

Once the goals are set, you must check their progress and revise your plan as needed. It is critical that you regularly monitor progress so that you adjust your plans and strategies when necessary. For some goals, like saving for a child's education, it is easy to evaluate the progress of your savings for this purpose. Simply compare accumulated savings against anticipated future costs and adjust your savings as necessary.

There is also a way to evaluate your financial progress overall. I call it the net worth approach to wealthbuilding. Many people tend to evaluate their wealth according to income earned. Instead, you should evaluate your wealth by net worth. Prepare a net worth summary each year and use it to measure progress every year. I have included a net worth calculator on the next page to help you.

SPECIFIC FINANCIAL GOALS

The starting point of all effective planning is to understand your goals. These goals can be long term, such as saving for your retirement, or short term, such as minimizing your taxes. Some goals can be of greater or lesser significance to you and, of course, these goals can change over time.

Here is a list of some goals shared by many people. Please identify your goals according to the time frame that you have in mind to achieve each goal. Add other goals that may be relevant to you.

	Relevant time frame			
	Short term (0-1 year)	Medium term (1-5 years)	Long term (5-10 years)	Greater than 10 years
Establishing adequate retirement income	❑	❑	❑	❑
Saving for your child's education	❑	❑	❑	❑
Purchasing a home	❑	❑	❑	❑
Taking a vacation	❑	❑	❑	❑
Lowering taxes	❑	❑	❑	❑
Purchasing a vacation home	❑	❑	❑	❑
Purchasing a car	❑	❑	❑	❑
Providing for survivors in the event of your death	❑	❑	❑	❑
Protecting against inflation	❑	❑	❑	❑
Taking early retirement	❑	❑	❑	❑
Starting a business	❑	❑	❑	❑
Other	❑	❑	❑	❑

Your net worth is the best number for evaluating your success with wealthbuilding. Logically, your net worth will rise as you pay off debts, increase assets, grow investments, and save extra income. By preparing a net worth statement, you can judge all aspects of your finances together, on one page, for a fair evaluation. In my opinion, your net worth should grow by at least 5% each year. If it doesn't, perhaps you are spending excessively, carrying too much debt, or saving insufficiently. Keep in mind that some of your assets (such as vehicles) will generally lose value, so take this into account when planning how to grow your wealth.

Self-Test

Calculate your net worth as shown for the last three years of your life.

Net worth today:

Net worth last year:

Net worth two years ago:

Is your net worth growing by at least 5% each year?

Calculating Net Worth

	Current Value You	Spouse	Joint
Assets			
Liquid assets			
Cash, chequing, and saving accounts	$ _____	$ _____	$ _____
Treasury bills, term deposits	_____	_____	_____
Canada Savings Bonds	_____	_____	_____
Other	_____	_____	_____
Investments			
Bonds	_____	_____	_____
Stocks	_____	_____	_____
Mutual funds	_____	_____	_____
Real estate (income property)	_____	_____	_____
Business assets	_____	_____	_____
Retirement plans (RRSP, RPP)	_____	_____	_____
Other	_____	_____	_____
Personal assets			
Principal residence	_____	_____	_____
Recreational property	_____	_____	_____
Other	_____	_____	_____
TOTAL ASSETS	$ _____	$ _____	$ _____
Liabilities			
Current debt			
Personal loans outstanding	_____	_____	_____
Credit cards	_____	_____	_____
Other	_____	_____	_____
Long-term debt			
Mortgage - Principal residence	_____	_____	_____
Mortgage - Recreational property	_____	_____	_____
Other	_____	_____	_____
TOTAL LIABILITIES	$ _____	$ _____	$ _____
TOTAL NET WORTH			
TOTAL ASSETS MINUS TOTAL LIABILITIES	$ _____	$ _____	$ _____

Chapter Two
Wealthbuilding and Your "Big Picture"

One of the most important concepts of wealthbuilding is what I refer to as "managing your big picture."

Long before you focus on specific strategies or products for your financial plan, it is essential that you start planning at the highest level first. This is what I refer to as your big picture.

Think of your personal finances as having varied levels of planning. At the bottom level is products. Products are purchased as tools to help you accomplish your goals. One level above products is strategies. Before you buy a product you need to develop the appropriate strategy to accomplish your goal. One level above strategies is goal setting. Before you buy products, and before you set strategies, you need to establish goals that define your needs. Goal setting is specific to certain areas of your finances. You

THE BIG PICTURE

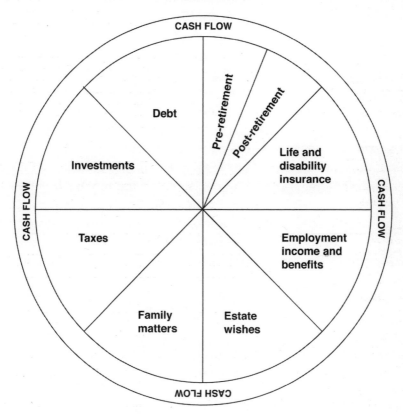

may have goals related to retirement, estate, insurance, investing, career, debt repayment, and family. And finally, one level above goal setting is managing your big picture. This is the highest level and the starting point for any financial plan at any phase of wealthbuilding.

Managing your big picture means taking an integrated planning approach to all areas of your finances. Since you have set goals, implemented strategies, and bought products for each goal that you set, you must integrate the different goals and resources to develop one overall plan. This involves prioritizing the goals, sharing resources (e.g. saving money for retirement or using the money to buy insurance) across different planning areas, and creating a logical gameplan. This is your big picture, and managing it effectively is ultimately the most important aspect of your planning.

When you think about your finances, do you immediately think of investing and taxes? Perhaps, but your personal finances consist of a lot more than that. When I speak about wealthbuilding and integrated and comprehensive financial planning, I mean that you need to manage the big picture: investing, retirement planning, living in retirement, employer benefits and compensation, use of debt, risk management and insurance needs, eldercare, legacy planning, cash flow management, and more. These areas comprise your total financial picture and interrelate through the sharing of cash flow. The money into and the money out of these different areas of your finances is the link between them. This relates to goal setting: if you only have so much money, you will end up making decisions on how to allocate it among these different areas.

By looking at your financial plans, issues, resources, and timelines, you can allocate your resources more effectively.

Here are some examples of managing your big picture by taking an integrated planning approach to decision making in your finances:

- Many people randomly buy stocks and mutual funds without examining how much money they have and how much they will need for retirement. The amount you save and how aggressively you invest should be based on a retirement plan with well-defined goals.
- When your tax return is prepared, the accountant should provide tax-planning ideas for your investment portfolio. After all, you pay tax on your investments.
- Investing without consideration of taxes leaves you with an incomplete investing process. Never buy a product without evaluating the tax consequences first.

- Before you buy that life insurance for your estate, make sure you won't need that money for your retirement! Few of us can predict what health care will cost in twenty years. Estimate and consider all of your future costs before you buy insurance.
- It may be better for you to take your annual bonus and pay down your car loan, instead of maximizing your RRSP, saving for your child's RESP, paying down the mortgage, or keeping the money in a bank account. The right answer depends on the pre-tax cost and return of each alternative.

As you can see from each of these five examples, determining what to do with your money involves a coordinated examination of your different financial issues. To invest or to buy insurance without examining your big picture first is foolhardy.

What complicates this further is that many financial advisors cannot or will not advise you on your big picture, despite its importance. For example, an investment advisor or portfolio manager may know nothing about taxes. An insurance agent may know little about your stocks. And your accountant may not understand your life insurance.

You have two choices. You can be the middle person who manages the big picture among all of your advisors. You are not an expert, however, and likely don't want to spend your time doing this. Or you can replace your advisors with one comprehensive financial planner. Not only will you get integrated planning and goal setting, it may save you time and fees as well.

Chapter Three
Wealthbuilding and Your Attitude

Very few of the people that need this book most will read it.

Many of them, sadly, care very little about the state of their wealth. They are happy to do nothing or continue to take a very product-focused approach: they make their RRSP contribution each February, file their taxes each April, and that's about it.

Their attitude is that money issues are boring, complicated, beyond them, or time consuming. Whatever the reason, it is their attitude that can get them into financial trouble in every stage of the wealthbuilding process.

Here is my take on Canadians' evolving attitudes throughout the phases of wealthbuilding:

Phase One: Emerging Wealth

People at this first phase often say, "I don't have any money, so why bother planning?" This attitude convinces them that they don't need an advisor either. I can see why it is easy to feel this way, but the reality is that taking time to plan at this phase is more important than all the other phases combined. In phase one you are trying to plant wealthbuilding roots—roots that need care and attention to ensure you get the desired results. Further, time is on your side at this phase—implementing financial strategies now can give you years of lead time.

Phase Two: Wealth Creation

In the early stages of wealth creation as the money starts to come in and you rise above your debts, the attitude is one of spend, spend, spend. Often you have young children at this phase, and between work and home life there is no time to focus on financial planning. You often have no idea about the status of your financial goals. There may be no accountability of financial advisors, and you may not know what fees they charge you. You may have RRSPs or bought life insurance when your first child was born, but now you have three children and you purchased more. You are accumulating wealth at a good rate, but still operate without a formal financial plan.

At the later stages of phase two, you wake up one morning and fear sets in. There are only five years to go until retirement and you don't have a financial plan. Your attitude changes to one of "no more fooling around" and it is time to get serious about your finances. However, it is too late. If you need $1 million for retirement and you are fifty-five, it is safe to say you won't meet that amount. You have taken too long to develop the right attitude.

Phase Three: Wealth Management and Preservation

In phase three there is a massive attitude shift related to your finances. If you have planned properly and arrived at financial security on your terms, your attitude often shifts to protection of what you have. The previous goal of growing your wealth is less important, with emphasis shifting towards preservation of the wealth you have accumulated. It is common to experience the following attitudes during this mature phase of wealthbuilding: fear that you will run out of money before you die; anger at the amount of income tax you may pay in retirement; responsibility for the financial security of your family and particularly your spouse.

As you move into retirement, you may finally get more involved in day-to-day financial management. This involvement, however, should really start at age thirty—not age sixty.

Phase Four: Wealth Transfer

In the final phase of wealthbuilding, we once again see a significant attitude shift. The underlying attitude of wealth preservation remains, but a new attitude of caring about estate planning and death is added— Will planning and giving assets to children or charities ahead of death. Giving money to grandchildren is popular. As children struggle with the same issues you did many years ago, many of us want to help. This caring attitude also extends to charity, where many of us volunteer while we can and leave legacies to favourites. The challenge is not to give away so much now that you run out of money for yourself!

In this final phase there is also some fear that results. The fear of being alone when your spouse dies. The fear of disease, nursing homes, and long lineups at hospitals. Even the fear of running out of money. In these last years, proper financial planning is a must to ensure peace of mind during the final phase of wealthbuilding.

Triggers

There are many triggers that can occur during our lives that can affect our attitude towards our finances. Some of these triggers can serve as a wake-up call and affect us immediately. Sadly, many of these triggers can have negative results and, because of poor planning, devastate your finances. Here are some triggers that I have recently encountered.

- A thirty-seven-year-old man lost his brother suddenly to cancer. His brother was married with three young children; his wife was a home-maker. At the time of his death he only had a small amount of group life insurance from his employer. That ran out after three months and the widow had to sell the house and move to an apartment. She now has two jobs and the children are in daycare everyday. The thirty-seven-year-old-man, who is married and has children of his own, bought $1.5 million of term life insurance after witnessing the experiences of his brother's family.
- After losing $200,000 in the stock market between 1999 and 2000, a do-it-yourself investor fired himself and hired a financial planner to help him establish goals and build a proper financial plan. His stress level has gone down, and his children are happy to have their dad back. Together they are building a common sense retirement plan coordinated with an investment program.
- A forty-five-year-old executive watched his boss retire at fifty-five and receive a pension that was equal to a quarter of his salary. His boss had to downsize his home and struggle to afford new cars and vacations. Desperate to avoid a similar kind of poor retirement, the forty-five-year-old executive purchased some retirement planning software as the first step to ensuring he has enough money for retirement.
- A seventy-five-year-old widow threw out her handwritten Will after the death of her best friend last month and makes plans to visit a lawyer. The deceased lady had prepared her own Will a decade earlier. When the estate was settled, the poor planning cost the family an additional $100,000 of income tax. Worse, two of her children resented the third child whom their mother had selected as the sole estate executor. The children fought and presently don't speak to each other. The handwritten Will is being disputed by one child and the lawyers estimate it will take two years and $40,000 of legal fees to resolve.
- A thirty-three- and thirty-four-year-old couple give birth to their first child. With a new dependant in the house, it is time to purchase life insurance as a safety net against loss of income.

It is essential that you have the proper attitude towards your finances and towards wealthbuilding. Here are some key attitude traits that I encourage you to adopt:

- Review the state of your finances for two hours every six months with an advisor who can provide an objective opinion on what you are doing.
- Be skeptical when you are hiring a financial advisor. Your trust should be earned—let them prove their worth to you. Call me if you would like a questionnaire that I wrote for interviewing potential financial advisors.
- Be in control and aware of the state of your finances. You should want to know the costs, know your goals, and know how your plan is progressing.
- Get a second opinion—it is natural and necessary. Get one today and get another one in three years before you make any major changes to strategies.
- No one cares about your money more than you. Delegating to a financial advisor should be limited, controlled, and monitored. Your life savings are too important to be careless.
- Keep an open mind towards wealthbuilding. New ideas, strategies, and products are constantly being created. Since your financial situation evolves, it warrants the updating of strategies and products.

You're attitude towards wealthbuilding is essential for wealthbuilding to take hold. There is no point in reading this book if you don't plan to act on it.

Besides attitude, it is also important that you adopt the right personal focus from the beginning. There are three wrong focuses to have and one correct focus.

The wrong focuses are: having no focus, which is self-explanatory; having a product focus (for example, buying RRSPs in February is all you do); or having an event focus (e.g. filing a tax return by April 30 but not tax planning). These are reactive, last minute reactions that ensure only the minimum is done, but that fail to plan for your big picture. I find many Canadians caught in a product or event focus in relation to their finances. Many will say it is all they have time for. I say it has to change if you want to prevent trouble down the road.

The right focus is to set goals and follow a process for addressing them—call it a goal and process focus. By creating a logical framework for financial decision making and ensuring it matches your objectives will leave little room for error and create greater control and peace of mind. And you know what? It doesn't take more effort or time to do it this way. It simply involves working with a financial planner that is focused on a goal-based planning approach or educating yourself (if you are a do-it-yourselfer) about a proper financial planning process. Every single Canadian should take this approach to their finances. Period.

Getting the Right Attitude:
Following the Canadian Financial Planning Standards

The Financial Planner Standards Council (FPSC) is a not-for-profit association that governs Certified Financial Planners in Canada. The FPSC requires the following rules to be heeded by all of their members (these rules can help you to): 1) follow a methodology for managing your own finances over your lifetime; 2) holding your financial advisor accountable by making them follow these rules; 3) find a financial advisor who is a member of the FPSC. Every Canadian should want a financial advisor that is governed by a professional association and held to a higher standard of professionalism. Are all of your advisors practicing members of the FPSC (not just associate members)?

Planning Standards for Certified Financial Planners in Canada (draft September 2003):

Rule 100: The terms of the engagement with a client must be defined, including the scope of services, time frames, compensation, and any conflicts of interest. This must all be written out in the form of an engagement letter signed by advisor and client together.

Rule 200 A: The financial advisor will discuss a client's goals, needs, and priorities before making any recommendations.

Rule 200 B: The financial advisor must gather background information about the client's personal situation before making any recommendations.

Rule 300: The financial advisor must analyze all client data to determine the client's situation and evaluate to what extent the client's goals can be met under the current situation.

Rule 400 A: The financial advisor will identify and evaluate relevant financial planning strategies that could help to achieve the client's goals.

Rule 400 B: The financial advisor will develop recommendations to achieve a client's goals and will communicate these recommendations in a fashion that the client understands.

Rule 500 A: The client and the financial advisor will agree on implementation action, responsibilities, and time frames.

Rule 600 A: The client and the financial advisor will agree on a time frame for monitoring and evaluating the financial plan.

Rule 600 B: The client and the financial advisor will review the financial plan to assess progress and determine if any plan revisions are necessary.

Chapter Four
Wealthbuilding and Your Taxes

For many Canadians, the largest single expense of their lifetime will be income tax. Therefore, tax planning should be a top priority. However, many of us spend less time on tax planning than we spend shopping for a vacation deal.

The top marginal tax rate is almost 50% in most provinces; finding even one small tax break can add up to a big savings. Canada has some of the highest tax rates in the world—taxes reach into every corner of our lives, affecting our income, investments, assets, or estates. In all wealthbuilding phases, you should have a tax advisor, a tax specialist that you visit once a year, or as needed, to advise you on tax-planning issues, opportunities, and rules.

Here are some examples of how taxes affect your life:

- Your salary or wages are reduced by income tax
- Your investment savings, both RRSP and other savings, are affected by three different types of taxation (tax on income, dividends, and gains)
- Saving for a child's future is impacted by income tax
- There are many estate tax issues when you die
- Marriages, births, and divorces have significant tax complications
- Life and disability insurance policies have different tax consequences
- Moving in and out of a province or Canada has tax issues
- In retirement, it is important to minimize tax in your pension money
- RRSP contributions should be carefully planned based on your marginal tax bracket

Tax touches all of your money issues, affecting every phase of wealthbuilding.

Let's examine how your approach to taxes may change as you evolve through the wealthbuilding phases:

Phase One: Emerging Wealth

Tax planning at this first phase likely consists of preparing your tax return by April 30 each year; you may even do this return preparation yourself. Here are some tax tips for this phase of your life: 1) Avoid using the Home Buyers Plan (HBP) to buy your first home. I feel that the HBP removes too much money from your RRSP and puts you further behind in your retirement planning. 2) Focus on paying down your non-tax deductible debt (student loans, car loans, and home mortgage, etc.). 3) Any money that you receive as a gift from a parent or a grandparent is not taxable as a gift. 4) Avoid the temptation to blow money in aggressive stock market investing. Instead, focus on maximizing your RRSP every year. Starting early in life will give your RRSP the chance for significant growth over many decades.

Phase Two: Wealth Creation

With a greater income and the start of faster wealthbuilding, your first thoughts about tax planning and tax minimization begin. Surely you can pay less income tax on all that income that you are generating? But as is so common in the wealth creation phase, many people don't have the time to properly seek tax-planning expertise. Instead, many go for a quick fix, purchasing high-risk tax shelters, labour-sponsored venture capital mutual funds, high-risk small business ventures, and natural resource limited partnerships. These quick fixes rarely work out, and are not the right way to approach tax planning.

You may engage a tax return preparer for the first time in this phase. Many people get too focused on cost and hire poorly trained tax preparers who have little tax-planning expertise to offer. Often, you get little more than tax return preparation, which is only the mechanical act of preparing your return.

Some key tax tips for phase two are: 1) Hire an established tax professional to prepare your tax returns and to meet with you each August to discuss tax-planning opportunities. 2) Make spousal RRSP contributions instead of contributing to your own plan if your spouse is in a lower tax bracket. 3) Write off child care and charitable contributions. 4) Switch to a self-employed relationship with your employer or start your own business, allowing you to write off your home office, your car, and much more. 5) Pay off your non-tax deductible debts and consider a new loan for investment purposes and write off the interest cost. 6) Consider some permanent life insurance for long-term estate planning tax minimization.

Phase Three: Wealth Management and Preservation

Tax planning in this phase can include the uses of trusts, holding companies, income splitting with family members, tax-smart investing, and more. With established wealth now in place, people in this phase often start helping their children get ahead. Sharing wealth between family members should be done very carefully, as divorce among children can devastate wealthbuilding. Tax planning, however, can be a success when you share wealth with children. See the strategies at the end of this chapter for two ideas. At this point in your life, your tax advisor may no longer be a generalist. Engage a tax specialist who can bring advanced tax-planning expertise to your finances. A tax specialist will have completed the In-Depth Tax Program in Canada.

Phase Four: Wealth Transfer

Tax effective Will planning, the use of testamentary trusts, permanent life insurance, joint ownership, and gifting before death are just some of the tax-planning maneuvers available to reduce taxes on death.

Tax planning is one area of your finances that is always important. However, as your wealth grows, so does your tax bill. As you purchase more assets, earn more income, rear your family, build a larger investment portfolio, and more, your tax issues and tax-planning opportunities grow.

Important Tax-Planning Strategies for People in All Phases of Wealthbuilding

Here are several tax-planning ideas that are well worth considering:

The Starting Point: Know the Personal Tax Rates Applicable to Your Income

You must have a basic understanding of the Canadian tax system before you can implement a tax strategy. There are three elements to taxation that I want to discuss:

1. Taxation of people
2. Taxation of investments
3. Taxation of investment income

The more you apply these three elements of taxation together, the greater the effectiveness of your tax-planning strategies.

Taxation of People

Canada has a progressive tax system. We pay an increasing amount of tax as taxable income increases. Each slice of taxable income for which the tax rate increases is known as a tax bracket. A higher tax rate is applicable only to the taxable income within that bracket and is called the marginal tax rate. Therefore, there are different tax rates applicable to different levels of your taxable income. Also important to note is that tax rates applicable to people vary by province.

Every Canadian with taxable income is taxed individually. The amount of tax we pay is dictated by the total taxable income we earn each year. Most of us already have a sense of our tax bracket and marginal tax rates, however, I would like to broaden your thinking. Instead of considering only your tax bracket, consider your entire family's—the tax brackets of your spouse, your children, your parents, your company, your trust. If the tax brackets of your family are different from your's, there may be opportunities to share taxable income and reduce family taxation. In other words, think family tax minimization instead of just your's alone.

Taxation of Investments

Bonds are taxed differently from equity mutual funds, which are taxed differently from GICs, which are taxed differently than real estate, which is taxed differently than foreign stock, and so on. The tax rates applicable to various types of assets are so different that selling an asset should not be done without a thorough review of the tax consequences on the sale. Focusing on after-tax value may lead to a completely different decision on what and when to sell the asset.

This line of thinking and tax effective evaluation is particularly relevant to your investment portfolio. Ensure that you understand the tax consequences of the various assets you own in your portfolio. You may be surprised by many unusual tax consequences associated with specialty investments in the market place today.

APPROXIMATE TOP TAX RATE ON ASSETS WHEN YOU SELL	
Stocks	23%
Bonds	23%
Canada Savings Bonds	0%
Primary home	0%
Cottage	23%
Mutual funds	23%
Permanent life insurance	23%
Rental property	
tax	23%
recapture	46%
Private business	varies

Taxation of Investment Income

There are at least five different types of investment returns you may earn: interest, Canadian dividends, foreign dividends, derivatives income, realized capital gains, and unrealized capital gains. Each type of investment return is taxed differently from the others. For example, in Canada today interest income is taxed at almost double the tax rate of capital gains realized in your portfolio. With such significant ranges of tax rates applicable to taxation of investment income, it is paramount that any investment income you receive is evaluated on an after-tax basis to ensure you manage the tax liabilities associated with your cash flow. Also, it is important to remember that tax rates applicable to investments and to investment income vary by province.

Employment income, along with interest income and foreign dividends, is the most highly taxed income type in Canada. Interest income is earned from bank accounts and from fixed-income investments like Canada Savings Bonds, guaranteed investment certificates (GICs), and government Treasury bills. Foreign dividends are earned from foreign stocks of foreign equity mutual funds.

Dividends are distributions of after-tax income paid by corporations to their shareholders. You may receive dividends from the mutual funds you own if the funds own shares of corporations that pay dividends. Canadian dividends generally attract far less taxation than interest, but more than capital gains.

Capital gains result when you sell an asset for more than its purchase price. The increase in value is a capital gain, and 50% of the gain (called a taxable capital gain) is included in your personal income for tax purposes. Capital gains generally attract the lowest tax rates of all investment income types, largely because only half the gain is taxable even before your marginal tax rate is applied. There are two types of capital gains: realized and unrealized. An unrealized gain consists of the accrued capital gain on an asset before the asset is sold. A realized gain generally results when the asset is sold. A capital gain is not taxable until it is realized. This means it is a tremendous tax advantage to earn unrealized capital gains since they face no annual taxation.

Note that interest income earned is usually taxable annually, whether it is received or not. Dividends are generally taxed when received. Capital gains, however, are taxable only when realized; you may be able to own an investment that has a growing market value and not trigger any tax until it is sold.

Your Marginal Tax Rates

Your marginal tax rate is the tax rate applicable to the next dollar of taxable income you earn.

Understanding marginal tax rates can be beneficial by:

- helping you to understand the tax paid on your income and how that tax may differ according to the nature and amount of the income you earn.
- knowing your own marginal tax rate is important in order to plan how to minimize the tax you pay on additional income.
- knowing the marginal tax rates of different investment income types

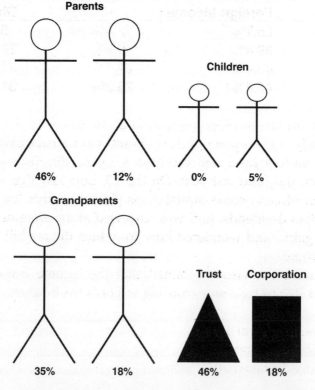

MARGINAL TAX RATE PLANNING

This family has eight different marginal tax rates that allow them to income split to minimize taxes. How many tax brackets is your family in?

These rates assume top tax bracket income.

permits you to reduce taxes paid by varying your investment mix.
- permitting you to calculate the tax savings on your registered retirement savings plan (RRSP) deductions. This knowledge may affect the way you decide to utilize your money.
- knowing the marginal tax rates of your family members can help you to assess who needs tax deductions the most and who can claim taxable income and pay the least amount of tax.
- knowing the marginal tax rate savings of tax credits and tax deductions allows you to better plan their use.

Below I have approximated the marginal tax rates for different taxable income levels in Canada (combined federal and provincial rates) on average. Keep in mind that each province has its own exact rate, which differs from those presented here. For our purposes, however, these approximations are practical.

Taxable Income Level	Wages, Interest & Foreign Income	Capital Gains	Canadian Dividends
$35,000	25.1%	12.6%	8.3%
$70,000	39.4%	19.7%	22.5%
$113,804	43.4%	21.7%	27.5%
Greater	46.4%	23.2%	31.3%

An Example for Greater Understanding of the Rates

Lori, who is in the top marginal tax bracket in Canada, owned a popular equity mutual fund and received a T3 for the distributions she received from the fund last year. On the T3, Lori saw that she earned some interest income, some capital gains realized within the fund, and some Canadian dividends. Lori was surprised at the amount of income and capital gains, and wondered how to reduce the tax bill associated with this income.

Lori's financial advisor explained that the income from the fund would be taxable as follows, according to Lori's tax bracket:

> Interest: taxed at 46%
> Capital gains: taxed at 23%
> Dividends: taxed at 31%

It was obvious to Lori that she should eliminate the interest and dividends income, so she wouldn't have to pay so much tax. Lori didn't need to live off that income. She started to examine what investments she needed to change in order to stop receiving high tax investment income.

Tax Planning with Your Spouse

One of the most common tax problems for couples in Canada is that one spouse has all of the income and assets in their name, while the other spouse has very little wealth in their name. For example, if one spouse works for thirty years, earns an income for the family, and invests the surplus in his or her name, while the other spouse chooses to stay home and raise the family without an income, their income levels and tax results may be very different. The spouse who earned the family income must declare that income, the investment income and the pension income all in their name, likely paying high income tax. The other spouse who has no wealth in their name, pays little or no tax. Many Canadian families are frustrated by this situation and wonder if there is a way they can shift some income to the lower earning spouse and pay less income tax.

This situation becomes a bigger problem as people move through the four phases of wealthbuilding. As a family accumulates more wealth in the higher income earning spouse's name, the tax rate applicable to that one person gets higher. Solving this problem early in the wealthbuilding process can save a family thousands, if not millions, of dollars in income tax by using some effective income-splitting techniques.

Here are some strategies that allow you to share income with your spouse:

- Get your low-income spouse involved in your career. Even part-time work as your assistant can permit them some income and save tax by effectively splitting income into a lower tax bracket.
- If your low-income spouse inherits assets from their family, use your growing savings to buy those assets (cottage, jewelry, other) from them for a fair market value. This will shift investment wealth into your spouse's name and they can invest it and pay less tax than you on the investment income generated.
- Contribute to a spousal RRSP if the chances are good that you will earn more than your spouse over the course of your working career. Note that a spousal RRSP provides you with a tax deduction and uses up your RRSP contribution room, but your spouse will be the one to eventually withdraw the money. If your spouse does earn any income, they will have their own RRSP contribution room and should

open a savings plan in their own name.

- The higher income earner can loan some of their accumulated savings to the lower income earning spouse. A formal loan agreement is drawn up, using the government prescribed interest, which is currently 3%, as of December 2004. Let's look at an example:

    - If today Dad has a $100,000 GIC earning 5% and pays 50% tax on it, Dad keeps only $2,500 of interest after tax each year.
    - But, if Dad loans this $100,000 to Mom at 3% interest cost, Mom can now invest the savings for the same 5% return. Dad must declare the loan interest as income, but Mom gets to write it off as an investment expense. More importantly, Mom can keep the difference between 5% return and 3% cost. So 2% investment return, or $2,000 each year, will now be taxed in Mom's name, at little or no tax cost. This can be a substantial tax savings each year to the family.

Before I leave the income tax section, I want to stress the importance of getting regular tax advice on your finances. Be careful who you engage as a tax advisor. And get a tax review every year. Never sell an asset without reviewing the tax results first. Never share wealth with family without examining the tax results first. Never invest your money without completing a tax-smart investing review. And don't prepare a Will without having a tax professional review it alongside the lawyer preparing the Will.

Tax Planning is Different from Tax Return Preparation

There is a big difference between tax-planning services and tax compliance services. One can be extremely valuable, the other is mandatory.

Tax compliance is a mechanical preparation whereby the government requires us to file a personal tax return that summarizes our taxable income and expenses for each year. This task requires little understanding of the Income Tax Act and can often be achieved in minutes using some of the tax software available on the market today. There is little value in tax compliance services. It is truly only worth the $65 you can pay to have it prepared by someone in a mall. There is no value because there is almost no likelihood that tax-planning opportunities are going to jump off your return and identify themselves. Tax return preparers may only be preparing the return, they may not identify any tax-planning strategies for you.

Tax-planning services are completely different from tax compliance and far more valuable. Tax planning is a profession: you sit down with a tax-planning expert, someone who knows the Income Tax Act thoroughly, and you tell him or her how you live your life. Chatting back and forth informally, the tax specialist will ask you many questions about how you (and your family, if applicable) live your life day to day. With this knowledge the tax specialist will relate your situation to the rules of the Income Tax Act to see if there are tax saving opportunities. This is personal tax planning and it can be tremendously valuable to Canadians.

I spent almost a decade working in public practice at one of the world's leading Chartered Accounting firms in Winnipeg and later in Toronto. During that time I completed hundreds of personal tax returns for a wide variety of Canadians. No matter how simple the return was, I typically charged $1,000 or more each time. My personal billing rate was well over $300 per hour. These costs may seem very high to someone paying $65 to have their return prepared. But I'll argue it's quite a deal.

For the last twenty years you may have prepared your own tax return or had a local tax service do it. I doubt that you uncovered many memorable tax breaks during that period because of the approach. That's just tax compliance—not tax planning.

But let's say that this year you did your return and then sat down with a qualified tax specialist for an hour to a) let them review your return for accuracy; and b) to chat with you about tax-planning opportunities based on your situation. I've done this recently where in ten minutes I found a tax break worth hundreds (potentially thousands) of dollars to the client, just from listening to how they live their life…

If I find a big tax break that you can claim this year, claim for the past three years by refiling, and claim well into the future, that could amount to thousands of dollars of savings. If that is the case, does my $300 per hour rate or $1,000 for a tax return seem so expensive? Not likely. The secret is in the tax planning!

Even if I don't find any tax breaks in your return, it is well worth the money for the validation that you are not missing opportunities. Since the Income Tax Act can be changed every week (not just during budget season as many people think), consider getting a tax-planning review on a regular basis.

How do you find a tax specialist? Here's a simple rule: the kind of tax specialist you want to sit down with will have a well-thumbed copy of the Income Tax Act in their office. And they will have a working knowledge of it. Before you sit down with anyone, ask to see his or her copy of the Income Tax Act. If they don't have one, find someone that does.

Investment Holding Companies

A private corporation is a separate legal entity that you create when you file legal documents to register it with the government. You can pick a name for your company, determine what to use it for, decide who the owners will be and how much stock they will receive, and set other parameters. Some companies are used to operate businesses such as restaurants or dry cleaners. Other corporations are simply empty shells that own shares in other companies. Private companies differ from public companies in that private company stock is not traded on a public stock exchange. There are many other differences as well, like tax treatment, that are beyond the scope of this book.

A private investment holding company is a corporation that exists solely to hold your taxable investment portfolio (excluding RRSPs, RRIFs, and all tax-sheltered assets). There is no active business operated by the company, because the investment holdings are not considered an active business. If you have a corporation that operates an active business or that blends investments with business interests, consult a tax professional about the specific tax characteristics.

There are a few important details worth mentioning about general corporation tax rules:

- In many cases, private companies are subject to tax rules different from those for public companies.
- The first $500,000 of capital gains that you earn on the sale of your private company shares is tax free, provided you qualify. Talk to a tax specialist about how to qualify.
- Assets can be transferred to a corporation on a tax-deferred basis. This means that you can move your entire investment account into a new corporation without triggering any taxes. Be careful, though—it doesn't work the same way when you try to get your assets out.
- Shareholders can remove earnings from their company in two ways: they can pay themselves a justifiable salary or pay dividends based on shares owned. Both methods have different tax implications.

Why Have a Private Investment Holding Company?

After reading the previous section you may be thinking that a holding company is too complicated to own. Yes, there are a lot of rules, but usually an accountant can take care of the filings and day-to-day work, leaving you with little else to do except manage the cash flow and the needs of the investment portfolio.

In the past, if you asked someone why he or she had a holding company, the reply was most likely "for tax reasons." Years ago, it was likely that your after-tax return was greater if you owned your investments through a holding company than if you owned it personally. Those days are gone. In many cases the tax savings are the same. If you have had a corporation for several years, you may want to revisit the reasons for having it. Today, there are new and different reasons to utilize a holding company:

- Private corporations can hold the investment assets of seniors. Since the investment income is taxed within the corporation, it is not included on seniors' personal tax returns. This will reduce their personal taxable income on their own tax returns, possibly increasing their Old Age Security (OAS) benefits or reducing the fees they have to pay to a nursing home.
- Private corporations can hold the investment assets of a disabled child. Since the investment income is taxed within the corporation, it is not included on the child's personal tax return. This reduces the child's personal tax on his or her own tax return, possibly enhancing the disabled child's government benefits.
- Private corporations can be established in Canada or offshore to guard against undesirable loss of assets from creditors. Corporations are considered separate legal entities, so they protect assets against challenges to your personal net worth. If you cause a car accident and someone files a lawsuit against you, a corporation would shield your assets from loss. If you are in a high-risk profession, a corporation would shield your assets from potential lawsuits. If you are faced with bankruptcy, a corporation would shield your assets from being taken.
- Private corporations can provide confidentiality. A public company must publish financial statements and even the salaries of key employees, but private corporations have no such obligations. Many of Canada's largest companies are privately owned, and the public never sees the financial details of their success.
- Private corporations can hold foreign real estate and foreign stock portfolios. Few are aware that their U.S. condo in Florida and their U.S. stock portfolio may be subject to U.S. estate taxes on their death, subject to the qualifying rules. Holding these assets within a corporate structure that you own historically will protect you against the

IRS, since U.S. estate taxes do not apply to qualifying corporations. If you have substantial U.S. assets, talk to a U.S. estate tax specialist as the rules are changing.

- Private corporations can be used to hold assets from your net worth and avoid probate fees on death.

Private investment holding companies can be a very effective planning tool. The rules for corporations are complicated and any discussion about holding companies should involve a lawyer or an accountant familiar with how they work.

Interest Expense

Generally, if money is borrowed to purchase an income-earning investment, any interest expense incurred is tax deductible for you. Here are the finer points of this tax break:

- Although you don't need to earn income immediately, you do need to expect to earn income in excess of the interest expense in the future. Income includes interest and dividends, but not capital gains.
- Interest expense incurred on borrowed money is tax deductible when used to buy common shares with dividends.
- If you realize a loss on the sale of an investment, interest expense that you were deducting will continue to be deductible if the loan remains outstanding.
- Interest on money used for contributions to an RRSP is not tax deductible.
- Interest on money used to purchase personal assets, like a home or a car, is not tax deductible.
- If you are claiming a tax deduction for interest paid, ensure that all necessary payments will be made by December 31.
- Convert non-deductible interest into tax deductible interest by using your available cash to pay down personal loans and mortgages and then borrow money to reinvest.

Capital Gains and Losses

It is important that every Canadian know a bit about what a capital gain is, how it comes about, and the many tax rules that surround it. Most Canadians will incur some form of taxable capital gain in their lives. At a very basic level, when an asset (investment, real estate, and so on) is sold for a price that is greater than its cost the difference is a capital gain. A capital loss results when the sale price is less than the cost. An example of a capital gain is when you sell a mutual fund that has appreciated in price over time.

Capital Gains Actually Relate to Dispositions

Technically, a capital gain or loss arises when there is a disposition of a capital property. Property includes tangible and intangible assets. A tangible asset is a real asset like stock or a cottage. An intangible asset is like goodwill of a company. A disposition includes the actual sale of an asset, but it also includes more than that. A disposition includes, for example, a gift or transfers to a trust and settlement of a debt.

There is a different form of disposition called a deemed disposition that can give rise to a capital gain or loss. The most common deemed disposition leading to tax consequences is death. Every Canadian, at the time of their death, faces a deemed disposition of all capital property and other assets they own. Deemed dispositions can mean large and unexpected tax liabilities—they should be well planned for. The most common story I hear is of the old couple with the ancient family cottage that, on the death of the last surviving spouse, faces taxation on a huge capital gain built up over fifty years. Unfortunately, the tax liability is not planned for and the family is forced to sell the cottage to generate the cash to pay the tax.

Getting Rid of Bad Investments Without Actually Selling

Many Canadians continue to hold one or more investments that just didn't work out. They bought the penny stock on a hot tip, but it just fizzled. Today, the stock still sits on their brokerage statements with a zero market value. Is this you?

If so, you likely have a capital loss since the cost is more than the current value. This capital loss can be used as a tax deduction against capital gains. To access the loss attach a letter to your tax return outlining an election to recognize the loss on the stock. You must also include specific details about the transaction and the stock (I would encourage you to talk to a tax accountant about how to properly complete the election). This election has specific rules as to how it will be applied. An advisor needs to be diligent in tracking losers in your portfolio, since aspects of this election to realize the loss only apply in the year the stock goes to zero or the debt goes bad. In some cases, if you miss the relevant year you may miss the chance to utilize the loss on your valueless holding.

How to Calculate a Capital Gain or Capital Loss

There are three elements that are combined to determine a capital gain or capital loss:

1. The proceeds of disposition
2. The expenses of disposition
3. The adjusted cost base

The proceeds of disposition are the actual sale price of the asset, or the deemed fair market value of the asset (market price) in the case of a deemed disposition where there isn't a real sale.

The expenses of disposition are any selling costs of disposing of the asset. These amounts are deducted from the proceeds on sale; they are not directly tax deductible on your tax return. These expenses reduce the size of the capital gain for tax purposes. Examples of such costs include real estate fees, legal fees, or advertising costs.

The adjusted cost base is the trickiest number to calculate when determining a capital gain. It can take many forms and include many variables. The adjusted cost base is the cost of the asset for tax purposes. In the most simple case, it is the original purchase price of the asset. Here are a number of factors that can complicate the calculation of a cost base:

a) Additional purchase costs incurred over time. For example, if you bought a cottage in 1995 for $150,000 and then built a garage on the property at a cost of $20,000 two years later, what is the adjusted cost base of the property when you sold it in 1999? The answer is $170,000. Additions to the property made over time are capitalized and added to the purchase price of the asset.

b) Identical properties. For example, if you bought 100 shares of ABC stock in 1996 for $10 per share, and then made another purchase of the same stock a year later at a price of $15 per share, what is the adjusted cost base of the entire lot of these identical shares? It would be the average cost of the purchase prices divided by the total shares. Every time you purchase a stock, mutual fund, or other asset you already own, you need to recalculate your average cost base.

c) Foreign exchange. Whenever you claim a capital gain or loss on your tax return it must be displayed in Canadian dollars. If the price of the underlying asset is originally denominated in a foreign currency, you will need to track down the exchange rate at time of purchase and the rate at time of sale. Calculate the cost in Canadian dollars at time of purchase. Do the same with the proceeds of sale at the time of disposition. Foreign currency can also result in additional capital gains or capital losses depending on the direction of currency changes. A good example is a U.S. dollar mutual fund. In order to keep track of an accurate adjusted cost base on this fund, you need to convert every purchase, sale, and reinvested distribution into Canadian currency as they happen. This may be more accounting than you hoped for. You may want to have your financial advisor do all these calculations for you.

A Potpourri of Issues and Strategies Related to Capital Gains and Losses

Gifts

There are special rules applicable to the gifting of assets. This is particularly relevant for assets gifted between family members. Generally, assets gifted between relations result in the recipient being deemed to have an adjusted cost base on the asset equal to the fair market value of the asset at time of the gift. A similar result happens with inheritances. This triggers taxation on any accrued gain that exists in the name of the giver.

It is important to note that this rule does not apply to a spouse. In the case of a gift to a spouse, the asset is transferred to the spouse at the adjusted cost base, not fair market value. There is further planning that is possible around gifting to a spouse that you should talk to a tax accountant about before making the gift.

Old Assets

The rules for capital gains have evolved, affecting the taxation of assets that you may have owned for the last several decades. It would be worthwhile to explore special tax consequences before selling a significant asset that you have owned for a very long time. For example, prior to 1972 there was no taxation applicable to capital gains or capital losses. If you sell a cottage today that you have owned since 1960, the first twelve years of appreciated value are not taxable and need to be determined. There are other special dates like this that need to be examined for applicability to your situation prior to selling an asset.

Rollovers

A rollover is a tax term that allows an asset to be moved between people or companies without triggering a capital gain or capital loss. In some situations this can be a very effective tax-planning maneuver. For example, some Canadians transfer their investment portfolio into a holding company at no cost (or tax!) to provide estate planning benefits.

Income versus Capital Gains Treatment

It is possible that despite all the rules, a capital gain or loss may not face capital gains taxation. The transaction may instead face taxation as regular income. The differences are big. A capital gain is taxed at only 50% of its value and the remainder is added to your regular income to be taxed at your marginal tax rate. Because only half the gain is taxable, the highest tax rates in Canada on capital gains are less than 25%. However, if the gain is taxed as regular income this is far less desirable. Regular income is taxed like your salary income, where tax rates can approach 50%. Clearly, it is advantageous to preserve capital gains treatment for tax purposes and not be forced to claim them as regular income.

On the reverse side, if you incur a capital loss, it would be more desirable to have this treated as regular income since you could claim the loss against salary to reduce taxes. Otherwise, a capital loss is also only 50% claimable and only deductible against other capital gains.

In an ideal world, you would want to have your capital gains taxed at capital gains tax rates and have your capital losses taxed as income, deductible against all other income. Unfortunately Canada Revenue Agency (CRA) doesn't allow this. It is either one or the other. Since most people hope to earn more capital gains than losses, most people stick with the capital gains taxation treatment.

In some cases, the nature of your activities will dictate whether you are taxed on transactions using capital gains rates or regular income rates. The classification of activities is a very contentious area of tax law between tax payers and CRA. There are dozens of court cases documenting how taxpayers fought for capital gains treatment of particular transactions when CRA decided the transactions get income treatment for tax purposes.

Here are two examples to highlight the above:

Marian Rose manages some of her own investments. Marian does a bit of research and buys the odd mutual fund. She was lucky last year and earned some capital gains. When she pays taxes on these capital gains, she will include 50% of the gain on her personal tax return, benefitting from the low taxation associated with capital gains.

Bev Durban is a day trader playing the stocks every business day. She considers stock market trading her career, following the markets and trading. At the end of last year Bev earned a modest income from the capital gains she earned on trades. In Bev's case, she would be taxed on her earnings as regular income (not capital gains) since the nature of her transactions were more of a business nature than of a capital account.

Preferred Tax Rates on Capital Gains

Tax rates applicable to capital gains are confusing, particularly with all the changes in recent years. The most important thing to note about capital gains taxation is that the entire capital gain is not taxable. An inclusion rate must be applied to the capital gain to determine what is taxable. Currently the inclusion rate is 50%, meaning that only 50% of a capital gain is taxable. This taxable portion is added to your other income on your personal tax return and taxed at your marginal tax rate. Tax rates applicable to capital gains are the lowest tax rates available on any kind of income you can earn.

Capital Losses

Here are a few comments on capital losses worth knowing:

- Since capital losses can be carried forward and used in the future it is important to keep track of capital losses realized but not yet applied. Either keep a schedule at home or track the amounts on your tax return software.
- Special rules, called superficial loss rules, exist around accessing capital losses in some cases. They exist to disallow losses that you may have otherwise thought were tax deductible. There are many different superficial loss rules, but here are two common examples.
  - Δ If you own a stock or mutual fund in a non-RRSP/RRIF investment account (also referred to as an "open taxable account") and it currently is in a loss position, you cannot use the loss if you move the stock into your RRSP as an RRSP contribution.
  - Δ If you own a stock or mutual fund in a non-RRSP/RRIF investment account and it is currently in a loss position, you cannot sell the stock and buy it back the next day, effectively realizing the loss for tax purposes. The loss will be disallowed. You have to wait at least thirty-one days before you can rebuy the stock in order to access the loss for tax purposes.
  - Δ As a general rule, before you contemplate selling an asset of any kind, buy some time from a tax expert to see if all tax-planning opportunities have been considered.

Chapter Five
Tax-Smart Investing and the Wealthbuilding Process

One of the greatest ways to reduce income tax is to focus on management of personal investments and being tax smart in your approach.

In this chapter, we will cover the many opportunities for tax-smart investing and how your planning should evolve as you move through the phases of wealthbuilding. I have a lot to say on this topic—my first bestselling book in Canada was called *Tax-Smart Investing* and provided more than fifty strategies on how to pay less tax in your investments.

ACCUMULATION OF INVESTMENT WEALTH DURING THE WEALTHBUILDING PROCESS

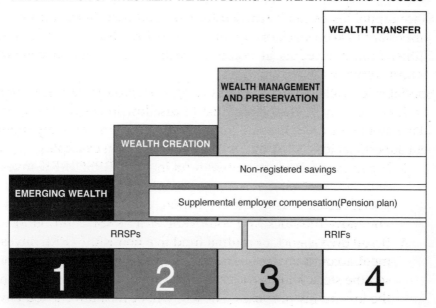

What Is Tax-Smart Investing?

Tax-smart investing is investing to maximize the after-tax return—it means looking at your investments the way you look at your paycheque, after tax; it means paying attention to the after-tax return, not the pre-tax return you see in the newspapers. Tax-smart investing is maximizing what you earn after paying income tax. In Canada, where tax rates approach 50%, tax-smart investing is the only way to manage your money. Regardless of the type of investing you do, tax planning and investment selection must go hand-in-hand every step of the way. Never purchase or sell an investment without a thorough tax evaluation built in.

Tax-Smart Self Test #1: The last time you purchased or sold an investment product, did you stop to ask key tax questions about the tax liability? Tax characteristics of the product? Tax characteristics of the income? Tax should be one of your most important investment selection criteria and one of the first few questions you ask about a new investment or before you sell an old investment!

Tax-Smart Self Test #2: Do you have a target rate of return for your portfolio? Is it a total return or an after-tax return? Pre-tax returns of products that you see in the newspapers are of limited use to an investor who pays taxes in Canada. You need to see after-tax information.

Achieving the after-tax rate of return you desire when you invest is a function of two related factors: buying an investment product that achieves a certain total rate of return and paying the income tax on the total return generated by the investment product. Many Canadians focus only on the investment product when they invest and neglect to consider the tax impact on their total rate of return. Remember, the interest income, dividends, and capital gains that you include on your tax return each year, and the tax you pay on this income, reduce the rates of return on your taxable investments. The tax paid on this investment income reduces the overall return or profitability of an investment product and warrants consideration before you buy the product in the first place.

Tax-smart investing means taking a different approach to strategies and products for your taxable savings account than for your RRSPs or RRIFs. After all, your taxable accounts are taxed annually, while your RRSPs and RRIFs are not. This requires different approaches to investing in the taxable accounts—an approach to maximizing after-tax returns.

What is After-Tax Rate of Return?

The best way to describe after-tax rate of return is by using an example:

Let's assume that last year you owned a mutual fund in your taxable (non-RRSP) investment account—worth $100,000 at the beginning of the year, and $103,000 at the end of the year. Let's also assume that at year end it generated a taxable distribution of $10,000 of interest income.

Your total return is calculated as follows:

$$(($103,000 + $10,000 - $100,000) / $100,000) \times 100 = 13\%$$

This total return is the number that you might see in the newspaper advertised as the return for the year. Sounds pretty good, eh? Think again! It is not your after-tax return. The distribution that was generated is taxable. It is included on your total personal income and a slice of tax is taken off. Let's assume that the distribution of $10,000 is taxable personally at a rate of 50% as you are in the top marginal tax bracket.

Your after-tax return is calculated as follows:

(($103,000+10,000-$100,000) − ($10,000 x 0.50%)) / $100,000) x 100 = 8%

On an after-tax basis, your return is only 8%. There can be a significant difference between pre-tax and after-tax returns. Canadians who pay taxes on investments should be focusing on after-tax returns, yet few are.

Who is Tax-Smart Investing Suitable For?

Every Canadian who pays income tax on their investment income should be focused on tax-smart investing. Since all of us will likely have taxable savings (savings in an open account), tax-smart investing is important to us all. Tax-smart investing is not age sensitive or gender sensitive. Children can often accumulate taxable savings from family gifts. Spouses can also accumulate taxable savings from inheritances, employment, or family income splitting. Tax-smart investing is not people specific. Individuals, trusts, estates, corporations, based in Canada and offshore, have relevant aspects of tax-smart investing that must be considered. Tax-smart investing is not only for wealthy Canadians. A student may be saving for a new car and has a taxable savings account. An elderly couple may have significant amounts of GICs and bonds outside of their RRIF. A granddaughter may have an in-trust account funded by her grandmother.

How is Tax-Smart Investing Applied?

Tax-smart investing consists of three different interrelated variables:

1. Tax-Smart Financial Advisor: Working with a financial advisor that understands taxation and investing on a technical basis, and has the ability to correctly apply tax-smart strategies to your situation is imperative. I'm not saying you need a tax accountant as your investment advisor, but you need someone who has a basic understanding, and passion, for tax-smart investing.
2. Tax-Smart Strategies: Arguably planning is more important than product, making the formulation of a tax-smart investing strategy applicable to your needs is an essential step. Formulation of a strategy requires knowledge of you and knowledge of tax-smart investment rules from which you can benefit.
3. Tax-Smart Products: It is critical that all investments products be evaluated with an eye to tax issues. An RRSP-eligible product may not be suitable for a taxable investment account. You need to know the differences!

Tax-Smart Investing and the Wealthbuilding Process
Phase One: Emerging Wealth

In this first phase of wealthbuilding, most people will try to start contributing to an RRSP, but they may not maximize their contributions and they may not save beyond their RRSP. This limits tax planning to tax-sheltered investments alone. Within your RRSP, if you are single, follow these strategies:

* Try to maximize your RRSP contributions each year.
* Take the corresponding RRSP tax deduction in the same year, unless you are in a low tax bracket and your income will go up next year. If this is the case, make the contribution this year, but take the tax deduction on next year's tax return.

Phase Two: Wealth Creation

In this phase of wealthbuilding, there are more tax-smart investing opportunities to consider. You may have company stock or stock options and you need to develop a tax-smart option exercise strategy. If you are married and your spouse is in a lower tax bracket, you may want to make spousal RRSP contributions instead of contributing to your own plan. Perhaps you are also borrowing to invest in the stock market and can write off the interest you pay on the loan. Near the end of this phase you are likely saving money outside of an RRSP and developing a growing non-RRSP investment portfolio; your investment planning takes on a new dimension of tax planning. It is important to put highly taxed investments in your RRSP and control the amount and type of investment income you earn each year.

Phase Three: Wealth Management and Preservation

In this phase you likely have a larger investment portfolio than you do an RRSP. With more real estate, stocks and bonds, and funds, you may be paying a lot of income tax on your investments. As you move into retirement, this income may become a large component of your retirement cash flow. In every case, tax planning becomes essential to preserving what you have and to maximizing your after-tax income when you no longer have employment earnings. For you, tax-smart investing is not an option, it is essential. The strategies discussed later in this chapter should be mandatory for your investment planning.

Phase Four: Wealth Transfer

Many Canadians won't hit their wealthbuilding peak until they die. This means they have the highest net worth of their life at the time of death. With so many assets, a variety of income sources, and a Will/estate that sends all this wealth in a number of directions, tax-smart investing continues to be essential for purposes of preserving family wealth. Taxable income levels can affect how much a person pays to enter a government nursing home in some provinces, whether your Old Age Security income is clawed back, and government benefits that you may like to receive.

Let's look at a host of tax-smart investing strategies that matter to all Canadians progressing through the four wealthbuilding phases.

The Six Dimensions of Tax-Smart Investing

1. Taxation of people
2. Taxation of investments
3. Taxation of investment income
4. Taxation of foreign assets
5. Legal ownership affects taxation
6. Taxation of fees

The six dimensions are fundamental principles that apply to every Canadian taxpayer. No matter what your income or in what phase of wealthbuilding you are, these dimensions should be considerations that you always make before you invest.

Taxation of People

Your annual average tax rate and annual marginal tax rate are two vital bits of information that you or your investment advisor needs to consider in order to properly build an investment portfolio. When I review client investment statements, I will review their last tax return as well. I can't imagine recommending an investment without knowing what level of taxes the investor pays. Chances are the investor is in a different tax bracket than a spouse, children, grandchildren, trust, holding company, or business. Looking at the tax brackets of you and your family together offers many more tax-smart investing strategies than by just looking at your own tax bracket. The reality is that many investors aren't even considering their own tax brackets when they build an investment portfolio.

Taxation of Investments

You should understand the tax implications of the different assets that you own. When you buy and sell various assets, including portfolio securities, you need to know the tax implications that you will trigger— even when selling one mutual fund to buy another. You should also be aware that a gift of an asset to a family member is considered a sale in the Income Tax Act (giving the cottage to your son triggers all of the built-up tax, due next April). Or that gifting a stock to your grandchild also causes a deemed disposition and nasty tax results. Don't sell or gift a major asset to anyone without talking to a tax expert first. Also, don't buy or sell sexy investment products like tax shelters and natural resource limited partnerships without understanding the tax implications. So many people buy and sell blindly, getting themselves into so much tax trouble. If your financial advisor does not or cannot explain the tax implications, consult your accountant for a second opinion or change your financial advisor to one who understands the importance of tax and who can advise you on it.

Taxation of Investment Income

Every February you receive tax slips in the mail summarizing your taxable investment income for the year. On your tax return you also have to list all the securities that you sold in the year. I'm suggesting that you pay a lot more attention to these slips as the tax you pay can be controlled. You can put a lot more of this money back into your pocket instead of with the government if you closely control the amount and type of investment income that you earn.

This is particularly relevant for retired Canadians. Last year I sat down with a lady whose OAS income was being clawed back. When I looked at her tax return, and suggested some tax-smart investing changes to her investment portfolios, we changed the type and amount of her realized investment income, reduced the tax she pays, and stopped the clawback of her OAS. Now that's tax planning!

Taxation of Foreign Assets

Many Canadians are not aware that they face taxation and/or annual reporting on foreign assets that they own. Whether you own real estate in England, have rental property in Germany, have a bank account in Hong Kong, or own stock in Brazil, the income from these assets is taxable annually on your Canadian tax return and the sale or gift of these assets will be taxable as a capital gain or loss when you dispose of them. Fail to report this income and you are breaking the law in Canada.

If you own U.S. stocks or businesses outside of Canada, you now need to report these assets on your tax return every year if their cost is greater than Can$100,000.

Even your RRSP is affected by foreign assets. When you own U.S. stocks in your RRSP, any dividends that you earn may face U.S. withholding tax of around 15%. This tax, because it is being incurred in your RRSP, is not recoverable and is essentially a fee. You may want to think twice about owning foreign equities in your RRSP or RRIF.

Even at death, if you own a large amount of qualifying U.S. assets your estate may pay U.S. estate tax of up to 55% of the value of the assets. This can be applied to your estate even if you are not American.

There is no doubt that international investing is an important part of a diversified investment portfolio. But so is tax planning related to owning these foreign assets. Don't overlook it.

Legal Ownership and Taxation

Opening an investment account in your name triggers different tax results than if you open an investment account jointly with another person. Holding your investments inside a trust account triggers different tax results than if you hold your investments inside a holding company. Be careful who's name you invest in!

If you transfer your investments into a holding company that you own, you can shift taxation of the annual income from the investments from your personal return to the company tax return and make your personal income less. This can reduce your personal taxation and even prevent the clawback of OAS benefits in retirement. It can also help you to avoid probate fees in your estate when you die. The tax savings can be in the tens of thousands just by paying attention to how your accounts are set up.

Taxation of Fees

Many of Canada's largest mutual funds come in two versions—one with no directly tax deductible fees ("A" or "I" class versions) and one with fees that you can deduct on your personal tax return ("F" class version). Both types are available for purchase from your financial advisor. Most Canadians are buying the non-deductible type. Purchasing the "F" class version of the fund in your non-RRSP portfolio can save you a significant amount of tax every year by making part of the fees that you pay directly tax deductible.

Tax-Smart Investing: Essential Planning For Canadians in Advanced Stages of Wealthbuilding

Now that you have a basic understanding of the key elements of tax-smart investing, let me review why it is so important through a quiz. Apply this quiz to your own investment portfolios and assess whether you are a tax-smart investor. If you are not, it may require a change of your financial advisor, or at least a change in your strategy, to get back on track.

1. Do you have the same stock, bond, or mutual fund in different investment accounts? This is a good indication that your portfolio is not tax smart.
2. Do you own the same mutual funds or stocks as your spouse or your children? Why? It may not be tax smart.
3. Do you improperly pay stock/bond commissions and mutual fund loads that are not tax smart? A tax-smart investor should prefer asset-based fees, where you pay zero commissions to buy and sell a product and, instead, pay an annually negotiated fee for service over all your investments. This form of fee is more tax deductible.
4. Are you controlling the type and amount of investment income that you get? By carefully planning the type of investments that you own with an eye to taxation, you can increase your after-tax investment income while lowering your tax bill. Alternatively, you can examine opportunities to use trusts and family holding companies to hold your investments to reduce income tax on income as well.
5. Are you controlling portfolio turnover? Turnover, or the rate of buying and selling within your investment account or within a mutual fund, is one of the key factors in controlling after-tax returns.
6. Are you incorrectly buying U.S. stocks thinking you are getting the Canadian dividend tax credit? You can boost your after-tax cash flow by buying Canadian dividend yielding stocks and dividend mutual funds. Stocks owned directly or through mutual finds can often offer attractively high dividends.
7. Do you have inappropriately hidden money offshore? As a Canadian there is nothing you can do to legitimately avoid tax through offshore investing.
8. Are you giving random gifts of money to you spouse? Taxation of investment income is attached to the person responsible for the source of the investment.
9. If you have a high income and a lot of wealth, do you need an RRSP at all? Have you explored the long-term result of this?
10. If you share investment money with a spouse, children, or grandchildren, have you explored all the after-tax investment planning oppor-

tunities that can be used among close family members? As you factor in more people, the number of tax-planning opportunities grows.

11. Are you reviewing after-tax rate of return on your investments each year? The published rates of return that you see in the newspapers for investments are pre-tax returns, not after tax. You need to review after-tax data to really judge value.

12. Have you purchased too many labour-sponsored funds such that your portfolio is full of poorly performing investments? Don't lose sight of the investment merits because you are overly focused on the tax breaks that these products offer.

13. When you buy and sell an investment product, are you closely evaluating its tax merits?

14. Do you understand the tax rules for all the investment products that you own today? If you regularly buy natural resource flowthrough investments, are you aware of the tax bite that can occur when you sell these products?

15. Does your current financial advisor have the technical background to assist you to focus on after-tax wealthbuilding as described in this book?

16. Do you feel that you have done everything that you can do to be tax smart in your investing approach?

The Tax Seduction of Specialty Products

There are many forms of specialty products that an investor can buy today for their investment portfolio. The purpose of this section is to inform you of what I consider to be specialty products, provide some basic background, and suggest a process for evaluating them.

Labour Funds

An important point about labour funds is that their tax credits have allowed them to achieve mainstream sales, where you see labour funds regularly in people's portfolios. Although labour funds are popular for their tax breaks, they are not popular for their investment returns. When evaluated on their investment merits alone, far fewer people may consider labour funds as a worthy investment. Make sure you evaluate labour funds for their investment and tax qualities equally.

Tax Shelters

Many tax shelters are structured in the form of limited partnership investments where, as an investor, you become a partner in this investment. A limited partnership is a flow-through structure, meaning that income and losses incurred by the partnership are allocated directly to partners involved. Ownership of a limited partnership investment will require complex accounting in order to keep track of your adjusted cost base of the investment over time.

Tax shelters are specialty investments that often get special tax breaks making them appear more attractive as an investment. The Canadian film industry, for example, is one industry that has been subsidized by the government. One of the subsidizations is a provision of tax breaks to those who invest in Canadian films and Canadian production. Often the benefits of these tax breaks have been passed on to the investors in the partnership. In recent years the government has been aggressively examining investments in tax shelters and disallowing tax breaks in some cases.

Private Company Investments

Investing in a private company (car wash, restaurant, automotive dealership, etc.) can be very risky, but it can also have tremendous payoffs. Some of the world's richest people have invested in their own private businesses and are billionaires today. Many more, however, don't survive. Some of the advantages of investing in a private company include the potential for high returns and tax advantages not otherwise available. The disadvantages of investing in a private company include the lack of liquidity if you need to get your money back and the outright risk of loss.

If you are contemplating investment in a private company, have the business plan reviewed by a lawyer and an accountant (at a minimum). If you do invest in a private company it is important to supplement this with an equal or greater investment in marketable securities, whether as part of your RRSP or open taxable account.

Income Trusts

Income trusts are included in this section just by the virtue of how new they are in Canada. From a tax-smart point of view, I see many Canadians buying income trusts for the high distributions that often appear to be tax effective as well. An oil and gas trust offering 12% distributions can be enticing compared to a 3% GIC. But don't be fooled—never cash in your relatively safe GICs for the high risk of an oil drilling company. Further, dig deep into the distributions of an income trust to assess what it is made up of. The money you are receiving may consist of some return, but it may also consist of some return of your own capital, which is not an investment return at all.

How to Protect Yourself With Specialty Investments

Below are a few tips to follow when faced with buying a specialty investment.

1. Get an objective accountant or lawyer to examine it thoroughly.
2. If it is going to cost you more than $10,000 to buy, get a second accountant or lawyer to examine it.
3. If it is a new type of product, be very cautious.
4. If it has been around for a while, how successful has it been? How many people have bought it? Have any articles been written on it by the media? Have any reputable accounting or law firms provided an opinion on the product?
5. Does the value justify the cost?
6. Has CRA put a stamp of approval on it for tax purposes?
7. Is it legal?
8. Does it fit with your personal financial profile?
9. Is this the right time in your life to be buying this?
10. What is urging you to buy into this and is that the right motivating factors?

Universal Life Insurance as a Tax-Smart Investment

A universal life insurance policy is a form of permanent insurance where the insurance component and the savings element are separate and distinct. The policy owners may have several investment options to consider for the savings piece of the policy, along with flexibility on the timing and amount of premium deposits. The investment options for the savings component can include fixed-income instruments, GICs, and equity-associated investments. Selection of the types of investments for the savings component of the policy should be made after careful consideration of your risk/return preferences and balanced with your total investment portfolio mix.

A universal life insurance policy can provide tax sheltering of death benefits paid out on the policy holder's death, if the policy qualifies as an exempt policy under the Income Tax Act. These death benefits will include the accumulations from the savings component of the policy, which can grow tax free inside the policy over the life of the policy. The investment accumulation can be added to the original death benefit amount. If, however, the accumulated savings are ever "cashed in" during the life of the policy holder, a taxable transaction can result.

Aside from tax, if you name an individual beneficiary for the policy, the proceeds of the insurance on death pass outside your estate and eliminate the need to pay probate fees on the proceeds. There may also be creditor-proofing opportunities associated with owning universal life insurance that are not available with non-life insurance company products.

So what should you be concerned with? For tax reasons, you should try to avoid cashing in the policy before death. That aside, when you are investigating universal life policies, factors to evaluate include the following:

- The number of investment options for the savings component of the policy. Consider a policy with options in a variety of asset classes.
- The company's rules and any fees for switching between different investments as your needs and risk tolerance change over time.
- The quality of the life insurance company. Purchasing a universal policy may be a fifty-year commitment, and you want the insurance company to be there in fifty years.
- The life insurance company's administration expenses, mortality costs, and other expenses. These costs may affect the success of your investment component if they are factored into the costs of the policy. The treatment of these and other costs may vary by company.
- Accountability of the insurance company. Will it provide minimum credits to the investment funds you invest in? The size of credits can be affected by the variables described in the previous point.
- The basis on which the insurance company pays bonuses into the investment component.

In addition to pure insurance objectives, universal life insurance can play a role in your estate plan (e.g. to provide tax-free proceeds to pay tax liabilities on death). Given the variety of uses, the wide selection of products available, and the tax and investment complications, careful evaluation of options should be made before purchasing. Consider seeking a second opinion from an accountant or advisor who has expertise with insurance products and can provide independent advice. Have a clear objective in mind when buying, and, most important, ensure that the policy is affordable. There is no sense in buying a policy that rewards death if the cost of the premiums hurt your lifestyle in the present.

Finally, it is important to remember that insurance is risk protection first. Risk protection against loss of income, against lack of liquidity, and other reasons. Buying insurance for investment reasons is unusual and should not be contemplated until you have paid off your debts and maximized your RRSP. Even then, carefully evaluate the strategy to determine if it this is right for you.

Chapter Six
Wealthbuilding and Investing

This chapter is framed in the form of a chart. Each of these sections will be covered in detail in this chapter, but this overview will help you to see how the approach to investing may evolve over time. Many of the bad habits identified in this chart will be addressed along with a discussion of a professional investing process that can serve as a framework for all investors, at every wealth level.

The Realities of How People Invest and How People Should Invest in Canada Today

Investment Characteristic	Phase One Emerging Wealth	Phase Two Wealth Creation	Phase Three Wealth Management and Preservation	Phase Four Wealth Transfer
Investing attitude	Maximize RRSP contributions, tax-driven investor	Maximize returns, risk taker	Maximize after-tax returns, cautious investor	Minimize loss, conservative investor
Investable wealth main source	RRSP	RRSP, pension plan, and stock options	Non-RRSP investments, real estate, small business	RRIF, non-RRIF investments, real estate, small business, life insurance
Investment product types people should use	Mutual funds	Pooled funds and exchange-traded funds	Individual stocks and bonds, pooled funds, and exchange-traded funds	Individual stocks and bonds, managed by different types of managers.
Investment results	Low risk/high cost	High risk/high cost	Low cost and controlled risk	Controlled cost and low risk
Fee Types	Commissions	Commissions and fees	Fees	Fees
Investing tax efficiency	Little	Some	A lot	Maximum
Potential flaws in the investing process	Tax-driven with no plan	Product-driven, hodge-podge of yesterday's winners	Investment plan disconnected from rest of finances	Little tax-smart investment planning
Proper investing process	Goal-driven, integrated financial plan	Goal-driven, integrated financial plan	Goal-driven, integrated financial plan	Goal-driven, integrated financial plan

Section One: Wealthbuilding and Investor Attitude

The investor attitude is how you think about investing. A big problem with investing is the failure to evolve one's thoughts and considerations properly or at all.

Phase One: Emerging Wealth

In phase one, investors are typically new at investing and have a small amount of savings. Most people first start saving through their employer's pension plan, or their own RRSP if they don't belong to a pension plan. Maximizing contributions to your plan may be tough to accomplish in the early years. At this phase, investor attitude is tax driven—Canadians will often buy RRSPs for the tax break each April, often rushing to get their RRSP contribution completed before the annual February deadline. After a few years, many Canadians have a variety of RRSPs with several institutions, and there is rarely a plan around it all.

Phase Two: Wealth Creation

As you move into the wealth creation phase, cash flow is going up, debt is going down, and you are creating wealth from several investment sources: an employer pension or savings plan, company stock or stock options, real estate (home), RRSP, and even the start of some discretionary savings. As investors gain discretionary income, many choose to become high risk takers with their savings. Many people purchase aggressive small cap stocks, tax shelters, questionable real estate ventures, new small businesses, and labour-sponsored venture capital funds. The attitude shifts towards maximizing return at all costs, with little worry of failure. Since cash flow is ample and retirement is often far off, investors may not be cautious—investing in almost anything without questioning the cost, purpose, risk, and development of a proper plan. Investment in phase two can be characterized by random investing or investing without a formal written investment plan. This can even be more of a problem compared to phase one, as you are likely tinkering with more money.

Phase Three: Wealth Management and Preservation

There is no pressure on investors in phase three to create more wealth. More wealth may be created, but the investor attitude shifts to a more conservative position of wealth preservation, moderate growth, cautious investment, and continued tax minimization. Investors may want more formalized planning for building a more structured approach to managing their finances because their net worth is more complex. Many investors can be scared into getting more and better professional advice at this stage, based on the sheer magnitude of wealth created.

Phase Four: Wealth Transfer

For the wealthy, the attitude towards investing may change a little. Their wealth is so abundant that the element of loss is insignificant. With little chance of spending all of their money, their attitude towards investing may always be consistent. For the less wealthy, the final wealthbuilding phase sees a change of attitude towards conservatism and a protection of assets. This may lead to significant changes in investing strategies, possibly propelled by fear and paranoia of loss. It is important to remember that you may live for forty years in retirement, and becoming excessively conservative can erode your standard of living over the long term.

Section Two: Wealthbuilding and Investable Wealth
Phase One: Emerging Wealth

Wealthbuliding is about accumulating capital, of which there are several kinds. In phase one of the wealthbuilding process, most Canadians will be limited to their RRSPs or employer's group RRSP as their sole source of wealth. Some people may also have a home, but it may be highly mortgaged, leaving very little equity or wealth. Within phase one I have several recommendations on how to start effective wealthbuilding:

- Get your RRSP started and make contributions of any amount you can afford each month off your paycheque.
- Borrow money from relatives if you have a large unfunded RRSP carryforward that you want to contribute to.
- Do not use your RRSP for the Home Buyers Plan to buy your first home. It ravages your RRSP at the time in your life that you need to leave it alone to grow.
- Buy an affordable home rather than rent, unless you have the ability to rent at a low cost each year.

Phase Two: Wealth Creation

As many Canadians hit their stride with their careers, they start to benefit from wealthbuilding options offered by their employer: company stock, stock options, and perhaps a pension plan. These perks can be significant wealthbuilders, and, when choosing a career path, companies that offer these compensation plans offer an advantage over companies that do not. Also, a defined benefit pension plan is worth a lot more than a defined contribution or group savings plan.

The temptation at this phase of wealthbuilding is to take this extra compensation and liquidate it in order to pay debts and pay for a lifestyle. Wait a minute. Company compensation plans can be one of the best ways to build long-term wealth—look at people who owned shares in Microsoft since its inception, many are multi-millionaires now. Before liquidating your options to pay down debts, evaluate the pre-tax and after-tax cost of paying off the debt versus leaving the investment in place. And before liquidating your options to spend the money on your lifestyle, make sure that you are leaving enough to continue an effective wealthbuilding approach. It is possible to carelessly spend your wealth by upsizing your life prematurely.

As your sources of wealth broaden, it is important to get expert advice on what to do with your wealth and to start putting some foundational wealthbuilding strategies in place. This is not the time to be a "do-it-yourselfer."

Phase Three: Wealth Management

At this point your wealth has typically accumulated in a variety of sources: a mortgage-free house and perhaps a cottage as well; a growing RRSP and/or a company pension plan; non-registered savings (which is where you are putting your extra cash each year); a large amount of company stock or stock options; and other sources, such as club memberships, antiques, and vehicles.

With significantly more savings and assets, your approach to managing your finances warrants a more sophisticated process. Integrated planning among the various assets and a more advanced approach to tax planning may be necessary. Tax-smart investing becomes more important, really for the first time, as you have accumulated a large amount of taxable wealth. Refer back to the tax-smart investing strategies from the previous chapter.

At this phase, you may be concerned about having too much wealth concentrated in company stock or stock options. After many years of accumulating company stock, chances are the amount that you have may be half of your total net worth, if the stock has performed well. It is necessary to develop an exercise and sell strategy, as the extra risk of carrying a lot of money in one stock may not be worth the extra return.

Phase Four: Wealth Transfer

At phase four, you will likely have the highest wealth level of your life and the greatest number of assets.

You may well be beyond $1 million in total wealth. It is not the time to cut corners with a handwritten Will, prepare your own tax return, invest in retail investment products like GICs or traditional mutual funds, or plan your retirement income off the cuff. With established wealth in place, and significant inter-generational family wealth transfer on the horizon when you die, take time to get expert advice in the areas of law, tax, investing, and financial planning. Make sure you do this before a health issue arises so that you are of sound mind and body to make the financial decisions you want to.

How About Some Numbers?

Defining the wealthbuilding process by age or by money level is dangerous. In my opinion, wealthbuilding is 50% state of mind and 50% financial situation. It is possible to reach the highest level of wealthbuilding with less than a million dollars of investable wealth, depending on the quality of life you prefer.

However, if I must provide some numbers to define the various investable wealth stages of the wealthbuilding process, here they are:

Phase One: Zero wealth to $100,000 of net worth
Phase Two: $100,000 to $750,000 of net worth
Phase Three: Greater than $750,000 of net worth
Phase Four: Transitional phase not defined by wealth level

If you use these levels to define your stages of wealthbuilding, reaching these milestones allows you to know the timing of all of the various strategies in this book, and coordinate the changes that you need.

Section Three: Wealthbuilding and Types of Investment Products
Phase One: Emerging Wealth

With small amounts of wealth, the diversification that mutual funds offer make them the appropriate product for small investors. Costs can be managed, choice is broad, and, most important, your money is pooled with that of others in order to buy diversified portfolios of stocks and bonds around the world.

Phase Two: Wealth Creation

With more free cash flow, it is tempting to start buying stocks and specialty investments. But investment in individual securities should be limited and controlled depending on your wealth level. With only a few hundred thousand dollars of savings, you lack the adequate savings amount to build a properly diversified portfolio. The use of pooled funds, indexed investments and "F" class mutual funds in a blended portfolio can offer the protective diversification that you need, while providing the excitement of some carefully selected individual securities. You should still be focused on building a solid investment foundation using blue chip investments. Save the sexy investments for your "fun money" account and limit the size of this portfolio to no more than 10% of your savings.

Phase Three: Wealth Management and Preservation

With $300,000 to several million in the bank at this point in your life, your range of investment products will include pooled funds ("F" class mutual funds), stocks and bonds, and exchange traded funds. With significantly more wealth, most people will engage professional money managers. A professional money manager is a discretionary portfolio manager, consisting of one of the more than two hundred such firms in Canada today.

Phase Four: Wealth Transfer

With your wealth now mature, your money should be managed by professional money managers, often specialized by asset class (bonds, stocks, U.S. equity, global equity, etc.). Few people will be doing their own investing at this stage, as you can get top money management at a reasonable cost, allowing you to spend more time on leisure and family. It is safe to say that many money managers lack the expertise, depth, and tax savvy necessary to manage wealth properly, so selection of money managers should be carefully done—especially when you consider that you may give them a million dollars or more to manage.

Section Four: Wealthbuilding and Investment Results

We all invest for similar reasons: to reach our goals. But how we get there and the risks we take vary. As you progress through the various phases of wealthbuilding, the characteristics of your investment plan change. This kind of analysis is something that you may not otherwise contemplate if you didn't read it here. Yet, by the time you finish this section, I trust you will agree it is important to consider.

Phase One: Emerging Wealth

Many Canadians will use mutual funds for their investment solutions as they start to save money. While these investment products are recommended for this phase, without careful evaluation of products, the costs can be high (3% or more per year). As discussed earlier, however, mutual funds offer a level of diversification and this risk control is important. For this reason, investing in this first phase of wealthbuilding can be characterized as "low risk, high cost."

Phase Two: Wealth Creation

In phase two, many Canadians get irresponsible with their excess cash flow and invest in aggressive stocks, often without any plan or care for cost, risk, or wealth. Investing is treated almost like the lottery, where investors hope to strike it rich on one ten-bagger stock. Sadly, this rarely works out and you are far better off building a proper investment plan with most of your savings. People's bad investing habits at this phase are characterized as "high risk, high cost" because of the uncontrolled investing habits and the total disregard for cost.

Phase Three: Wealth Management and Preservation

Investors in phase three can characterize their investing as "low cost, controlled risk." With more money comes more clout to negotiate lower costs for active money management. And, with retirement and estate goals in sight, a more formalized plan is finally developed that consists of proper diversification and the use of professional money managers. Through development of a carefully designed plan, risk can be controlled to a level that you prefer, while also addressing your goals.

Phase Four: Wealth Transfer

The final phase of wealthbuilding is often highlighted by low-risk investing and controlled cost. Investors are willing to pay higher fees for the peace of mind that their money is safely guarded. Risk is low because it is no longer about growing wealth, but about protecting what you have.

These characteristic conclusions for the four phases of wealth management do not match everyone's profile. However, in my experience, I have found that many Canadians are setting up their investment portfolio to follow these guidelines. The message from this analysis is this: none of the characteristics of the four profiles above match what you should really be doing. Yes, all four are wrong. At any stage in the wealthbuilding process you should be following a "controlled cost and controlled risk" approach. Everyone deserves an investment plan that is written, focused, and speaks to your individuality. Even if you are too busy to build a personalized investment plan, your financial planner should be more than capable to prepare such a plan for you.

Section Five: Wealthbuilding and Fees Types

This section is about investment fees related to full-service advice and products.

Phase One: Emerging Wealth

Mutual funds and GICs are often the tools of choice for new investors. While GICs appear to have no purchase commissions, I would argue that getting an inferior interest rate compared to a bond from the bond market is a fee. If I sell you a GIC at 3% instead of giving you 3.25%, that extra 0.25% return lost is a fee.

There are three ways to purchase mutual funds: rear loaded, front loaded, and no load. Rear load means you pay no purchase commission and instead agree to remain in the mutual fund family for up to six years, so the mutual fund company can charge you fees over time. If you sell out of the fund family before your six years is up, you will face a redemption fee that declines to zero over time. Front load means you pay an agreed upon commission (usually 2%) up front to buy the fund and no fee to sell. This approach offers the most flexibility. No load means you don't pay purchase or sell commission for the fund. While this appears to be a superior approach, no load often provides no compensation to a full-service financial planner, and if you wish to engage them for services, you need to agree on a payment amount and method.

Besides the costs to buy and sell, mutual funds have internal fees called management expenses and operating costs. The management expense ratio (MER) can range from 0.25% per year to more than 3% per year. And finally, within the mutual fund portfolio of stocks and bonds, you will pay buy and sell commissions as the mutual fund manager trades securities within your fund.

In phase one of wealthbuilding, you may also pay an annual RRSP trustee fee of up to $137.50 to the dealer or firm that you hold your RRSP account with.

Phase Two: Wealth Creation

As you save more money, you should move towards new investment products and fee levels. Also, with more wealth you get more clout to negotiate lower costs. With several hundred thousand invested in your RRSP or other savings, your fees evolve as follows: stock and bond commissions to buy and sell that range from 0.5% to 3% per trade; no load mutual fund or commissions to buy and sell; mutual fund MERs that are closer to 1% per year than 3% per year; and indexed investments with MERs of 0.25% per year and little or no annual RRSP trustee fees.

Phase Three: Wealth Management

By phase three, you should not be paying commissions and fees for investing should be asset based. Asset-based fees are a percentage of the investment account or the investment. These fees are tiered (they decline as your account grows). They are often based on the investment portfolio totals, eliminating all product biases that are often the concern with the commission fee approach. This objectivity from separately paying for advice and paying for products aligns your objectives with that of your advisor. Asset-based fees are tax deductible for non-RRSP investment portfolios. Investment commissions (e.g. paying $50 for a stock trade) are not directly tax deductible. So asset-based fees can result in a lower after-tax cost compared to the old commission approach. Asset-based fees for investment accounts greater than $500,000 will range from 0.5% per year to 2.5% per year.

Phase Four: Wealth Transfer

At the time of your maximum wealth level, often $700,000 to multi-millions, you should be paying asset-based fees for professional advice. This is the fee approach of high net worth Canadians for the last one hundred years. Since much of your wealth will be non-RRSP money, asset-based fees will be fully tax deductible against other income on your tax return. Fees can range from 0.5% per year to 1.5% per year. Very large accounts may negotiate lower fees.

Fee Strategies for All Four Phases of Wealthbuilding

The investment fees that you pay are an important factor in wealthbuilding and warrant careful consideration. Some principles about fees go beyond specific phases of the wealthbuilding process, and I'd like to provide my opinion on these overriding principles below.

1. Know the amount you pay. By far, the most concerning fact about fees when I speak to Canadians is that most, if not almost all, don't know the amount they pay for investment fees in a year. In a society where we will go across the city to get a sale price on laundry detergent, many Canadians make little effort to understand the costs of investing.
2. Base your fee preferences on value, not on lowest cost. The financial press in Canada can often be seen as obsessively focused on low-cost investing. While I am thankful for their commitment to educating the public on this important topic, I don't appreciate the often one-sided

and narrow point of view they take on fees. In my opinion, it is not about getting the lowest fees, it is about paying for desirable value. For example:

a) financial planner who spends twelve hours creating a written financial plan that you value deserves to be paid more than a broker who doesn't do this.

b) financial planner who meets with you six times a year in your home deserves to be paid more than an advisor who meets with you once a year in their office.

c) A financial planner who helps you with estate matters, retirement planning, tax planning, and more, deserves to be paid more than an advisor who only helps you with investing.

3. Decide whether you are buying products or services. When you pay $29.95 to buy a stock at a discount brokerage, you are paying a transaction fee to buy a product. You get little or no financial planning, no personal meetings, and no caring relationship. You cannot expect a discounted fee when you are paying for the advice of an expert and all the time they will spend helping you. When you engage a financial planner, just like an accountant or lawyer, you are paying for their professional expertise and the time they spend on your file, not just the time meeting with you.

4. Prefer a fee-based approach to your investing costs, instead of commissions. Most Canadians incur a commission when they buy a stock, bond, or mutual fund. I am suggesting that you should purchase all of your investment products with zero commissions and, instead, pay separately for advice, achieving several powerful advantages:

a) A fee charged separately, whether an hourly rate, a flat fee, or a percentage of the investment account managed, is tax deductible every year if the advice is provided over non-RRSP or non-RRIF assets. When you incur a stock commission or a mutual fund load, it is not directly tax deductible. Most Canadians don't take advantage of this tax write-off. Most brokerages in Canada can offer you both ways.

b) Asset-based fees calculated as a percentage of your account (e.g. 1% per year x the market value of your portfolio) better aligns your advisor's goal with your own. Now you are both motivated to grow your total wealth since the advisor only makes more fees if the account grows. However, when commissions are levied on product sales, the advisor makes money whether you do or not.

c) Asset-based fees are often tiered, where commissions may not be. So, it is possible for larger accounts to pay much lower fees than smaller accounts. With traditional product commissions, you may not always get a price break for larger accounts.

Section Six: Wealthbuilding and Tax Efficiency
Phase One: Emerging Wealth

As you start into the wealthbuilding process you may find it difficult to invest money beyond your RRSP. For many Canadians, building their RRSP is their top savings priority for their early investing years. Since the RRSP is tax sheltered, there is a limited amount of tax-smart investing that you can practice. However, I do have a few great strategies for you to consider:

- Minimize fees charged inside your RRSP to preserve the tax-sheltered value. For mutual funds, refer back to the previous section where we reviewed the fees saved on "F" class versions of most mutual funds. With "F" class mutual funds, you can avoid having more than 1% of the total fees charged against your RRSP account, and, instead, pay this cost outside of the plan by cheque.
- Be aware that buying U.S. stocks inside your RRSP may trigger U.S. withholding tax on any dividends that you receive. And, because this is your RRSP, you cannot claim a foreign tax credit on your income tax for the U.S. tax paid. This withholding tax becomes a very expensive fee, as the tax is 15% to 25% of the dividends paid. You may want to hold your U.S. stocks outside of your RRSP or RRIF to avoid this.
- If you don't have the cash to maximize your RRSP contributions, consider a short-term loan. Use the loan proceeds to make the RRSP contribution and then pay back some of the loan with the tax refund you get. You should pay back the loan in a year or less.

Phase Two: Wealth Creation

As you develop taxable savings outside of your RRSP, and perhaps savings in your spouse's and children's names as well, you now have several tax-smart investing dimensions to consider. You and your family may all be in different tax brackets, presenting a number of tax-smart investing opportunities:

- Hold bonds and fixed-income investments inside your RRSPs to defer high taxation of interest.

- Maintain very little selling of investments outside of your RRSP to defer capital gains tax.
- Invest in Canadian stocks and dividend mutual funds to generate lower taxed dividend income.
- Note that U.S. dividends do not offer the same low taxation as Canadian dividends.
- Consider corporate class funds for non-RRSP money as a tool to defer more income tax. Review my previous book *Tax-Smart Investing* for a greater understanding of corporate class funds.
- Consider preferred shares, with their lower dividend taxation as a substitute, for some of your corporate bond portfolio.

Phase Three: Wealth Management

As your savings outside of your RRSP likely now exceeds your RRSP savings, tax-smart investing is more important than ever. Planning your investments should include a close review of your annual tax return to analyze what kind of investment income you are receiving and what the tax implications are. Pick your investment products and investment managers with an eye to taxes, inquiring about their tax-management techniques along with their investment philosophies. Avoid money managers that say tax doesn't matter. Many of Canada's most established money managers don't pay enough attention to the tax impact of their investment strategies. Look at Schedule 3 of your personal tax return each year: a lot of trades on this schedule may result in excessive and unnecessary capital gain taxes. To avoid excess portfolio taxation, hire money managers that don't trade as frequently to manage your non-RRSP and non-RRIF savings.

Keep your eye on the number of T5 and T3 slips you get every February. These slips are much more than a summary of investment income—they are a treasure chest of tax-planning opportunities. Redesign your investment portfolio to convert to lower taxed income types and investment amounts.

Phase Four: Wealth Transfer

At the end of your life, the biggest tax-smart investing strategies relate to avoiding death taxes and probate fees and taxes. Some of the tools you can use to avoid these costs include:

- Family trusts: They can be set up while you are alive or upon death through your Will. Besides tax-planning advantages, they offer legal protection of assets against divorce or bankruptcy.

- Holding companies: Any Canadian with a business should maintain a second Will covering only their small business shares. In many cases, you can avoid paying probate fees on this asset (a savings of as much as 1.5% of the value of the shares) on death. A holding company can also be utilized to hold your stocks, bonds, cottage, and more.
- Life insurance can't help you to avoid tax, but because it pays out tax free on your death, it will offset the impact of taxes. If you purchase permanent life insurance (instead of term), it is possible to create a tax sheltered component to the policy and further avoid taxation.

Section Seven: Wealthbuilding and Potential Flaws in the Investing Process

Do you ever wonder how Canada's largest pension funds invest the money they manage? Pension funds worldwide are some of the most sophisticated and wise investment managers. Generally, they utilize a logical investing process that is focused on their goals. Their plan is written down, focused, measured, disciplined, accountable, cost and risk sensitive, tax wise, and regularly monitored and adjusted.

You can use the same investment principles and follow the same methodology to be as successful at investing. Much of the high net worth community in Canada has been following this process of investing for decades.

Let's start out with an examination of some of the flaws of investing made at the different phases of wealthbuliding.

Phase One: Emerging Wealth

Investing at this stage is often nothing more than reactionary—a last minute rush to buy RRSPs and labour funds to avoid tax. The process is no process at all, it is simply a rush to buy products without a plan.

Phase Two: Wealth Creation

For many investors, phase two is a continuation of the bad investing habits from phase one, except now with more money. Costs are often ignored and commission based, offering poor tax efficiency. Many Canadians will end up with a portfolio of yesterday's hot products that can best be described as "hodge podge." When asked why they own the various products, few know why.

Phase Three: Wealth Management

Many Canadians at this established wealth level fail on many fronts: they often still have investment products that were suitable for them ten years ago, and they have failed to evolve to more appropriate solutions for their higher wealth levels. Further, they are paying costs that are often double what they should be for their wealth level. They lack any integrated financial planning, so there is no comprehensive strategizing occurring between taxes, estate, retirement, debt, investing, and more. Their accountant, broker, and insurance agents never speak together, so advice is fragmented and there is no overall plan. With major milestones, like retirement, only a short while away, it can often be too late to sort things out.

Phase Four: Wealth Transfer

The poorest investing habits that I regularly notice in Canadians at the highest wealth level and at the pinnacle of the wealthbuilding process are:

- Still buying retail versions of investment products when they have the clout to access institutional style professional money management.
- Paying fees that are too high for their wealth level.
- Lack of tax-smart investing strategies. Many affluent investors implement no tax-smart investing strategies at all, often because they utilize advisors that don't understand this aspect of investment planning.
- Failure to use specialized wealth advisors, instead of retail brokers, insurance agents, and financial planners. At the pinnacle of the wealthbuilding process, with more money than ever before, a specialist is needed.

The Professional Investing Process: Developing Your Own Carefully Crafted Investment Plan and Evolving It Through the Wealthbuilding Process

Why is it that before we buy a car, we decide what type we want, budget how much to spend, shop around for the best deal, and compare value? We do all this because we want to want to reach a goal of having a positive experience at a fair price.

Many Canadians, however, do not follow a similar process with their investments. They think that investing is about buying products and nothing else matters. Unfortunately, many financial advisors also rush to sell you a product when they meet you. Placing product ahead of process is clearly inappropriate. How do you know what to buy without having a blueprint or personal plan, first?

Discussing investment products is the last step you take after defining your personal goals, examining needs and resources, reviewing your financial "big picture" issues, and setting timelines around your plan.

Steps to Building a Proper Investment Plan:

Step 1: Goals
Define and prioritize your goals.

Step 2(A): Financial Plan
Examine your financial "big picture" and integrate all needs before focusing on investments.

Step 2(B): Cash Flow Analysis
Assess your current and future cash flow needs.

Step 3: Asset Allocation and IPS
Prepare an IPS (Investment Policy Statement) that serves as a blueprint to your investment profile, summarizing your risk tolerance, cash flow needs, target returns, liquidity needs, tax situation, and timeline for investing.

Step 4(A): Macro Investment Analysis
Examine the appropriate types of investment products suitable to your situation.

Step 4(B): Micro Investment Analysis
Examine specific products for your needs.

Step 4(C): Rebalancing
Develop a transition plan to move towards your new portfolio as set out in your IPS.

Step 5: Monitoring and Evaluation
Regularly measure and monitor the ongoing quality of your investment program for continued appropriateness.

Step 6: Review
Annually review the integrity of your financial solutions and new issues. Adjust your plans as required.

Step 1: Goals

Set goals and prioritize them. Then regularly evaluate progress towards your goals.

For example, if a fifty-year-old couple with one teenage child were to set some financial goals, they may tell you their goals are as follows:

- Save for a fruitful retirement in twenty years
- Pay off the mortgage by the end of this year
- Buy a new car next year
- Early retirement in fifteen years
- Fund the child's university education starting in five years

The goals are starting to take shape and are more clearly defined. However, there are many goals, and uncertainty remains about whether cash will be available for them all. Next divide the goals into essential and non-essential.

Essential: New car, university funding, and retirement planning.
Non-essential: Quick mortgage payoff and early retirement

Now the couple has a clearly defined set of goals that are prioritized. The next step would be to start examining cash flow resources and needs, and to strategize how to achieve the prioritized goals.

Investment Returns as Your Goals

Many Canadians use investment returns as their goals. I'm sure you've heard someone say, "I expect to get 12% a year from my investment portfolio." It's pretty easy to fall into this trap, since much of the mutual fund advertising highlights big return potentials, leaving us conditioned to want to strike it rich with big rewards. Chasing big returns is the wrong way to plan. First, big returns are rarely consistent. Second, along with the potential for big returns comes big risk. You can't expect to earn 30% a year without accepting the potential to lose 30% as well.

The most important question to ask about investment returns is: What annual target return do you need to earn in order to achieve your financial goals? You may be pleasantly surprised to learn you don't need to earn 15% a year to hit a financial homerun. You may only need 6% to easily reach your financial goals.

Step 2(A): Financial Plan

In my opinion, most Canadians fragment their personal finances in two ways:

1) As Canadians we are a pretty paranoid bunch. When we think about our investments, we tend to spread money around among several different institutions, because we don't want any one institution to know about everything we have. I support the idea of hiring several different minds to manage your money, but you can often do that through one institution. By fragmenting your investments among institutions you are hurting yourself in several ways:

- Not one of the institutions is in a position to give you advice on your entire financial situation because you have not told any of the institutions about the others.
- Hiring several institutions to manage money leads to piles of investment statements and a mess of uncoordinated investments.
- Many investment products today are priced according to the amount of money you invest in them, with lower fees applicable to larger investments. Also, some investment programs have high minimum investment amounts just to access them. If you are fragmenting your investments, you are likely paying more in fees, and you may be restricting yourself from accessing some of the best investments.

2) Canadians also fragment their personal finances by zeroing in on investments and failing to think about all aspects of their personal finances. Back on page 27, you saw a wheel where I have summarized all the aspects of one's personal financial picture: sometime in your life, some, all, or a few of these different aspects of your finances will come into play. Some, like taxes, you interact with everyday. Others, like life

insurance, only come into play at certain times. They all fit together to form your financial picture and must be integrated to properly maximize your opportunities. Together, these areas are bound by cash flow (the lifeblood of the system). Overall, it is essential that your financial picture is examined as a whole, not in pieces.

When Canadians think about their finances, they tend to think about their investments alone. Worse, they immediately focus on investment products without building a plan. But this fragmentation—where investments are examined without considering the other wedges around the circle of your financial life—leaves you making plans without fully considering all the variables. At least once a year you need to view your entire financial situation and examine the "big picture," whether you are cross-integrating goals and resources between different areas of importance, and whether you are progressing towards your goals in the different sections of your personal finances. Only by taking this integrated (not fragmented) approach, can you hope to take full advantage of all the opportunities.

A simple way to test whether you are a "fragmenter" is to count how many advisors you have. Do you have a life insurance agent, a couple of investment institutions that hold your money, an accountant to do your taxes, a lawyer for estate planning, a banker, a mortgage lender, and yourself? Have you ever put all these people in a room together and said, "Okay, talk to one another?" Doing that would put you on the road to integrating your personal finances. Alternatively, take steps to build a properly integrated financial plan with one competent advisor who can coordinate it all for you.

Step 2(B): Cash Flow Analysis

The second step to building a disciplined professional investment program is the preparation of a cash flow forecast. Cash flow, or money in and out of your daily spending and savings, is the lifeblood of your personal finances. Deciding where to spend your money daily, whether it be on expenses, life insurance premiums, savings for children, your RRSP, taxes, your mortgage, etc., binds these areas of personal finance together and forces you to evaluate them as an integrated plan, each topic dependant on cash flow.

To complete your cash flow forecast, have your financial planner assist you or do it yourself using a software package or a financial calculator. This basic exercise determines whether you will have enough money to achieve your future financial goals. In the case of planning for

A PROFESSIONAL INVESTMENT PROCESS

STEP 1 — GETTING TO KNOW YOU

OBJECTIVES
- Goal focusing and prioritization

PROCESS
- Assess financial and non-financial needs
- Clarify goals, constraints and preferences
- Establish relationship parameters
- Collect detailed personal data

RESULTS
- Establish expectations
- Build infinite knowledge of client

STEP 2 — EVALUATING YOUR "BIG PICTURE"

OBJECTIVES
- Cash flow optimization and integration of your financial issues and resources

PROCESS
- Cash flow forecasting and "what if" analysis
- Integration of investments with overall personal finances
- Regular monitoring of progression towards goals

RESULTS
- Cohesive, multi-layered financial plan where opportunities are maximized across your entire personal financial spectrum

STEP 3 — BUILDING YOUR FINANCIAL BLUEPRINT

OBJECTIVES
- Liquid reserves calculation
- Constraints assessment
- Tax analysis and minimization
- Volatility profiling

PROCESS
- After-tax optimization of your financial profile
- Development of a written personal financial blueprint (called "Investment Policy Statement"), serving as the infrastructure to your professional investment program

RESULTS

STEP 4 — IMPLEMENTING YOUR BLUEPRINT

OBJECTIVES
- Macro portfolio design
- Micro portfolio design
- Investment search and selection

PROCESS
- Determine appropriate types of investments for you
- Evaluate current investments against up to ten criteria
- Assessment of rebalancing requirements (short term and long term)
- Implementation of a new money manager search and selection process

RESULTS
- Action plan to move to a desired investment policy benchmark over an agreed upon period of time
- Multi-manager specialists hired for specific portfolio mandates

STEP 5 — KEEPING YOU INFORMED

OBJECTIVES
- Proactive annual monitoring analysis and communication

PROCESS
- Ongoing measuring and monitoring of financial solutions for continued effectiveness
- Constant behind-the-scenes money manager due diligence

RESULTS
- Regular personalized reporting of results
- Proactive personal contact and communication on results, progress and new opportunities

STEP 6 — KEEPING YOU ON TRACK

OBJECTIVES
- Proactive annual review and update on progress towards goals

PROCESS
- Complete annual review and analysis of all program aspects and personal finances in general for continued applicability and effectiveness of strategies and products

RESULTS
- Identify new opportunities
- Manage strategies and products and revise as necessary to keep you on track towards goals

retirement, you would examine your current savings and compare this to how much money you would like to live off each year in retirement. In completing the calculation, you need to account for inflation, annual savings, unusual cash flows, the time value of money, and assume an investment rate of return annually. You'll also need to calculate the impact of taxes on all the cash flows. It sounds hard to do, but this exercise can be completed in a few hours using the right tools.

- You will be able to conclude whether your current savings levels are adequate to reach your future goals.
- By re-doing the calculations using different investment returns, inflation rates, and savings levels, you can examine several "what if" scenarios to determine how you can improve your chance of reaching your goals.
- You will end up with several simple rules to live by all year long, such as a target rate of investment returns or a minimum level of savings each year. These simple targets are easier to keep track of and strive towards.

Unfortunately, many Canadians never do a cash flow forecast of their finances. They prefer to head towards their financial goals (e.g. retirement) with their eyes closed, planning to live off whatever they accumulate until then and hoping government benefits will help out. These people often discover that their poor planning requires them to live retirement in a constant cash crunch situation where they are forced to live off one-third or less of what they had been used to, so that they can't afford to take vacations or buy a new car. It doesn't have to be that way.

If you are wondering if you are headed down this disastrous road to retirement, here's a test: Do you know, based on what you have accumulated, whether you have adequate funds to live the retirement lifestyle you want? Do you know what you need to earn from your investments annually to ensure this future lifestyle? If you don't know the answers to these questions, I strongly urge you to find out. Don't just invest blindly—make sure the "math" that underlies all of your finances adds up.

Use Sensitivity Analysis

There are a lot of people today doing their own financial planning or utilizing financial planners. This is a great step towards organizing your personal finances, assuming the financial plan is done properly by someone appropriately qualified.

One shortcoming of many financial plans is a lack of sensitivity analysis around cash flow forecasts. Some clients are shown fancy forecasts by advisors or salespeople demonstrating what their financial future will look like based on a high annual compounded rate of return of 12% or more. Often this same sales pitch is given when consumers are being sold permanent life insurance, leveraged investing strategies (borrowing to invest), retirement planning, and systematic withdrawal plans out of your investment savings. Showing optimistic returns is only half the story.

Never make a purchase of an investment or insurance product without doing a cash flow forecast that examines what is called "a worst-case scenario." In other words, what is the risk if you don't achieve fantastic investment returns, if you can't save as much as planned, and so on? I call this balanced examination of all the scenarios—best-case, worst-case, and most-likely sensitivity analysis. It involves examining a series of different situations and results by adjusting the variables involved for possible outcomes.

For example, if you are forecasting your savings into the future to see how much you will have accumulated by age sixty-five, you would want to see the total savings you will have if you earn 10% per year, 8% per year, 6% per year, and so on, to better understand the range of possible results. When you review any financial forecasts, it is very important to examine several different possible outcomes in order to prepare you for a range of results.

Ultimately, performing sensitivity analysis on your cash flow forecasts will help you determine the minimum annual rate of return you need to earn, help you set a target rate of return, and let you dream about the possibilities by examining the best possible returns. Sensitivity analysis is a risk management technique that helps you determine what you really need your money to do for you, and then incorporate financial strategies that include only as much risk as you need to get you where you want to go.

Step 3: Asset Allocation and IPS

Before you can decide what investments to buy, you need a master plan, or blueprint, to follow—a plan that is uniquely you, such that your investments are custom made to match your financial needs. It is only after the creation of this financial blueprint that you can start examining the investment products needed to fill it.

Strategic Asset Allocation: The Backbone of Your Investment Plan

Strategic capital allocation (SCA) is the opposite of market timing (called tactical asset allocation). To understand SCA, let's define market timing. When an investor market times, they move their money in and out of the stock and bond market frequently, as they try to "time" the area of the market that will be the next big winner. Market timing is exciting, because you are always chasing the next big payoff. But do you ever catch it?

Here are a few quick reasons why you shouldn't try to market time:

- Research has proven that market timing is almost impossible to do successfully over the long term.
- If market timing was easy, all the world's brokers would be million-aires lying on a beach in Mexico with a fruity drink in their hand...they wouldn't need to manage your money!
- In addition to poor performance, market timing results in more frequent buying and selling of securities (which creates greater investment fees and commissions), time consumption, greater taxes from any gains realized on sales, and more aggravation as you stress out trying to make money but never seem to get there.

SCA, on the other hand, is the process of building an investment plan according to each investor's personal financial situation. Each investor has their own unique investment-print, like a fingerprint, that is unique to them, and, because of this individuality, their investment plan must be created to match their situation. Often when I look at an investor's portfolio, I ask them how they decided to put certain amounts of money in particular asset classes? Most often, investors don't have a clear answer. And that's what this strategy is all about—there should be specific reasons as to why you have invested in a particular asset class. The investment plan based on SCA is summarized in an Investment Policy Statement (IPS), and it should serve as the blueprint or infrastructure to your overall investment plan

The percentage that is invested in each asset class must be determined after an evaluation of some basic questions, like:

- What is your investment timeline for this money?
- Do you need to keep a lump sum aside for a short-term purchase?
- Do you need an annual income from this portfolio?
- What is your tax bracket, and do you have taxable and non-taxable investments?

- Are you married, and, if yes, does your spouse have investments that should be included in this plan?
- What is the level of your investment knowledge?
- What is your risk tolerance? Can you tolerate short-term investment losses and, if so, how much?
- What is the target return you need from your cash flow plan in order to meet your financial goals?

Once you have formulated answers to these and other questions, you and your financial planner will be able to put the major investment asset classes together in proportions that are unique to your situation. This is the only correct way to build a portfolio in my opinion. The sum of these proportions should add up to 100%, and the plan should incorporate all of your investment accounts, taxable and non-taxable, as well as those of your spouse.

Risk-Managed Investing

A risk-managed approach to investing is taking on only as much investment risk as one needs. Unfortunately, this is often lost among Canadian investors as they often underestimate their ability to stomach short-term losses, or worse, ignore risk completely as they shoot for double digit returns.

Building a risk managed investment portfolio simply means two things: 1) assessing your risk tolerance (how much money you can stand to lose should the markets tumble over the short term); and 2) setting a target annual investment return based on cash flow forecasting of future needs. Both of these factors should be put together to create a portfolio where the expected return (historical results per asset class as well as future expectations) and risk (measured through volatility of returns using standard deviation, or more simply, the number and extent of past losses) are put together in proportions that match your needs and tolerances.

Creation of an Investment Policy Statement: The Written Blueprint for Your Plan

Think of an Investment Policy Statement (IPS) as your blueprint for building an investment plan and purchasing investment products. The IPS consists of three written parts. It is prepared long before you consider buying any investment products. After all, how can you build anything without a blueprint?

The first part of the IPS is a summary of your personal financial characteristics and risk profile. You should define personal net worth; investing timeline; marginal tax rate on taxable income; needs for ongoing cash flow from investments; risk tolerance for investing; liquidity needs from investments; and any other notable factors about personal finances. It should also include your determination of a target rate of return from your portfolio.

The second part of the IPS consists of listing all the major asset classes and the recommended percentage of your investable wealth that should be invested in each asset class for the long term according to your personal profile from section one. Your entire investable wealth should include all the money in your and your spouse's RRSPs, your investment accounts, real estate holdings (except your main home), pension plans, corporations, trusts, and other savings. Don't make an investment plan for each spouse—you should think of everything as one big plan.

Once the percentages are assigned to each asset class and the total adds up to 100%, some financial planners will assign ranges around these percentages to allow for some variation. For example, if any investor assigns 20% of their money to be invested in U.S. equity investments, a range of 18% to 22% may be tolerable. These ranges are put in for two reasons: to allow for some minor market timing if you can't give up the thrill of market chasing completely and as a re-balancing mechanism. As the markets rise and fall, the original percentages invested in each asset class will change. Setting ranges of variation serves as a trigger for rebalancing the portfolio to the target policy by selling investments in asset classes that are too high and buying those outside of the set ranges.

The third part of the IPS consists of signatures. The IPS can serve as a written contract between you and your advisor, you and your money manager, or just for your own records. The signatures bring accountability to the parties involved. You, as the client, sign it, and all other parties involved sign it as well. In many cases, failure to follow an established IPS can be grounds for legal action.

The IPS tells you what proportion of your money you need to invest in each major asset class in order to meet your preferences and financial goals. Without it, you are buying investment products without any organization or discipline, without being able to assess progress or judge value. Having an IPS links your personal finances with your investment selections in a logical methodical way that makes sense. I'm not sure how anyone can properly invest without one.

STEP 4(A): Macro Investment Analysis

Once your IPS is developed, it is time to purchase investment products according to the policy you have created. Step 4(A) examines investments from a macro point of view. In other words, before purchasing one of 5,000 mutual funds or 2,000 stocks, do you know if you even belong in mutual funds or stocks in the first place? There are a variety of products out there to choose from.

Selecting the Right Product Type for You

Macro investment selection consists of sorting out the types of investments that best suit you. Mutual funds are one type of investment. GICs and wrap programs are others. Direct stock investment is another type. You can also index invest. There are other options too. Considering the right types of investments before purchasing specific brands is something that is often overlooked as Canadians buy investment products.

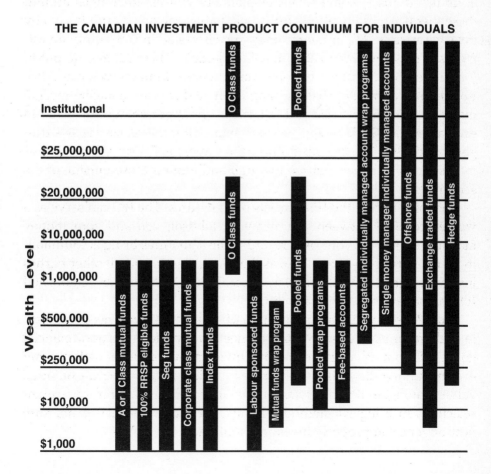

THE CANADIAN INVESTMENT PRODUCT CONTINUUM FOR INDIVIDUALS

I have included a decision tree chart that displays many of the different types of investments available in Canada today. Regardless of who's selling them, they are included on this chart. Depending on how you answer some basic questions about your investing preferences, you can follow a logical path to finding the type of product best suited to you. Almost every type of product sold in Canada today can fit on this chart, regardless of what institution offers them.

To find out where you belong on the chart, prioritize the following criteria according to your own personal preferences—1 being most important and 6 being least important.

- Minimize fear of losing some of your money due to market volatility and investment risk
- Minimize total annual cost of your investments
- Tax efficiency to minimize your tax bill on your investment returns
- Simplicity in owning an investment solution that is easy to manage and follow with low time involvement
- Direct access to money managers buying your investments so you know what is going on daily

Owning Individual Stocks

I don't think the average investor should build their own stock and bond portfolio because there are several variables that, once considered, make this the improper approach. Below are two such variables:

- Fees: A single investor with a small pool of cash to invest will pay higher trading commissions and get poorer investment choice than a huge institutional money manager investing billions of dollars of people's money together.
- Risk: A single investor with a small pool of cash to invest may only have enough money to buy a few stock positions. Should one or a few of these positions blow up, the small investor's finances could be devastated. Small investors are better suited to mutual funds where their money is combined with other investors' to allow all investors to buy many stock and bond positions, reducing the likelihood of significant loss if one stock falters.

There are only a few situations, in my opinion, where Canadians should be buying individual stocks versus funds and pools. Here are some of those situations:

- Where an investor has $1 million dollars or more such that there is enough money to purchase adequate amounts of stocks and bonds in several asset classes, using more than one money manager to manage the money. Purchasing twenty stocks in each category ensures adequate diversification to balance investment risk. Having adequate cash to buy larger quantities of each stock ensures a more reasonable commission price on trades. And using several different money managers offers varying management styles to also minimize risk of loss.

- It's okay to tinker with a few stocks as part of a "play money" account if the account total is a small portion of your overall portfolio—say less than 10% of the overall market value. Since I know many people want to have a little fun in the markets, many of my clients maintain a separate account for themselves to invest and to "go crazy" with. Buy all the technology stocks you want, but limit the account size to a low enough level such that a complete loss of the funds would not be a financial setback that you can't recover from.

- Senior executives and employees of some companies can purchase or are gifted shares or stock options of the company they work for. This can be a very lucrative road to wealth if the shares shoot up in value or the company goes public very successfully. That is what the employees wish for, but it may not always end up that way. One of the drawbacks of holding your company's stock is that you may have a lot of money tied up in one stock. Often an employee is faced with deciding what to do with excessive amounts of company stock: the high investment risk of having all your money in one stock; the possible political risk of following management's expectations to hold the stock; and potential for future returns and the tax implications of selling now. There is no magic answer about the best route to follow—it depends on the employee. A conservative strategy is to sell a little bit of the company stock each year and reinvest in a diversified portfolio. Another strategy is to never let the value of the company stock exceed 35% of the total value of your savings. If it does, sell the excess and reinvest in a diversified portfolio to reduce risk.

- Finally, it is fine to hold a selection of stocks if they are mixed with a properly diversified portfolio of mutual funds or pools (active or indexed) as well. This ensures a diversified portfolio overall.

Indexing

If you ever watch the news on TV at night, you may hear the broadcaster mention that the TSE 300 rose or that the Dow in the U.S. went down. Both indexes are a collection of powerful companies in Canada and the U.S. collectively tracked and used as a measure of the progress of an economy. The TSE 300 is the 300 leading companies in Canada representing most of the major industries in Canada. All of these companies trade daily on Canada's stock exchanges and their values changes daily.

There are mutual funds that exist that purchase the same investments as the indexes, called index funds. Importantly, these index funds rarely trade the companies they own because they must match the index and the index only changes when a company in Canada's big 300 goes bankrupt, merges with another, or a smaller company grows bigger than one of the 300. This is called passive or indexed management because of the low turnover rate and lack of active money managers managing the funds. Non-index funds have active money managers and researchers running the funds, and they regularly change their investments as the fund money managers try to pick stocks that may outperform the market or indexes. The dilemma for you is which to own—active managers or indexed products?

In my opinion, every Canadian should own a combination of active and passive products. Here's some of the reasons why you should consider some indexed products for your portfolio:

- Indexed products can sometimes be purchased at a fraction of the cost of the average actively managed funds. In some cases a fee reduction of 2% per year is possible, an extra 2% that stays in your pocket every single year!
- Most indexed products have naturally low turnover since the stocks in the indexes rarely change. With little changes to the portfolio each year, your annual tax bill decreases and after-tax return increases as compared to some actively managed portfolios.
- The cost reduction, coupled with lower taxation, means index products generate after-tax returns that, over longer time periods, can be superior to many actively managed products.
- Since indexed products are broadly invested across all major industries of a country (oils, forestry, consumer products, high tech, industrials, etc.) they offer broad exposure, like a blanket across a country's economy. This extensive diversification reduces your downside if only one part of an economy decline. Actively managed products can also protect investors during down times by holding larger amounts of cash than indexed products.

By combining both active and passive investment products, you will create an overall investment portfolio that is risk managed, cost effective, tax efficient, and where the performance is stable.

No One Needs GICs

You are being penalized if you buy a GIC. You always have been. Canadians have purchased GICs for the last fifty years because of the attraction of that $60,000 CDIC (Canadian Deposit Insurance Corporation) guarantee, where the government guarantees you won't lose your $60,000. Now I'm telling you that coverage from CDIC is actually a penalty. That's because it is a federal organization that is offering to protect you for $60,000 because you are investing with a Canadian financial institution, instead of investing with the government directly. But they are only prepared to cover you for $60,000. Had you invested with the government directly by buying a Government of Canada bond, for example, there would be no $60,000 limit, and you would be insured for your entire investment amount, whatever it is. You would, for example, be insured for $1 million if you bought a Government of Canada bond. So why would anyone ever buy a GIC that only offers a partial guarantee?

There are even more reasons to buy bonds or bond funds, instead of buying GICs:

- Market traded bonds offer one- to thirty-year maturities, while GICs only offer one- to five-year maturities. Bonds offer more flexibility in planning your finances.
- The bonds I am telling you to consider are market-traded bonds—not Canada Savings Bonds. Market-traded bonds fluctuate in daily value based on market interest rates, and they come in all varieties: federal government, provincial government, corporate, international, etc. Since these bonds are market traded, should interest rates fall in comparison to the bond you own, there is the potential to enhance your return with an additional capital gain on top of the interest income. That's how many of the bond mutual funds have obtained double digit returns in the 1990s, through a mix of interest return and capital gains. GICs do not offer this extra return potential.
- Bond portfolios should be diversified just like equity portfolios. GICs offer only one type. An investor can purchase bonds from around the world, in all varieties. This diversification of your bond portfolio can help to enhance yield, while managing risk. This same kind of diversification is not possible with GICs.

In my opinion, there is rarely a good time to purchase a GIC instead of a bond like a Government of Canada bond. The only advantage a GIC offers is that they are available over the counter at the local bank, while bonds require you to open a brokerage account. This small inconvenience, however, is well worth the advantages of owning bonds instead of GICs.

Bonds or Bond Mutual Funds

A lot of people buy bond mutual funds thinking they can't lose money because they are buying bonds. On a short-term basis, in many cases, you can lose money on bond funds depending on market interest rate fluctuations. Bond funds generally consist of a collection of market traded government and/or corporate bonds. The bond manager managing the fund tries to anticipate changes in interest rates and actively trades in and out of a variety of bonds to enhance returns. If she/he is successful the investor will earn a capital gain in addition to the interest income from the bond. If he/she is unsuccessful, the investor will be left with a capital loss in addition to the interest income.

Bond funds generate two kinds of return for an investor. There is the interest rate on each bond, commonly referred to the coupon rate, and it is this type of return that Canadians are most used to when they thinking of fixed-income investments. In addition to this, active buying and selling of bonds by the fund manager can also generate capital gains and capital losses depending on interest rate movements and other factors. It is this active trading that can lead to big returns from bond funds when bonds on their own are left far behind with just an interest return.

In my opinion, you should own both bonds and bond funds.

A bond fund should be held by investors who have greater than a five-year timeline to invest in. This time frame will smooth returns on average. Since bond funds are actively traded and bring an element of risk to investing, ensuring you will hold them for several years should protect against the odd negative return or less than expected return.

Consider owning individual bonds (instead of bond funds) when you need the money in less than five years. When you hold bonds to maturity you eliminate the market risk associated with active trading and get less sleepless nights. In other words, you know exactly how much money you will get on maturity and with each interest payment. Consider a series of bonds, each maturing one after the other annually, to be used for your short-term cash flow needs.

Here are a few examples:

- If you are middle aged and retirement is twenty-five years away, go with bond funds for long-term enhanced returns compared to just buying bonds.
- If you are sixty-five and retired, you are five years away from drawing on your RRIF, take the fixed-income portion of your portfolio and hold half of it in diversified bond funds and half in bonds directly. Have several bonds maturing each year to fund any liquidity needs or larger cash flow needs in the following five years.
- If you are thirty-two and saving for a home purchase in two years, invest all your home deposit savings in a single bond, maturing around the time you plan to purchase the home.

RRSP Foreign Content

Technically, the foreign content limit on RRSPs and RRIFs is still limited to 30% (based on original cost of the investments in the account) according to the Income Tax Act.

However, several new mutual funds, called clone funds, have been developed in the last few years that qualify as Canadian content for your RRSP or RRIF (not contravening the foreign content rules), while the return generated by the fund is linked to a foreign investment giving you foreign returns.

These clone funds use derivatives such as forward contracts to replicate foreign returns while not actually investing in foreign investments. A forward contract is a contract within your mutual fund that offers a return equal to the change in a specific foreign investment without actually investing in that investment. With derivatives some of your money is invested in these contracts, while most of the money in the fund is held as cash (or near cash securities) as collateral for the contract. In this way, the fund is technically never over the 30% foreign content limit due to the large cash reserves, yet the return you earn is completely foreign based since it is generated from the forward contract on expiry. This serves to provide you with foreign diversification using a Canadian based asset.

There are lots of clone funds available today for your RRSP or RRIF, a simple way to find them is to examine the title or name of a fund company's mutual funds. If the fund has "RSP" in the title, it usually means it is a foreign fund that is 100% RRSP eligible. Use these funds to maximize your RRSP foreign content far beyond 30%. Most Canadian fund companies now offer these clone funds.

However, be cautious. First, these funds often charge a higher MER as the price for greater foreign content. Select these foreign clone funds wisely to justify any increased cost. Second, the return on these clone funds is taxed as regular income and does not receive the tax benefits that a similar non-cloned fund would offer if it generated dividends and capital gains. Given this, use the clone funds only for RRSPs and RRIFs where all tax is sheltered, and use the similar real funds for a taxable portfolio so that you have to access the preferential tax aspects.

Discretionary or Non-Discretionary Investment Management

The difference between discretionary and non-discretionary investing is based on whether you want your investment manager to be able to trade (buy and sell investments) without your permission, on your behalf, or with your consent.

A discretionary account is one where the money manager has the authority to trade securities on your behalf without your transactional authorization. Normally you provide them with investing guidelines or they assess your needs and tolerances, build a portfolio and make changes to it on your behalf. Mutual funds and their money managers are really discretionary money managers, since you have no say as to what they put in the portfolios you buy from them.

A non-discretionary account is one where the money manager cannot trade anything without your understanding and complete approval. If they traded without your authorization you could potentially sue them for this violation. Most brokerage accounts are non-discretionary accounts and that's why your advisor must consult you on all trading.

Deciding whether you want discretionary or non-discretionary accounts depends on your personal preferences. If you want greater control over your money management to the extent that the trader needs to call you every time they want to transact in your account, so be it. But if you would rather not be involved to this extent, discretionary accounts may be more appropriate for you.

Many people settle somewhere in the middle by owning mutual funds that offer discretionary money management and by hiring a financial advisor to assist them in fund selection according to their financial profile, to monitor the funds and money managers, to ensure the portfolio is tax effective and meets their financial planning needs, to communicate results, and to discuss portfolio changes with them.

Step 4(B): Micro Investment Analysis

In the previous section you sorted out the "type" of investments best suited to your financial profile according to your IPS. Now it is time to consider the actual investments to purchase to fill in the IPS.

In Canada today, many investors (and advisors as well) buy products without detailed background analysis. It is critical that investors figure out what they need first, set some guidelines, and then analyze all the choices according to their needs.

Selecting Products

Let's assume that your savings are $20,000 and you are best suited to own mutual funds in general, on a macro basis, as determined in the last section. Deciding what funds to purchase is a two-step process. First, you need to determine what your needs are according to your financial profile—what types of funds match your tax position, risk tolerance, cash flow needs, investing timeline, and need for liquidity in your portfolio. Second, you need to evaluate all the funds according to several criteria. Consider these criteria as a filter that you will use to "weed out" all the poor quality funds of a particular type.

Below are my criteria for evaluating funds—qualitative and quantitative. It doesn't matter what fund you look at, the criteria never change, so comparisons are easy:

Qualitative Criteria

Far more important than performance are the factors that create the money management organizational infrastructure and the company culture. If these factors are put together appropriately, they help to repeat the long-term consistent performance we all want. So it's these qualitative factors that are more important, and they often require visiting the investment product's or money manager's premises and asking them to complete the evaluation.

1. Research capabilities of the money manager managing the fund. Teams of highly qualified researchers located around the globe are generally preferred to managers reading research reports while sitting in a glass tower in Toronto, Canada.
2. Profitability of the money manager managing the fund. A well-financed money manager means lots of money for research, equipment, and happily paid employees.
3. Size of the money manager's pension fund business. If a manager has a huge pension clientele, it usually means the pension funds have approved of the manager. Pensions are often shrewd investors.

4. Ownership structure of the money manager's company. Money management companies that offer share ownership in the company are preferred as they ensure employees stay put.
5. Rate of turnover of employees at the money manager. A large employee turnover is a bad sign, especially if money managers and researchers are leaving.
6. Money manager's style and philosophy about investing. It is important to understand the manager's approach to investing—you don't want a bunch of managers all picking stocks the same way.

Quantitative Criteria

1. Five-year or ten-year historical performance. A shorter time period may not give a fair evaluation of a manager's ability over complete business cycles.
2. Risk-adjusted return. It is necessary to analyze a manager's historical returns according to the amount of risk that has been incurred.
3. Number of years the money manager has managed the fund. If a fund has a great track record, is the current manager the one responsible for it?
4. Annual cost and MERs. Add load fees to MERs to see what you will pay in total and then comparison shop.
5. Portfolio turnover. In your taxable portfolio it makes sense to have low portfolio turnover of 25% a year or less to maximize after-tax returns. Check what your portfolio turnover is—the rate at which the manager buys and sells inside the portfolio.

One Money Manager or Fifteen?

Never place all your money with only one money manager—one money manager can never consistently outperform year to year. When dealing with your wealth, the stakes are higher than ever because it is your life savings, warranting a risk managed investment plan in all cases.

Investing with several money managers allows you to benefit from different management styles, different expertise, different perspectives, different research capabilities, and so on. By owning more than one, you still have another to offset any negatives.

The exact number of managers you need depends on several factors, including how much you have to invest and your personal financial objectives. Here are several factors to consider in deciding how many managers you need to hire:

- If one of your concerns is to minimize your investment risk, consider investing with several money managers that vary according to asset class mandates, geographic mandates, sector mandates, investment management style mandates, and so on. Having a little bit of your money invested with managers who take a slightly different perspective, lays your money across the broad market, limiting your exposure to a significant loss in any one area.

- In some cases, your wealth level affects your access to quality money managers. The number of money managers you are able to hire may be affected by how much money you have to invest, and how much money you give to each manager.

- If you own several money managers in one asset class (e.g. Canadian equity), you need to be sensitive to excessive duplication within your portfolio. It may not be wise to own the same stock seven times within seven different mutual funds or investment accounts. This level of detail is not always explored by investors, but needs to be.

- As a rule of thumb, the average investor would be well served by up to ten different mutual funds or other money managers, each hired for a specific role within your portfolio. However, depending on your investor profile (as defined in your IPS), you may be adequately served with fewer or more managers.

- Ensure each money manager or product in your portfolio plays a specific role. Know exactly why you own something—there should be a disciplined and professional reason for every product you own. If you don't have a reason, this could be the first indication that you lack a professional investment plan. (Note that buying a specific product because a sector is "hot" is not a competent reason to own something.)

- Beware of a money manager that says you only need him/her to manage all your money. Remember, they have big personal financial incentive to say this to you. Also keep in mind that if their financial house is burning down behind closed doors, they may not tell you this because they don't want you to leave. Having a personal financial advisor to help monitor your money managers can add a level of objectivity to your investment plan that is worthy of consideration.

- Put a financial advisor between you and your money managers. Someone needs to objectively evaluate your money manager solutions on a regular basis for the reason mentioned in the previous point. Having a professional advisor on your team representing you is a powerful ally to keep your money management solutions consistent with your needs and expectations.

How To Buy Investments

There are many organizations through which you can purchase investments and the investments of competitors. The landscape in Canada for purchasing investment products is becoming a collection of financial supermarkets where you can buy everyone's products through one "store." Sorting out which store you should deal with is a matter of prioritizing services that matter to you.

Who to Hire

Financial Planner; Investment Specialist; Private Wealth Consultant; Financial Advisor; Insurance Advisor; Registered Financial Planner; Certified Investment Manager; Private Client Advisor; Investment and Insurance Consultant; Certified Financial Planner; Personal Financial Advisor; Registered Investment Consultant; Broker; Insurance Agent; Personal Wealth Manager—I could go on and on as to what you may see on your financial advisor's business card today. And then there are the business card designations: CA, RFP, CIM, FCSI, LLB, BA, CGA, CFA, CIMA, PFP, CFP, CHFC—the choice is overwhelming!

The following criteria will help you to evaluate financial experts:

1. Academic background. Ask potential advisors about their schooling. Give more weight to a four-year university degree in finance or economics than to someone who is taking three months of night courses on the world of investing.
2. Work experience. Ask potential advisors to outline their experience dealing with clients just like you.
3. Professional development. Advisors continue to attend training until they retire, and they have to report what they do each year to their professional association. Question your potential advisor about the associations they belong to and what courses they took this year to maintain their credentials. If they have done nothing, or don't belong to a professional association, don't hire them.
4. Client referrals. Ask for twenty client referrals for you to investigate. Don't ask for just three like many people recommend. By asking for twenty, you can select three for yourself, and have a greater chance of getting objective testimonials.
5. How are you paid? You definitely want an advisor and a company that can offer you investment products from their company and other companies as well. Avoid an organization that just wants to collect all your money and put it in their products alone.

6. What is your specialty? Beware of advisors who can do all your financial planning, fill all your investment needs, provide tax tips, complete an estate plan, and sell you insurance. Each one of these areas is a full-time career, so an advisor will likely know a little bit about each, but will lack a depth of understanding for each topic.
7. Research their credentials. All the designations on a business card have been issued by an association. Call the association to find out if your proposed advisor is registered in good standing. And ask them what the designation means.
8. Don't hire an advisor based on a friend or family referral. Many Canadians hire advisors based on word-of-mouth referrals. Don't rely on others to find your advisors—everyone's preferences are different, so do you own hunting.

Full Service or Do It Yourself?

The key criteria to deciding if you should hire a financial planner is whether you want a helping relationship or not—do you want someone to give you buy/sell advice, to monitor your investments and recommend changes, to assist with your cash flow needs, to reduce the time you spend on your finances, to offer some financial planning, and to "hold your hand" through rocky investment times?

If the answer is yes, then you want a "full service" advisory relationship and should be willing to pay for it. The fair going rate for an ongoing advisory service is no more than 1% per year on the market value of your investments. This fee may be tax deductible in some cases.

If the answer is no, then you may be a do-it-yourself investor. With the emergence of personal finance on the Internet, financial planning software, and discount brokerages in Canada in the 1990s, many Canadians are moving to a more self-empowered approach that has them doing their own investment research, reading books on financial planning, and buying investment products on their own.

As discount services and full services clash in the fight for investors, the cost of investing has begun to decrease. Advice has become a commodity, where many investors expect it for free. This is unfair to advisors as clients try to apply discount prices to full-service advisors.

Although being a do-it-yourself investor is admirable because of the control you exert and the involvement you have with your finances, don't get so involved that:

- you start spending six hours a week on your investments. Hobby or not, get a life! You should not be a prisoner of your money. Hire some-

one to ease the burden and get you back on the golf course.
- you think that a second opinion from an experienced advisor can't help you. If you have a regular job and tinker on your investments on Sunday evenings, you can't possibly know all the investments out there, recent changes to tax laws, new estate planning strategies, and so on. On a regular basis, seek a second opinion from a qualified advisor so that you know you are on the right track and not missing anything. Be prepared to pay for this opinion, whether they find anything wrong or not.

Step 4(C): Rebalancing

You need to assess the quality and suitability of your existing portfolio(s) within your new investment plan.

Here are a number of criteria for you to consider while completing this analysis:

- Past performance: Have your portfolio investments performed better than a similar passive index? Have they been better than a collection of similar managers managing similar investments? Has the current manager been responsible for the entire period of good performance?
- Future performance: Does the same infrastructure that resulted in positive performance at the money manager company remain in place (same people, process, management, research, etc.)?
- Cost: Are the annual and other costs of the product reasonable?
- Fees to dispose of: Can you exit or sell the current products without incurring a lot of fees? If exit fees are high, it may warrant holding the investment longer until fees decline.
- Tax efficiency: First, is a sale of the product going to trigger a large tax liability that could be deferred if you didn't sell today? Second, is the investment tax effective to own on an ongoing basis in your taxable portfolio?
- Risk: Are your current investments too risky or not risky enough, based on your current financial profile and risk tolerance? This requires an examination of the type of investments you own, as well as the investments themselves.
- Appropriate type of investment for your needs: It is critical that you end up with the right type of investments, long before you buy an investment. If, for example, you own stocks, you may realize it is more appropriate for you to own equity mutual funds based on your wealth level and other variables.

- Duplication: If you own six Canadian equity mutual funds, for example, you may own th same six shares of the XYZ Bank. This is a potentially costly duplication that needs to be minimized.
- Suitability to your new plan: Depending on what your new plan involves, your existing investments may fit or not. Don't rush to sell every one of your old investments because someone tells you to. Some new investment programs today require you to transfer in cash only. Think twice about going into these programs if it requires you to sell what are otherwise solid investments.
- Ability to easily purchase: Some new investments are highly desirable, but just not practical to purchase for one reason or another. It may be a personal decision as to whether you want to go this extra mile.

There are generally two schools of thought when it comes to the timing of placing trades in your portfolio:

1. Wait until it feels right. Maybe markets are too high today and you'll plan to invest right after the next crash.
2. Invest immediately regardless of market conditions.

I support the second philosophy in most cases. Trying to guess which markets will be hot and when is nearly impossible to do consistently. Research has shown that had you ignored the short-term fluctuations of the market, you would have made far more money by just putting your money in the markets (stock and bonds) and leaving it there. If your timeline for investing is long enough it really doesn't matter what the markets are like today or tomorrow.

The "invest now" philosophy is difficult to swallow because investors left on their own let their emotions get involved with investing. Working with a financial advisor ensures that logic and reason are not clouded by sudden emotion. The facts clearly show that, historically over the long-term, there is no need to worry about what happens today or tomorrow if you are going to be invested for quite a while. No one knows when the markets will go up or down, but most experts believe that markets will generally go up over the long term.

Step 5: Monitoring and Evaluation

No matter how good an investment is, there are many variables that can effect it—the manager can die, jump to a competitor, or simply fall out of favour and underperform. You can never just buy something and then forget about it. Even the best investment solutions require an ongoing "watchdog" who will measure and monitor the products to ensure they remain excellent investments, and that they match your changing needs. Further, the rapidly changing financial landscape in Canada is resulting in thousands of emerging investment products. Investors need to be proactive in examining these new opportunities for their situation.

Regular Checkups

The state of financial services is evolving very rapidly in Canada. Here are some examples of how the times are changing:

- Hundreds of new mutual funds now exist since this time last year.
- The Income Tax Act can change daily, adding new rules and opportunities for tax planning. While many Canadians associate tax changes with the annual federal budget, the government can, and often does, put forth new tax rules each week.
- Court cases can occur to change laws that affect a Canadian's estate planning wishes.

Once a year, consult financial experts for a "checkup" on all the different aspects of your personal finances: retirement plans, investment programs, estate wishes, children's savings, tax plannings, and others. It will take only a few minutes to highlight changes that may impact your situation and result in more money in your pocket. Here are a few simple pointers:

- Consult a tax accountant for a quick review of your personal tax situation for new opportunities.
- Consult a life insurance agent for a quick review of insurance levels you have and their appropriateness.
- Consult an investment advisor semi-annually to review your overall asset allocation and risk profile, as well as the quality of your investments.
- Consult a lawyer to consider changes needed to your Will/power of attorney based on changes to your personal wishes or to laws affecting your wishes.

Between annual reviews, you want to review your personal financial strategies for life events. A life event is when something abnormal (good or bad) occurs in your life, such as marriage, death, births, changing jobs, moving out of the country or province, buying a home, and so on. These are events that are different from your everyday life, and thus warrant a special look at your personal finances.

For example, if someone gets married:

- Their tax situation may be significantly affected due to the sharing of some tax credits.
- Their estate situation is affected with a new spouse potentially becoming the Will beneficiary.
- Their investment situation is affected since they will want to explore joint investments and spousal RRSPs.
- Their insurance situation is affected since one spouse may be dependant on the other, calling for increased insurance.

Very often, Canadians fail to proactively review their personal finances, forgetting that their situation may have changed or that the landscape and rules may have changed. It is in your best interest to spend a couple of hundred dollars each year for a tune-up to ensure you are maximizing opportunities.

Regular Reviews

Any great money manager can fall apart anytime. As soon as tomorrow you could learn that the entire management team of your favourite mutual fund is leaving the company to start up their own company with new mutual funds, and the fund you are in will now be managed by Junior Greenhorn, just out of university. Not quite who you had expected to manage your life savings. It can happen. It has happened. No money manager is a guaranteed safe investment.

Fees are another factor worth considering when you revisit your investment plan regularly. It is important to have the flexibility to buy and exit from investment products inexpensively, should the need arise. Make sure you research any product fees that may hinder your flexibility with your investments.

Overall, you need to proactively monitor and evaluate all investment solutions on an ongoing basis because:

- good investments can go bad.
- new investments may evolve and be more suitable for you.
- investment rules and government regulations may change that affect you.

- your investment profile may change (e.g. you become more/less risk tolerant, or your portfolio cash flow needs change).
- good or bad market conditions may warrant rebalancing in your portfolio to move the mix of investments back towards your desired investment policy.
- other aspects of your personal finances may change requiring adjustment to your IPS. For example, new tax rules may come out affecting the tax-effectiveness of your investment strategy.

Staying on Track With Your IPS

In earlier sections I talked about how every investor should have a written IPS that matches their personal profile. So, for example, someone might have a profile for all of their and their spouse's investments that looks like this:

Asset Class	Percentage of Wealth Allocated	Permitted Range
Cash	5 %	0% to 10%
Fixed Income	45 %	40% to 60%
Canadian Equity	10 %	5% to 10%
U.S. Equity	30 %	30% to 40%
International Equity	10 %	5% to 20%
Total	100%	

The permitted range outlines the acceptable levels that each asset class can rise and fall to before rebalancing should occur to bring weightings back to the policy recommendations.

So now, let's say six months later, due to rises and falls in the markets your asset mix looks like this:

Cash	4%
Fixed Income	38%
Canadian Equity	12%
U.S. Equity	42%
International Equity	4%
Total	100%

This means that if you put 30% of your total wealth in U.S. equities and the market rises high enough that the percentage of U.S. equities according to market value became 42%, your profile would dictate that you should rebalance back to your original IPS since this level is outside your permitted range.

Rebalancing has a positive impact on your portfolio in several ways and rebalancing should be considered whenever your asset class weightings exceed the recommended ranges.

- Rebalancing ensures your portfolio never gets too risky or too conservative based on your IPS, which is a reflection of your risk tolerance.
- Forced rebalancing makes you sell high and buy low, which is a desired effect, but few of us seem to do this in a disciplined way.

Many institutions offer a rebalancing service for your portfolio that can be done manually or automatically by a computer. These can both be useful services, however be wary of the extra fees charged for the process. I'd rather see you do it yourself, at no extra cost, so evaluate the services available to you, or shop around.

Unfortunately, rebalancing may trigger taxes if you are selling an asset with accrued tax liabilities attached. While triggering taxes from investing is something I usually try to minimize, tax concerns are less important than risk issues. Failure to rebalance a portfolio may result in excessive risk of financial loss due to extra high weightings in some asset classes. Always rebalance if the risk in your portfolio exceeds your comfort levels. Your fears of loss overshadow taxes and fees.

STEP 6: Review

There are many reasons why you need to review your investments, and all other parts of your personal finances on a proactive basis, at least once a year. Here's why:

- Changes to the Income Tax Act can occur any business day of the year and may impact the level of taxes you pay, highlight new tax-planning strategies for your situation, or affect the tax you incur on your investments.
- Your money manager or your investments can explode overnight, such that constant monitoring of your portfolio is required. Solid investment picks one day can breakdown over time.
- If you add more money to your investment portfolio, an annual review may be the time to examine new investment considerations for this money. And even if there is no new money, new developments in investments require a constant re-evaluation of whether some of the new products are better suited to your needs than current holdings.

- As you age, your financial profile may change, warranting adjustments to your portfolio holdings. For example, when you retire, often your portfolio changes from being growth oriented to income oriented, since in retirement you now will need to draw an income from your portfolio. This change in profile usually requires a significant change to your investment portfolio.

- Market conditions will make parts of your portfolio rise and fall, moving your original asset class allocations away from your IPS benchmarks. Regular rebalancing of your portfolio is required to move the portfolio back to your IPS.

- On a regular basis it is necessary for you to evaluate progress towards your financial goals or retirement. This is accomplished for your retirement by annually forecasting your savings growth into the future using assumed rates of return and inflation to predict how much money you will have to meet your goals. This exercise can be accomplished at your annual review.

- Changes to your financial profile because of life events may warrant changes to your portfolio or other financial planning work. It is important to note that if these major life events can occur at any time, so don't wait for your annual review to deal with them. Deal with them immediately.

- Financial performance of your investments should be reviewed more often than once a year, but perhaps at your annual meeting a more thorough evaluation of your investments can be conducted.

Chapter Seven

Wealthbuilding and Use of Debt

Most Canadians will use debt as a means to get ahead at some point in their life. In this chapter, we will examine how the use of debt evolves as you evolve through the wealthbuilding process.

EVOLUTION OF DEBT USAGE THROUGH THE WEALTHBUILDING PROCESS

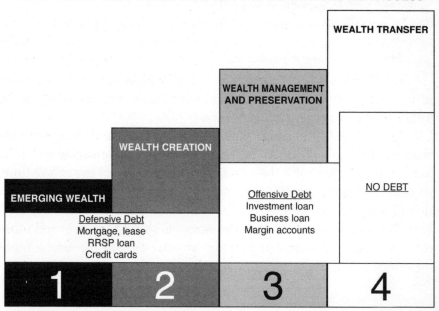

It is important to understand defensive debt and offensive debt (sometimes referred to as bad debt and good debt). Defensive debt is debt that you must have to accomplish your goal. For example, if your goal is to buy a home and you cannot pay cash for it, you need a mortgage that may take you twenty years to pay back. I call this form of debt defensive debt for two reasons: 1) it is not incurred by choice—you are being forced to incur this debt and the cost is set by the lender, not you; and 2) this form of debt is not tax deductible. Other examples of defensive debt are car loans, student university loans, and credit cards. It should be everyone's goal to eliminate defensive debt as quickly as possible.

Offensive debt is debt that you incur by choice. While many people strive to be debt free and not incur any new debt, many wise investors use good debt to build wealth effectively. Offensive debt has two characteristics: 1) the interest expense you incur is tax deductible; and 2) the loan is invested to create more wealth than the loan amount. Many of the world's most successful companies and the world's wealthiest people have all used debt to create wealth. In fact, if you don't use debt offensively over the course of your life, chances are you will never be truly wealthy. Debt levers your ability to grow your wealth many times over by using other people's money, at a reasonable cost, to magnify wealthbuilding results beyond what you could ever do with your own money. Examples of offensive debt include investment loans, margin accounts, company loans to purchase shares, and mortgages on rental properties.

Let's look at how both defensive and offensive debt should be used over the wealthbuilding process:

Phase One: Emerging Wealth

In this first stage you may have the greatest percentage of your net worth as debt compared to any other time in your life. With a mortgage, student debt, car loans, and credit card debt, you may be struggling to get a foothold in the wealthbuilding process. Look for opportunities to consolidate all of your debts into one low-cost loan. This will keep your costs of lending low and make it easier to manage debt payments. Make it a priority to eliminate this defensive debt as fast as possible.

Most people will not incur offensive debt at this point in their life as they are busy focused on paying off defensive debt. Because defensive debt is often more costly than offensive debt and even more costly than building your savings, eliminating all defensive debt should be a top priority.

Phase Two: Wealth Creation

As you progress into phase two of wealthbuilding, you start to pay down your defensive debt and generate more cash flow. Defensive debt will often exist in your life into the latter stages of phase two and this can be a problem. As debt levels go down, many Canadians will rush out to buy a bigger home or more expensive cars, incurring more defensive debt. Your desire for nicer assets needs to be balanced with your total wealth creation plan. It is important to eliminate non-essential debt as early in phase two as possible and make sure it doesn't come back.

In phase two you will also likely have offensive debt. You may borrow money to contribute to your RRSP. This is a wise move as long as the loan is paid off within a year. You may also borrow money to purchase the company stock of your employer if they offer it. Often these purchases are made at a discount and can be a good source of wealthbuilding.

Phase Three: Wealth Management

At this phase, you should have no defensive debt left. You've paid it off and life is good. Now, you are incurring offensive debt as a proactive technique to expand your wealth at a faster than average rate. This is good wealthbuilding, since you are using other people's money to grow your own, and you are claiming the interest cost as a tax deduction. Examples of common examples of offensive debt are:

- Purchasing rental units with a mortgage whereby you can write off the mortgage interest against the rental revenue
- Purchasing a business with arranged financing.
- Buying a limited amount of stocks and bonds with an investment loan or margin account.

People that don't use debt offensively to grow wealth often do so out of fear of loss, or a cultural barrier that teaches that debt is bad. In fact, if you understand the risks and you use debt in moderation, it can be an effective wealthbuilding tool.

Phase Four: Wealth Transfer

Phase four is often the only phase that contains no debt. With your wealth in place and life winding down, priorities shift to life simplification. In fact, your wealth may spill over to your children where you start giving them money to pay down their own debts. I'm not a fan of this gifting, as you still have a lot of life to live and may need this money yourself. On the other hand, if you still have debt in your life at this phase, consider it trouble. It may indicate that you have a spending problem and that you are struggling to grow your wealth.

Some Key Debt Strategies
Borrowing to Invest in the Stock Market

If you have never borrowed to invest before, taking a large investment loan may be beyond your comfort level. Try a little bit of leveraged investing before you try a lot, because it can be very scary if the markets don't always go up.

Borrowing to invest is called many things: leverage, margin, or just plain borrowing to invest. This strategy is quite aggressive, but can add significant wealth to your bottom line if it works. Here are some of the aspects to consider before borrowing to invest:

Why Your Leveraged Portfolio Needs to Be Equity Based

If you take out a loan to invest in a taxable portfolio, the interest expense on the loan may be tax deductible for you. So, for example, if your cost of borrowing is 6%, assuming a 50% tax bracket, your true after-tax cost of debt is only 3%. However, we need to examine your investments as well, and give them a tax-effected return. If you invest the borrowed money in bonds, but only return 5% a year in a 50% tax bracket, you will only keep 2.5% after tax. This is less than the cost of debt, and doesn't make borrowing to invest very wise. If, however, you invest the borrowed money in some stocks or equity mutual funds that offer the long-term return potential of 10% per year on average, borrowing to invest becomes more feasible. A 10% pre-tax return can be an 8% (or more) after-tax return if you earn all capital gains on your equities. In this case borrowing to invest is making you money.

But it is also important to remember that if you are going to buy equities with borrowed money, you should have a plan in place for ten years. If your time period is shorter, you may be exposed to some volatile and negative returns that can result from equity investing, and this may be hard to tolerate.

Tax Treatment of Interest Expense on Borrowed Money

Interest expense on money borrowed to invest in a taxable portfolio of stocks, bonds, mutual funds, or a small business will generally be tax deductible. However, interest expense on money borrowed to invest in an RRSP, a car, or home, is not tax deductible.

An Example of the Power of Leverage

John borrows $90,000 at 6% to invest in a portfolio of equity mutual funds. This is on top of $10,000 of his own money that is also invested. What is John's overall return if he achieves the following actual investment returns on the invested money?

a) If he earns 10% on the investment in one year. John's return will be 10% of $100,000 or $10,000 less interest cost on the debt of $5,400 for a net return of $4,600. John only invested $10,000 of his own money, so his overall return is 46% (4,600 / 10,000). This is very good.

b) If he loses 10% on the investments in one year, John's return will be a $10,000 loss plus the cost of interest of $5,400 for a total cost of $15,400. Since John only invested $10,000 of his own money, his overall loss is 154%!

Be warned folks. Leveraged investing works well when the market goes up. When you lose money on the investment, you have lost the investment, but you still have to repay interest and a loan.

If you are considering leveraged investing, start out with a small loan amount and have a long timeline. Ensure your investments reflect your investor profile as defined by your IPS. Evaluate the after-tax cost of your debt against the after-tax returns you hope to make to see if the economics of the strategy make sense. Stay true to a plan and leveraging as a strategy can be very effective.

Borrowing Money to Contribute to Your RRSP

Borrowing to contribute to your RRSP can make sense, but only if you pay off the loan within a few years, and don't do the same thing year after year. Here's why:

To evaluate the pros and cons of this strategy, you need to compare the cost of the debt with the investment returns you make. This is not easy to do because the loan interest is paid with after-tax dollars (your bottom line paycheque) while the investment earnings grow tax sheltered inside your RRSP (pre-tax dollars).

If we assume that you can get an RRSP loan today at 6% and you purchase investments inside your RRSP earning 9%, is this a smart move? Maybe, maybe not. That's because you have to compare the pre-tax cost of both the debt cost and the asset growth to see whether you are getting ahead. Within the RRSP your pre-tax earnings are 9%. However, the loan at 6% must be grossed up by a tax factor to convert this into a pre-tax cost of debt. If we use an average tax rate of 20%, your interest expense on the debt, pre-tax, is really 7.5% (6% / 1 - 20%).

The analysis is not yet complete, however. The cost of debt in my example above will last only as long as the loan exists, maybe a few years at most, while the benefit from the investment will last the life of the RRSP, maybe forty years.

I'm going to ignore the tax refund point because only some Canadians actually reinvest their refund cheques and because the value of the tax deduction that led to the refund reverses itself when money is ultimately drawn out of the RRSP and becomes taxable. But clearly there is a time value of money advantage here that pads the argument for contributing to your RRSP using a loan.

But let me focus on the pure RRSP borrowing versus investing argument. Two points are worth making:

- If you don't earn an RRSP tax-sheltered return each year that exceeds your pre-tax cost of debt, borrowing to invest may be foolish for you. Historically, it has been shown that to get a high investment return has meant investing in a large amount of stocks or equity mutual funds. Ensure this approach would match your risk tolerance before borrowing to invest in your RRSP.
- If you borrow for your RRSP and pay it off within a year, you don't have to worry about the cost of debt exceeding the investment returns each year. However, the types of Canadians that typically borrow to contribute to their RRSPs are the types of cash-strapped Canadians that will need to borrow next year, and the following year, and the year after that. This means they may never escape the debt burden of their RRSP loans, in a way that borrowing to invest for their RRSPs may always be a losing strategy.

Borrowing to invest can be a good strategy for many Canadians, but the appropriateness of this approach needs to be evaluated according to your unique financial situation. If you don't earn enough investment returns over the long term, or if you lengthen the loan payments over several years, the only person that may end up making money is the financial institution that made you the loans!

Prioritizing Your Debt to Repay

When you have several different types of debt that you (and your spouse, potentially) are trying to pay down, it is important that you prioritize the costs of each and pay down the most expensive ones first.

Let's look at an example to better understand how to pay down debt in an effective manner.

Mr. Smith currently has the following types of debt: a mortgage for $150,000 at 6%, a car loan for $10,000 for 6.5%, an investment margin account with a negative balance of $22,000 at 8%, a student loan of $3,000 at 9%, and one of his credit cards has been overdue by $4,000 at 15% for two months. Assume Mr. Smith is in a 50% marginal tax bracket.

What is the best way for Mr. Smith to tackle his debt problems? To answer this question we need to calculate the after-tax cost of each debt. You can't just look at interest rates and pay down the lowest since, in some cases, some of the loan interest is tax deductible. This changes things.

1. Pay down the credit card debt first. At an after-tax cost (meaning you

pay this out of your net pay after tax) of 15%, it is outrageously high. Just by paying down this debt you can essentially earn a return of 15% by wiping out a negative return of 15%.

2. Next, focus on the student debt at 9% as the next most expensive after-tax cost of debt.
3. Then the car loan at 6.5%.
4. Then the mortgage at 6%.
5. Last, pay down the investment loan or margin account. It's after-tax cost of debt is only 4% since the 8% interest cost is tax deductible (at a 50% tax rate), reducing the cost to only 4%.

I should note that if you can't afford to pay down debts quickly, consider refinancing the most expensive debts. For example, you could have your local financial institution pay off your credit card bills for you and set up a term loan for you to repay at a lower interest rate. A debt still remains, but the interest cost will likely be one-half to one-third of what the credit card companies charge. Take the reduced interest cost and pay down the debt faster.

Another good option, if you have the choice, is to have your parents pay off your debts through a gift to you or through a loan. No doubt your family will give you more favourable interest rates on debt than a credit card company. I would encourage you to consider a loan instead of a substantial gift in case your marriage breaks down. With a loan, there is more protection of your money against divorce and other life risks.

Chapter Eight
Wealthbuilding and Personal Insurance

Life and disability insurance are financial products that most Canadians will own at some point in their lives. In the last fifty years, these products have evolved tremendously—the days of the door-to-door insurance salesperson are long gone. Insurance products have become sophisticated tools relevant to some of the most important planning needs in your life.

In this chapter we will cover how your insurance needs should evolve over the wealthbuilding process. Perhaps here, more than in any other chapter, you will see how your need for insurance and different types of insurance change over the course of your life.

EVOLUTION OF PERSONAL INSURANCE DURING THE WEALTHBUILDING PROCESS

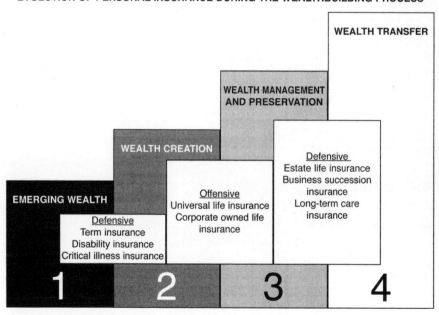

Phase 1: Emerging Wealth
Life Insurance

At this stage of wealthbuilding, you have little or no need for life insurance if you are single and have no dependants. Frankly, if you died, no one would be left with a financial burden. Your family might miss you, but financially they are no worse off.

If, however, you are married with children, your premature death could devastate your family's financial position. You cannot afford to let that happen, so it is necessary to purchase life insurance to protect your dependants for as long as they are dependants. This may be twenty years are more, until your children are finally in the workforce themselves.

Once you need life insurance, you need to decide what type. At this stage of your life, getting the right amount is more important than getting the right type. This means you should purchase ten- or twenty-year term insurance, since you can purchase large amounts for the lowest cost. In my opinion, a young family should plan on $500,000 to $2 million of term insurance on the life of the primary income earner. Work with a financial planner to complete a written needs analysis to determine how much you need. You will likely need a twenty-year term instead of a ten-year term if you have young children who will be dependant on you for more than ten years. Keep in mind the coverage can be cancelled at any time, and to buy more coverage will cost you more in the future than it does today as insurance gets more expensive with age.

I have to mention group life insurance offered by employers to employees. This insurance is provided by your employer and many Canadians are lulled into a false sense of security with their group coverage. Let's be clear: group coverage is not controlled by you and can be changed or cancelled by your employer at any time; it may be more expensive than coverage on your own; it is not personally designed for your needs; and you will lose this coverage if you leave your employer or you are fired.

Disability Insurance

Disability insurance is essential and more important than life insurance. If you fall down the stairs in your apartment and end up in a coma for two years, or you get cancer and can't work for two years, you need an income to pay your bills and buy food. Disability insurance provides this income when you cannot work. Unfortunately, many Canadians choose to ignore their disability insurance needs, despite the risk of being disabled, which is far greater than the risk of death.

Once again, your employer likely provides basic disability insurance coverage and many Canadians rely on this, often weak, group coverage. It may only cover half of your salary, excluding any annual bonus. The payments may be cut off as soon as you can work again. Once again, please consider a separate policy that you buy on your own—you can buy a base policy or buy a top-up to your employer's group coverage. It will be expensive, but it is a safety net that you cannot afford to live without.

Other key points about disability insurance you should know:

- Use your own money to pay the premiums. If your employer pays the premium using pre-tax earnings, any benefits you get when you are disabled will be taxable. If you pay the premiums yourself, the benefits would be tax free.
- You can control the cost of your premiums by tinkering with the features of your policy. For example, many policies will have a thirty-day elimination period. This is the amount of time before the policy would start paying benefits if you were disabled. By increasing your elimination period to a longer period, say ninety days, you can decrease your premium cost. Note that you would need to live off your savings for the first ninety days.
- Understand the different types of coverage, known as any occupation, regular occupation, and own occupation. If you have any occupation coverage, it means that as soon as you can re-enter the workforce doing any work at all (e.g. janitor in a school), the insurance company will cut off your coverage. Own occupation coverage means that the insurance company will pay you benefits until you can resume the same career that you had before. Many doctors have own occupation coverage. Many executives have regular occupation coverage. However, many group policies offer only any occupation coverage. Do you know what you have?

Phase Two: Wealth Creation
Life Insurance

As you evolve into phase two of the wealthbuilding process and start to generate cash flow due to a higher salary, you will start to go through a transition. As your wealth grows, your need for protectionist life insurance as a safety net for your family declines. As you build net worth, you effectively self-insure yourself such that if something happened to the primary family income earner, there is enough wealth in place to live off for the rest of the family's life.

It is very possible that by the end of this phase of net worth growth, you may no longer need life insurance for purposes of protecting your family. But, you better have well over a million dollars in the bank before you consider canceling your coverage!

With your debt on the decline or gone completely by the end of phase two, it is now time to look upon life insurance as a wealth creation tool and no longer a family protection safety net. It would be very easy to ignore life insurance at this stage in your life and spend your money on vacations and expensive cars, but the clock is ticking and every year the cost of insurance rises as you get older.

Your focus should be shifting from term insurance to permanent insurance as your need is shifting from protection of your family over a limited number of years to long-term wealth creation and protection over the remainder of your life. While term-to-one-hundred insurance does exist, permanent insurance costs about the same for a basic policy, but offers far more planning flexibility over the long term.

As you consider permanent insurance, understand your goals for buying this type of insurance: permanent insurance allows you to put money into a tax-sheltered policy and grow it tax free over the rest of your life. This is a wise wealthbuilding strategy. In many instances, you can grow wealth faster within this policy than you can by investing on your own. The money that you contribute to a permanent policy has to be money that you won't need in your lifetime. So, unless you know what your health care costs will be when you are ninety, be very careful about committing money to an insurance policy for the long term!

Disability Insurance

As your income and quality of life rises through phase two, your need for good disability insurance is greater than ever. Your income is higher than ever before and if you have children your spending needs are greater. You may not yet be wealthy enough to financially survive a short-term disability and still require good disability insurance. Chances are that your employer's group coverage is more inadequate than ever. With more money in your pocket, it is more important to buy top-up disability insurance to provide proper coverage. You may only need it for another ten years, but having a financial setback could completely change the financial outcome of the rest of your life. It is not the time to cheap out.

Phase Three: Wealth Management and Insurance
Life Insurance

By phase three you should be financially well-off, perhaps even retired or close to it. With a substantial net worth created and no debt, there is no need for term life insurance as a safety net. You now have no life insurance, or you are focused on regular contributions to a permanent life insurance policy for long-term wealth creation that pays out when you die. The more money that you contribute to such an insurance policy, the more money your estate will have.

Here are two of the reasons that Canadians consider permanent life insurance at this point in their life:

- Liquidity: Individuals who are business owners should use insurance to structure a tax-free transition of share ownership from their names to their children's names.
- Net worth growth: Individuals with lots of free cash flow can purchase permanent insurance and tax-shelter wealth beyond what they can do outside of an insurance policy. For Canadians focused on leaving their heirs as much wealth as possible, a permanent life insurance policy is an important planning tool.

Disability Insurance

If you have a sizeable net worth (and potentially you are retired at this point in your life as well) you have little or no need for disability insurance.

Here is an example of things to watch for. Recently, I met an executive with thirteen life insurance policies, mostly term insurance. He was fifty-eight with no debt and large investment savings. His children were grown up and moved out. He had bought every insurance policy ever sold to him and had never changed the coverage. He is a good example of failing to evolve his insurance coverage as he evolved through the wealthbuilding process. He is over insured and has the wrong kind of insurance. Worse, the amount of money he was paying in premiums every year was affecting his quality of life. We consolidated policies, reduced coverage, and replaced term with permanent insurance, designed to focus on his long-term estate goals, which were now important to him. His premium cost was reduced significantly, and his present quality of life was enhanced.

Phase Four: Wealth Transfer
Life Insurance

With the maturity of your wealthbuilding can come the most important need for insurance since you were young with dependant children.

Permanent life insurance can be used for three purposes in this phase: 1) offsetting income taxes on death; 2) providing liquidity to fund a transaction at your death; and 3) transfer wealth intergenerationally with no income taxes. Here are some examples of these purposes:

- As the last surviving spouse, your RRSP or RRIF will face 46% taxation, leaving your estate with only half as much as you have today. Purchasing life insurance that will pay out tax free on death can offset this tax liability and leave your heirs with more money.
- If you own a cottage or business with a large accrued tax liability, life insurance will provide the money on your death to buy out your shares in the company or pay the tax liability on the cottage. Without this money, your family may have to sell the business or the cottage to pay the taxes due on your death.
- When you die, your estate will face income tax and possibly probate fees that could be in the thousands of dollars. This will have to be paid before your heirs receive their inheritances. By converting your wealth into an insurance policy today, the tax-free payout on death can be passed directly to a beneficiary, bypassing your estate and avoiding income tax and probate fees.

Disability Insurance

There is no need for disability insurance in this final phase of the wealthbuilding process.

Critical Illness Insurance

Critical illness insurance is the new insurance on the scene. In a country of crowded hospitals and long waits for treatment, critical illness exists to help you cheat sickness.

Critical illness is life insurance that pays you a lump sum while you are still alive. It will pay out if you get one of a long list of major illnesses like cancer, stroke, heart attack, and Alzheimer's. The idea is that this cash from the insurance will assist you to pay for drugs and expensive medical treatments in Canada or the U.S. Equally important, critical illness will provide a financial benefit where disability insurance will not. While disability insurance provides a basic monthly payment to let you pay your bills while disabled, there won't be much money to keep the kids in private school, contribute to RRSPs, make car payments, and pay for other extra expenses. Critical illness insurance provides a chunk of money to ensure your quality of life continues. With the extra cash, you can make sure your family's quality of life continues at the level you are accustomed to. Many people will view critical illness as a substitute for disability insurance. I hope that from my explanation above, you can see they are not replacements, but complimentary coverages providing different protection.

Variations of Critical Illness Coverage

Would you believe that critical illness coverage can be a good investment in some cases? Yes, an investment. It is possible to buy a critical illness policy with a return of premium rider. This rider means that if you do not get sick and cash in the insurance over a certain period of time, the insurance company will pay you all of your premiums back. This means the insurance really leaves you with little downside—if you get sick the insurance pays off and you get the money; if you don't get sick, you get your money back all at once. Your only real cost under this scenario is the time value of money while your premiums are in the hands of insurance companies. This is worth looking into!

Amounts of Coverage

Critical illness insurance is expensive, particularly when you include the return of premium rider. How much you should buy should depend on your ability to pay and also upon the quality of life you need to preserve.

At What Age To Buy Critical Illness Insurance

Like other areas of your personal finances, critical illness coverage can evolve as your wealthbuilding evolves and your life progresses. At a most basic level, I would suggest a $100,000 policy, but much larger coverage could easily be appropriate if your financial needs are greater. Many critical illness policies end at age seventy-five, but I'm a fan of the coverages that extend for life. You'd hate to get cancer at age seventy-six and know you could have used the critical illness money for surgery in New York!

Permanent Insurance as a Million Dollar Gift for Your Children When You Die

There are several variables you need to consider before you should buy life insurance for death planning purposes.

What are your goals? If you are strongly motivated to maximize the value of your estate you may want to consider life insurance as one means to do that. Do your kids agree with this goal or would they prefer to see you live your life more fully with greater cash flow now instead of paying insurance premiums? Do your kids really care whether they get more cash after you are dead, or would they rather see you enjoy your money while you are alive? Or maybe they are prepared to pay the insurance premiums for your policy?

Can you afford the insurance? Since the cost of insurance premiums is going to come out of your cash flow, are you prepared to sacrifice your current standard of living to contribute towards a policy that will pay out a benefit after you are dead? Some people think their children will be happy to pay the life insurance premiums on their parent's policies. Maybe they will. Maybe they won't. It comes down to an evaluation of their personal situation.

Have you taken advantage of other forms of savings first? Don't consider an insurance policy for death planning until you have fully maximized your RRSPs each year. It is generally considered more advantageous to contribute to an RRSP.

Do you fit a target market that estate insurance suits best? People with very high income levels, people that own small businesses that they want to keep in the family, and people with cottages they have held in the family for decades (and want to continue to) are some of the categories of individuals that are well suited to life insurance as an estate planning tool. Estate insurance can be suitable for the broader consumer as well, just make sure the policy is a size that is easily affordable.

Once you decide you are going to buy, how much insurance do you need? How much you should buy depends on what you can afford, what your goals are, what your family wants, and what makes sense according to your financial situation. Further, if you decide you are going to buy a lot of insurance, then think about how solvent the insurance company may be. In other words, will they survive another twenty years to be able to pay out the policy on your death? The size of the policy you buy should be carefully thought out—seek opinions from multiple insurance agents before you purchase one.

When it comes to product, pay attention to cost! Permanent life insurance policies have a cost of insurance and you can also contribute to a tax-sheltered savings plan inside the policy. Make sure you understand the amount of fees taken each year and how these fees can fluctuate. The growth of your investment pool inside the insurance policy may also be affected by dividends credited to your pool by the insurance company and this may be affected annually by their company costs. Make sure you examine worst-case scenarios in checking out costs. Look at historical costs and dividends credited to the policy. Compare these between insurance companies. Stay away from variable costs that can rise and fall each year.

Watch out for slick sales presentations on the benefits of life insurance—numbers, numbers, and more numbers make life insurance sales charts confusing for even the most analytical accountant. Just remember, the attractiveness of the results from life insurance product forecasts are a function of the assumptions made by the agent and the insurance company. Make sure the assumptions from the presentations are reasonable with respect to investment returns, costs, dividends, bonuses, and other variables that affect long-term performance. Unreasonable expectations can leave you with an optimistic view of the future that may not occur and leave you paying insurance premiums long after you expect to. Always examine worst-case scenarios to understand how bad it can get with these products as part of your evaluation process.

Life Insurance: Lessons to Learn From

In the course of my travels as a financial advisor, I meet a lot of people with stories to tell about insurance. Here is an important one, selected because of the lesson learned that we all can benefit from:

Jane, an executive aged fifty-seven, bought a universal life insurance policy eight years ago, convinced of the tax and estate planning benefits that the policy offered. Today, expecting to pay premiums for only two more years, the insurance company informed her that because of poor investment performance within the policy she can expect to pay premiums for approximately another six years.

Jane was devastated as she was planning to retire in three years. But she will not be able to afford the cost of the insurance premiums if she retires and lives off her pension only. She was distressed and didn't know what to do. She is facing a part-time job in retirement just to pay the insurance premium, and she doesn't even know when she will be able to stop paying.

Well, there is hope. But, first here is a point about the purchase of the policy. Make sure the policy is affordable under all scenarios and that you understand how the policy works and what the risks are. In this case, the premium payments cross over a major life change where financial cash flow can be much different compared to working years. When you buy, examine what will happen to the policy under the worst possible economic conditions to get a feel for what you will have to pay in the future. You may decide you don't want the policy when you see the range of possibilities.

But, if you have the policy and you are in Jane's scenario, there are options. First, she could continue to pay the premiums until the policy is paid up. This may require her to work longer and, in my opinion, isn't the right way to go. Her second choice is to convert the insurance to term insurance. Depending on the cash value of the policy, the built-up value within the policy will pay for an amount of term insurance for her for a set number of years. This stops the need for future premiums, but when the term insurance expires the insurance will be cancelled. Her third choice is to convert the existing policy to "paid up." In this case, the insurance company can provide a quote on the amount your policy must shrink today for you to cease paying premiums. In other words, they look at the cash you have in the policy and estimate the size of life insurance policy you can afford at no future cost. This keeps the insurance in place, although through smaller policy, but stops the premiums when you can no longer afford them.

Evaluate a Life Insurance Trust

An insurance trust is a trust that receives the proceeds from your life insurance policy on your death. Rather than having an insurance policy pay out to your estate or your beneficiaries, the proceeds are instead paid to the trust. The money is then held inside the trust and either invested by the trustees or distributed according to the rules of the trust. The value of using a trust in this case is that if the insurance policies are large, e.g. $1 million or more, the benefits are as follows:

- Because the trustee is the named beneficiary of the policy (as opposed to your estate), the insurance proceeds do not form part of your estate and are not subject to provincial probate fees (if applicable).
- The insurance proceeds are protected from creditors, divorces, and unreliable children.
- There is more flexibility than simply naming a individual beneficiary in the life insurance policy. You can set out a plan for distribution in your Will; it can be to various individuals and over a period of time, and you can provide the trustee with discretion on how the amounts will be paid out. Part of the insurance proceeds can even be directed to pay taxes that may be due on your death.

The insurance trust does not actually become a legal trust until the insured person dies and the insurance proceeds are paid to the trustee. As a result, the insurance trust becomes a testamentary trust on death and, as such, it can benefit from lower graduated tax rates and perhaps pay less tax as a trust than you would receiving the money personally.

One Final Insurance Primer: A Lifetime of Life Insurance Needs

The following chart summarizes a lifetime of life insurance needs. My intentions are not to over-simplify the need for life insurance. Rather, I want to provide you with a reference to help you understand all insurance better as you search for products to suit your needs.

When You Need Insurance	What Kind of Insurance	Purpose of the Insurance
Before age twenty-five	None	You have no dependants, no debts, no one who will suffer should you die.
Get married	None	You were both fine before marriage, why would you all of a sudden need insurance?
Buy a home	None	If you died your spouse could pay the mortgage or just sell the house. Consider some basic term insurance for the amount of your mortgage if you really must.
Have children	$1.5 million of 20 year Term Insurance (more or less depending on your needs) from the child's birth to age 21.	Now you have dependants. You need enough insurance that if you died, the insurance proceeds could be invested to generate adequate after-tax income to replace what is needed to take care of your dependants. If your spouse is also working, you may need less insurance.
Spouse stays home to take care of children	Same as above.	You now need insurance to provide an income to your dependants in the event of your untimely death.
Get a new job	You will likely get group term insurance from the employer.	Group policies can be expensive, poorly crafted, an inadequate amount, and are non-transferable if you leave your job. Don't count on group coverage—buy your own for more control.
You have specific death planning goals to maximize your estate, and you can afford to do it.	Permanent life insurance: purchase it in your fifties or sixties. Buy it younger if you can afford to.	Offset taxes on death to preserve or enhance estate value by using an insurance policy that pays out on death.
Own a successful family business that you want to pass to the next generation.	Universal life insurance purchased on the lives of the business owners.	To permit shareholders to transfer share ownership by using the proceeds to buy out the shares of the dead owner.
Own a long-time family cottage with a big accrued capital gain; few other family assets of value exist.	Permanent life insurance purchased by the parents or by the children who will get the cottage.	If there is no cash available to pay the death taxes on the cottage, insurance can be used to generate needed cash.

Chapter Nine
Wealthbuilding and Compensation

Over the course of your working career, whether you are an employee, a professional, or a business owner, the type and amount of compensation that you will earn over your life will vary. Accordingly, the financial planning that you need to do related to this compensation should adapt as you evolve through the wealthbuilding phases.

EVOLUTION OF COMPENSATION DURING THE WEALTHBUILDING PROCESS

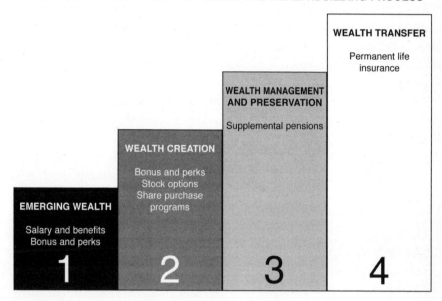

WEALTH TRANSFER

Permanent life insurance

WEALTH MANAGEMENT AND PRESERVATION

Supplemental pensions

WEALTH CREATION

Bonus and perks
Stock options
Share purchase programs

EMERGING WEALTH

Salary and benefits
Bonus and perks

1   2   3   4

Phase One: Emerging Wealth

As you join the work force your compensation consists of a salary, perhaps an annual bonus, and group benefits, such as dental coverage, and some insurance. These basic components of your compensation will likely remain the same throughout your working career, although the amounts will change.

Some basic strategies to consider at this phase are:

• Have your employer make your RRSP contribution for you. They will make the payment directly to your RRSP on a pre-tax basis, and there will be no tax withholdings. This will keep more money in your hands instead of the CRA's.

- Have your disability insurance coverage paid by you personally, or by your employer on an after-tax basis. By paying for the premiums on an after-tax basis, the benefits would be tax free if you ever draw them. This will leave you with more money in your pocket at a time when you really need it.
- Take the minimum amount of group life and disability insurance and buy separate coverage on your own. This ensures that your coverage won't be lost since group coverage is usually not fully portable if you leave your employer.

Phase Two: Wealth Creation

As your salary rises, and your bonus grows, you may become entitled to other perks like a company car, stock options, and the ability to purchase company stock at a discount. There are many important compensation strategies to enhance your value:

- Prefer to get your bonus on January 1, not late in December. A few days difference means that you can pay tax on that amount an entire year later.
- Ask your employer for more non-taxable perks. Having them pay for courses and conferences. Even an MBA can be tax free if the content is relevant to your career. The same applies for memberships in professional associations and clubs.
- Putting a lot of personal mileage on a company car can lead to a big taxable benefit included on your T4 slip. One way to keep the cost down is to leave the vehicle with the employer, not at your home, if you go on vacation for a few weeks. Part of the taxable benefit is based on availability for use during the year.
- Stock options are powerful wealthbuilding tools if the company stock rises in price over the course of your career. Stock options have complicated tax implications and need to be monitored. A stock option exercise strategy should be developed. Many executives just exercise and sell the stock when they need money. This can be dangerous. Considerations like the tax liability created, the risk of holding a large stock position for too long, and future potential of the stock need to be evaluated prior to exercise.
- One of the greatest sources of wealth for an employee and one of the greatest dangers for an employee is the build up of a large amount of company stock. Sometimes it is gifted to you each year, and some-

times it is purchased. Either way, the amount of money an employee maintains in this one stock should be controlled. Why? Think of an Enron employee who had their entire pension based on Enron stock. With six months until retirement the stock is crushed and their entire retirement pool of capital is gone. No one wants to be in this situation, so we all need to limit the amount of money kept in a single stock. As a general rule, never hold more than 20% of your total investment portfolio in one stock or one investment.

- Executives should seek a form T2200 from their employer, giving them the ability to write off a home office, supplies, and even a salary to a spouse. Keep in mind that the employer must agree with the business case of providing this to you.

Phase Three: Wealth Management

Phase three of wealthbuilding is often reached at the mature stage of a career. Early retirement may be a reality whether you want it or not. You may have changed careers one or more times before you reach this stage. And you have more options for wealthbuilding than ever before through your compensation:

- Individual pension plans, retirement compensation arrangements, and supplemental pension plans are tools that offer ways to provide a senior executive or valued employee with extra compensation, tax deferred or not, beyond what most employees would get. They can offer tax breaks and are highly desirable by executives. If you have the ability to influence your compensation levels, these compensation structures are well worth considering.
- Within five years of retirement ensure your company stock and stock options are winding down, as the last thing you need is the stock to blow up a year before retirement.
- Remember to arrange personal insurance coverage if dental and drug coverage do not extend into retirement.

Phase Four: Wealth Transfer

In the final phase of wealthbuilding, it is important to understand the implications of your various compensation structures on death and arrange proper planning. A company pension will likely offer a reduced survivor benefit for your spouse if you have one, otherwise the pension benefit will be gone when you die. Individual pension plans and supplemental compensation structures will remain the property of the estate, but face various tax consequences. Any remaining company stock that you have likely has a large capital gain because you have held it so long, and will face capital gains tax in your estate.

Important Thoughts on Compensation
Pension Plans

Gone are the days of juicy pension plans for most Canadian workers. Defined benefit pension plans, where a guaranteed amount of pension is provided to long-serving employees, can now only be found in the government and a select group of primarily large, older companies. These old plans have been deemed too expensive by most companies and have been replaced with defined contribution pension plans or group RRSPs. Now pension benefits for employees are based on contributions to the plan by you, the company, and any growth over time. You are also now responsible for deciding the investments that you buy with the money.

In my opinion, most employees don't know the weakness of a defined contribution or group RRSP. Many employees are incorrectly believing that their employer is taking care of their retirement plan. Many employees will not accumulate enough in their company pension plan to provide for the standard of living they desire in retirement. And, since few of these employees are doing proper retirement planning, they are heading for a lower standard of living in retirement and don't even know it. Yes, these are strong words, but I see so many employees that don't even understand their employer's pension or savings plan. They have trouble choosing the investment options, rarely question how they are doing, and, without a union, they lack the combined strength to demand more from the employer. The reality is that most employees need to supplement their employer savings with more personal savings on their own. Exactly how much they need to save should be determined by creating a proper retirement plan with a financial planner.

Professionals and Business Owners versus Employees

Professionals, like dentists and accountants, and business owners of all types have extra opportunities to plan their compensation through the wealthbuilding process. They can take advantage of income-splitting opportunities with their spouses and children, by involving them in the business operations even in a minor way. By paying a salary to a lower income family member, the entire family's tax burden may be reduced significantly.

If the child or spouse can have considerable involvement in the business, paying a salary up to $91,600 will result in income tax below the top rate, maximizing Canada Pension Plan (CPP) credits for retirement, and maximizing RRSP contribution room.

And then there is equity ownership. If your family can own shares in your business, you have the ability to pay dividends to them and provide a $500,000 tax exemption to each family shareholder on the value of their shares. If you currently own 100% of the shares of your business, consider an equity reorganization to bring family members in as new owners.

Employee versus Self-Employed

Every Canadian should prefer to be self-employed rather than be an employee. And you don't necessarily need your own business. You may be able to restructure your current employment relationship to one of contractor instead of employee. The advantage of being considered self-employed is tax breaks. As a contractor you can write off your car, your tools, your technology, your home office, and much more. As an employee you usually cannot write off any of this. Even with the same gross income, your after-tax take home income is much higher as a contractor because of the tax write-offs. But take note, there are several tests to pass to determine if you qualify as a contractor under the Income Tax Act. Speak to a tax expert about your particular situation.

On the flip side, I see many employers overusing the contractor status with new or part-time employees as a way to avoid paying benefits, CPP, Employment Insurance (EI), and income tax withholdings. If, in fact, the person is an employee in substance, the employer can face significant penalties for the incorrect treatment.

Employee Benefits: Tax-Smart Income Planning

In today's corporate world, there is a competition to find and keep the best employees. Employers are upping the stakes, by offering key employees more perks as part of their employment package. As you head into phase two of the wealthbuilding process, your compensation increases and the range of benefits you get from your employer grows.

The following is a list of benefits often provided by employers and how the tax impact affects you. Clearly there are some benefits that are more preferable than others—use this list to create a more tax effective benefits package if you can influence your employer's choice.

- Contributions by your employer to a registered pension plan on your behalf are tax free.

- Life insurance premiums paid by your employer on your behalf are taxable benefits.
- Private health care premiums (except in Quebec) are tax free; employer paid provincial health care premiums are a taxable benefit.
- Employee discounts, subsidized meals, and uniforms provided by an employer are tax free.
- Personal use of frequent flyer points that were earned on business travel is a taxable benefit.
- Athletic or social club memberships where the employer is the primary beneficiary of your membership is a tax-free perk.
- An employer-provided vehicle is a taxable benefit as it relates to the personal usage.
- Tuition for courses is tax free if the course is primarily for the employer's benefit.
- If your employer pays for your tax return preparation or any financial counseling prior to retirement this is a taxable benefit.
- A reasonable per kilometer allowance for business usage of your car is tax free.
- Most interest-free or low-interest loans provided to you by your employer are taxable benefits.
- Travel costs for family members when they travel with you on a business trip are taxable benefits if these costs are paid by the company.
- Stock option benefits are taxable benefits.

Stock Options Require Careful Planning

Stock options are financial instruments provided by employers that give employees the right to purchase company shares at a specified price (exercise price) within a specified time period. When the options are exercised, the employee pays the exercise price in exchange for the shares, which generally are worth more than the exercise price. In the last few years, stock options and equity ownership from an employer have been attractive forms of compensation provided to employees. Everyone has read the stories of the receptionist of a little tech company who earned some stock options and later cashed them in for millions. Companies themselves often like to hand out options and equity in the company as a form of employee remuneration because it instills a greater sense of value to the employee if they are a shareholder, and because the employer can avoid paying the employee cash compensation. Stock options and equity paid to an employee cost the employer nothing in terms of real out-of-pocket cash.

With stock options the amount of money an employee may eventually receive is tied to the success of the company as measured by share price increases—the higher the share price rises, the greater the difference between the market price and the exercise price, the more money the employee makes. Many corporations, therefore, like to see employees hold their stock options for the long term to benefit from a rising share price, and many companies apply delayed vesting periods stating the minimum holding period an employee must hold the options before the options can be exchanged for shares and ultimately for cash. It is not uncommon for an employee to receive options one year, but not be able to execute them for another three years. This is an effective way to bind an employee to a company and discourage them from leaving and forfeiting their options. It also promotes a buy-and-hold approach that can enhance the employee's ability to make money from their options.

The Politics of Stock Options

In some cases, executives of a company may have significant stock option holdings in their employer or significant stock in the employer. Sometimes the company encourages executives to continue to hold these positions for "political" reasons. Generally the company likes to see the executive be a supporter of the company by hanging onto their equity interests. This corporate expectation may, however, conflict with some employees' desire for a balanced investment strategy.

Many senior executives may hold significant amounts of options and company shares, which may create excessively risky portfolios since their portfolios may not be well diversified. If the company stock takes a nose dive, so potentially does a significant part of the executives' life savings and retirement plan. This can often result in a conflict for the employee or executive, where they must balance corporate expectations against their own financial security and a comfortable retirement.

Stock Options and Investment Strategy

The value of stock options and company stock should be included in an evaluation of the appropriateness of your broader investment portfolio and financial strategy. If your employer is a small private company, the options and stock that you own should likely be considered as a higher-risk equity component of your portfolio. If your employer is a blue-chip public corporation like a large Canadian bank, the options may be considered less risky in comparison. Discuss the appropriate risk level of your company with a financial planner and evaluate it accordingly in assessing your overall investment strategy for your savings. Overall, your employer's options and stock should not make up an overwhelming portion of your investment portfolio, but rather should comprise a portion of the portfolio that meets your risk tolerance and asset mix expectations. This may require you to exercise some of the options, sell the stock, and re-invest in a more balanced investment selection in order to achieve this balance. That's where it gets difficult, in that you must assess the pros and cons of diversifying your options and stock into something more diversified. See below for a further discussion on investment strategy.

Stock Options and Tax Strategy

Taxation of stock options is a complicated topic. In this section I will only discuss taxation of options on public companies and will not deal with taxation of options on private company stock.

Rules on Taxation for Public Company Stock Options

The 2000 federal budget changed the tax rules on the first $100,000 of qualifying employee stock options every year for public company stock options.

The Old Rules

From a tax perspective, under the old rules, the difference between the exercise price of options (cost of shares at time of purchase) and the market price of the shares at the time of exercise was taxed as employment income in the year the employee exercised the option. However, the taxation of this amount could be reduced by one half if: 1) the shares are normal common shares of the company; 2) the exercise price is not less than the fair market value of the shares at the time the option was granted; or 3) you are independent within your company.

After exercise-and-purchase of the stock, you could choose to continue to hold the stock of your company for a period of time. If the stock price rises during this time, you will earn a capital gain on the stock.

Any stock owned that accrued a large capital gain would be taxed when the stock is sold and the gain is realized. The capital gain is calculated as the proceeds on sale less the exercise price less the taxable benefit that may have been realized on exercise.

The New Rules

The same rules apply except that you can elect to defer the taxable benefit that may occur on exercise until the date you sell the shares. You can defer up to $100,000 per year of taxable income in this way, provided you meet the qualifications. These qualifications are: you must be a resident of Canada, be independent within your company, and not be a significant company shareholder. Additionally, the total of the amounts payable to acquire the shares cannot be less than the share's fair market value on the date the option is granted.

It is important to note that the $100,000 amount applies to the year that the options vest, yet the annual limit is based on the fair market value of the shares on the date that the options are granted. It is the employee's responsibility to ensure that the $100,000 limit is complied with when the deferral election is made. The employee has only one $100,000 limit for each investing year.

Employees wishing to claim the deferral on qualifying options must make an election with the employer, or other parties responsible, by filing a form by the following January 15 in which the share was acquired. Employees with deferred stock option benefits must file Form T1212 with their tax returns each year.

For More Tax Rules on Options

There are a variety of additional tax rules involving stock options of public and private companies. If you have any kind of stock options, seek professional tax advice before you exercise any options in any year. There are significant tax-planning opportunities that exist related to options, and a tax-smart investor should explore these breaks well in advance of exercise or sale.

Strategies for Employees Not Near Retirement

Selecting a strategy to provide you with financial peace of mind requires you to balance your preference for tax deferral with your investment risk tolerance, while considering your cash-flow needs and any corporate expectations of you to hold options or own company stock. Does this sound like a juggling act? The following points are worth considering.

The first priority is to develop a balanced investment portfolio and manage your equity portfolio such that the amount of stocks or equity funds you own lets you sleep at night. Taking steps to protect your retirement nest egg is more important than paying some tax today. This may mean reducing your holdings of options and stock and paying the tax now. This can be completed by:

- a lump-sum exercise of some invested options, sale of the resulting stock, and a reinvestment of the after-tax cash into other investments, or
- an annual exercise-and-sell strategy that produces a more gradual move toward a balanced portfolio. One attractive approach is a series of exercise-and-sell and reinvestment strategies where you can buy other investments with the after-tax stock option proceeds over a period of time at regular intervals, hopefully avoiding buying at a market high. Making interval sells and purchases over time is an effective strategy that reduces the risk of significant losses compared to buying all at once. This series of exercise-and-sell strategies is attractive because employees can partially continue to share in the success of their companies during the period of exercise but at the same time wind down their company equity.

Strategies for Retiring Employees with Options

Employees who are retiring and will no longer be "plugged into" the company may prefer to sell all their holdings before they retire. Some companies require employees to exercise all their options before retiring. Most employees consider their options and company stock part of their retirement savings, making it necessary to put a retirement strategy in place for the options like you would for regular retirement savings.

Overall, it is very important that, within the ten years prior to retirement, an employee implement an option exercise-and-sell strategy that starts soon and that ends by retirement. The worst thing that can happen is that an employee leaves their options alone until only days before they retire. Sure enough, the day before the planned exercise, the company's stock price dives, wiping out thousands of dollars of value off the employee's retirement savings. It is critical that stock option exercise-and-share sale is not deferred too long, and that a strategy to rebalance the portfolio starts well before retirement.

Company Stock versus Stock Options

Whether you hold stock options or stock directly, I still suggest that an exercise strategy be put in place, likely a tiered sale and reinvest strategy as discussed above. With the new tax rules in place, it appears that you may as well exercise your options as soon as you can, given you can defer taxation until the sale of the stock. At least by holding stock you own a real security and this may give you more flexibility and comfort.

However, either way, I am not a fan of large concentrated stock positions. Everyone has read of the possibility of striking it rich betting on one stock—rarely does this happen in real life. It is nice to play roulette sometimes, but not with your retirement finances. Implement a gradual exercise-and-sell strategy that allows you to keep some of your company stock for that big win that may happen someday, but hold enough money elsewhere in a diversified portfolio just in case.

Individual Pension Plans (IPPs)

An IPP is a defined benefit pension plan for one person. This plan resembles the complex pension plan that the government offers employees in Canada, and they are sometimes available to business owners. Generally, an IPP is suitable if you are a business owner, over age fifty-three, and earning a base salary greater than $100,000.

An IPP is also worth considering if you belong to an existing group registered pension plan and you would like to enhance the benefits.

Briefly, here are the pros and cons of an IPP. Clearly, they are not for everyone.

- You may be able to make higher contributions to an IPP than you would be able to within your RRSP.
- An IPP is creditor-proofed, while many RRSPs are not.
- You may be able to make some past-service contributions, further enhancing the tax-sheltering value of the plan. This is particularly attractive if you have been an employee for many years and have not been contributing to an RRSP or a pension plan.
- An IPP will eliminate your ability to income split with a lower income spouse, as you cannot make spousal contributions.
- Contributions to an IPP will be locked in until retirement according to pension benefits legislation.
- The regulatory environment for IPPs is complicated and costly—get an actuary to value your pension plan every three years.

Retirement Compensation Arrangements (RCAs)

RCAs operate outside of a registered pension plan system. A custodian accepts money from an employer on behalf of an employee, manages this money until the employee is retired or terminated, and then make payments to the employee from this pool of money. The employer receives a tax deduction for contributions to the plan, but a 50% refundable tax applies to contributions to the RCA. This tax is refunded when the money is paid out to the executive. The employee doesn't report the money on their tax return until it is received. RCAs are particularly useful as a savings strategy when the employee plans to retire in a lower taxed jurisdiction than where they live today.

The Incorporation of a Small Business

During the wealthbuilding process, many individuals will switch from being employees to owning their own business. Owning your own business has long been an established method for growing wealth successfully, in many instances much faster than by being an employee. When you look at the wealthiest people in the world, most of them are owners of their own business. While starting your own business may be intimidating and involve great risk, the rewards can take you to high levels of wealth that otherwise may not be possible.

Many small businesses start out as unincorporated ventures—the business is run without a legal company (no "ltd." or "inc.") and is simply an extension of your personal finances. On your tax return each year you simply add up the revenues and expenses and claim the income on your personal return. For a new business with little risk, starting as an unincorporated venture is likely the best way to go. It is less expensive to start and if you incur losses in the early years they can be claimed against any other income that you may earn.

But once your business becomes more successful you can grow the retained earnings of the business, or if the business is in a high-risk industry from the start, you will want to consider incorporation. Here are some of the advantages of incorporation:

- Incorporation can limit your personal liability by keeping your business assets and your personal assets separate.
- Incorporation can permit you to defer taxation on some income and accelerate tax write-offs.
- An incorporated business can choose a non-calendar year-end, permitting a tax deferral of income for a full year. A year-end other than December 31 may also be more practical for your business cycle.
- An incorporated business gives you access to the small business tax rate which can be less than 20% on the first $300,000 of active business income.
- An incorporated business allows you to hire your spouse and children as employees, pay them an income for work performed, and effectively split income for tax purposes among your family. This can reduce your overall family tax bill.

- If you sell your business you may be able to claim the $500,000 capital gains exemption, avoiding a huge tax liability on the sale.
- Once incorporated, you can implement a registered pension plan and a group health benefits program whereby the cost is tax deductible and can cover various family members.

How to Remove Money from Your Corporation

Did you know that there are up to five different ways to remove money from a corporation? It is important that you examine the methods that are best for you every year in order to minimize your overall tax liability. Here are some of the methods you can use:

- Dividends. Dividends are a distribution of the company's profits to its shareholders. Dividends are not tax deductible to the company, but are taxable to the recipient.
- Salary and bonus. Payment of a salary is tax deductible to the company and taxable to the employee. A salary is also subject to CPP and EI deductions. Depending on the year-end of the company, you can declare a bonus at year-end, pay it out within 179 days, and defer taxation of this income until the following year for the employee that receives it. This is a common tax-planning strategy.
- Shareholder loan repayments. If you are a shareholder that has lent money to the company at some time, this money can be repaid at any time without tax implications.
- Capital dividends. Any amount of a capital dividend can be paid out to shareholders without any tax implications. Capital dividends accumulate when a corporation incurs capital gains. It consists of the non-taxable portion of the capital gain.
- Repayment of capital. Any amount that is less than the company's paid up capital may be paid out to shareholders, generally with no tax consequences. Paid up capital is usually the amount of money contributed to the corporation in exchange for its shares.

Note that there are other ways to take money out of a company that can be problematic if not managed according to the rules:

- Loans to shareholders
- Share redemptions leading to deemed dividends
- Shareholder appropriations
- Shareholder use of corporate assets (e.g. cottages and vehicles owned by the company)

Chapter Ten
Wealthbuilding and Your Children

The range of financial issues that affect your children are huge as you progress through the wealthbuliding process. There are real opportunities to build wealth across your family if you recognize and take advantage of them.

EVOLUTION OF WEALTHBUILDING AS IT RELATES TO FAMILY

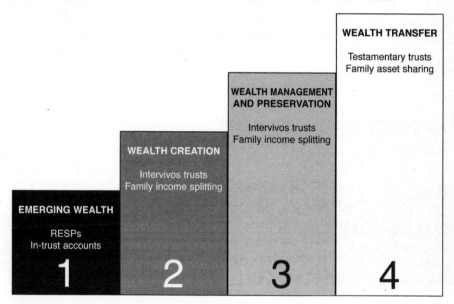

Phase One: Emerging Wealth

Open properly structured in-trust investment accounts for minor children (under eighteen) and invest the accounts to generate capital gains, thereby transferring the tax owed to the children and not you. If the child has no other income, you may save a significant amount of tax as a family.

Don't rely on group life insurance provided by your employer to protect your family. Buy separate coverage that would remain in place when you change employers.

Even when your income is lower it is important to start contributing to a Registered Educational Savings Plan (RESP) for your children. RESPs are a government sponsored savings plan where your contributions grow tax sheltered over the life of the plan. The money can only be used for the child's post secondary education after high school, and allows a parent or grandparent to accumulate up to $42,000 per child towards this purpose. The government also contributes $400 per child per year for every $2,000 you put in the plan—that's a guaranteed 20% return each year and too good to turn down! While you put money in the plan, the child pays tax on the earnings when the money comes out, reducing the tax burden on your family if the child is in a lower tax bracket.

There are two kinds of RESPs: individual and pooled plans. Stay away from the pooled plans which are often sold through magazines, flyers, or door-to-door. These plans are too restrictive, the fees are too high, and the investment choice is limited. Your child may not get all the money that you put in, and these plans are too confusing to even understand. Individual RESPs available from banks and investment dealers are simpler to use, cost less, and offer easier access to the money when the child needs it.

Note that grandparents can contribute to RESPs for your children if you are short of money, or if they want to do something nice for your children.

Child Care

With children typically at a young age during this phase of wealthbuilding, the cost of child care may be a large annual expense. Child care costs are tax deductible and include babysitting, day nursery services, day camps, boarding schools, and camps. For child care costs to be claimed, they have to be incurred while a spouse is working outside the home and earning an income or going to school full time. The tax deduction is limited to $7,000 multiplied by the number of children under age seven at the end of the year, plus $4,000 multiplied by the number of children aged seven to seventeen. This deduction is also limited to two-thirds of your earned income in the year.

Phase Two: Wealth Creation

With RESPs maximized, and with more income to spend, parents should consider additional methods to put money in a child's hands. Properly structured in-trust accounts are informal trusts where a contributor can put money in trust for a minor, invest the money, and have it taxed in the child's name. If the child has no other income, the investment income will result in little or no tax. This may be a bigger advantage than if the income is taxed in a parent's name. However, if the investment earns interest or dividends it is attributed back to the giver and taxed in their name. If the investment generates capital gains returns instead, it is taxed in the name of the child. So you want to buy stocks or equity mutual funds that generate gains in order to shift taxation to a minor child. Once the child turns age eighteen, they can pay tax on any kind of investment income without attribution.

If your children are teenagers at this stage of wealthbuilding, and they have part-time jobs, file a tax return for them even though their income is too low to pay taxes. They have earned income, and filing a tax return starts the tracking of RRSP contribution room for them. When they turn eighteen, they'll be able to open an RRSP, make a contribution of money that will grow tax-sheltered, and start their retirement savings years ahead of their peers.

Tuition Fees and Older Children

Tuition fees for admission to a post-secondary education facility, laboratory and library charges, examination fees, computer service fees, and the cost of books qualify for a tax credit on the student's tax return. Fees paid to private schools for grade school or high school will not entitle you to a federal tax credit. However, religious private schools may be able to provide a tax receipt for some of the cost if they treat the amount as a charitable donation made towards the school's religious instruction. Putting children through private school is not something that should be done at all costs. Parents need to balance the affordability of private school against the importance of debt repayment and planning for their own retirement. Note that only certain types of school, camp, and day-care costs can be written off for tax purposes.

For students that don't earn enough income to use all of their tuition tax credits in a given year, they can carry forward the unused tax credits for use in a future year when they are employed. The student can also transfer up to $800 per year in federal credits to a spouse, parent, or grandparent, permitting the elder to claim this tax credit on their tax return. Since a parent is often in a higher tax bracket, this transfer is advisable.

Phase Three: Wealth Management

When you reach phase three of the wealthbuilding process and your wealth is substantial, income-splitting with children for tax minimization is a priority. However, with children often adults themselves at this point, your concerns often shift to protection of your money. Perhaps the children are spendthrifts or too young to be financially responsible. Perhaps the children are getting married and you wish to protect money against a potential future divorce. Often an intervivos or living trust will be implemented, where you will contribute money or assets, like a cottage, to the trust. Your children will be the beneficiaries and a trustee will control the funds in the trust according to the trust agreement that you design. A trust is an ironclad tool for protecting wealth and allowing it to transfer to your children over time, according to your preferences.

If your marriage has failed and perhaps you have remarried, ensure you have your Will redone. Remember to update life insurance and RRSP beneficiary paperwork otherwise your ex-spouse may end up with some of your estate. Take steps to provide for your children, as your new spouse may not leave your wealth to your children if you die first.

Cut back on your employer benefits if you had signed up for extra dental and health coverage when you were younger. If the kids are gone, you no longer need this. Wind down expensive term life insurance if your family is no longer financially dependant on you. Even if you still wish to maintain insurance coverage, consider permanent insurance policies instead of term insurance for superior long-term value.

Take steps to educate and include your spouse in the family finances. If he or she regularly avoids investing, taxes, and other money matters, leaving it up to you, bring him or her to a few meetings with your financial planner to ensure they know the basics in case something happens to you.

At this point in your life you may also wish to start gifting money to your children or grandchildren. Before you start buying them houses or paying off their mortgages, it is important to ensure you won't need the money yourself for costs in old age like health care or nursing homes. Teach your children to be financially responsible by limiting the amount of money you give to them each year. You will teach them to be better money managers if they appreciate the effort required to pay off their own mortgage or cover other costs.

Two effective ways to give some money to children are to pay down their debt and gift them money to contribute to their RRSP. If you pay down their debts, you will save them the interest cost which can be 7% or higher. If you are only earning 4% in a GIC with the money, the savings between you and your child are clear—you save 3% as a family by paying off the 7% debt. With RRSPs, helping children contribute to their plans gives them a headstart on their retirement planning, and tax shelters investment income that you are currently paying tax on. Again, as a family unit, you are better off.

Becoming a Caregiver to Elderly Parents

In Canada today, middle-aged people are often referred to as the sandwich generation. Often they are financially supporting their children while also supporting their elderly parents by providing some form of personal care or financial support.

Canadians who are assisting their parents should be aware of the many different tax breaks available that address the challenges and costs of caring for the elderly. Starting five years ago, these tax breaks have grown and evolved and warrant a second look. Here are some of the benefits:

- Disability tax credit
- Attendant care tax deduction
- Caregiver credit
- Medical expense tax credit

Did you know that if you modify your home to permit an elderly parent to live there that these costs may qualify as a tax credit on your tax return?

Phase Four: Wealth Transfer

As your life winds down, and you look over a wide array of assets and wealth, your thoughts will turn to your children and wealth planning more than ever before. Now you must plan inter-generational wealth transfer, or the passing of your wealth to your next generation. This can be accelerated if you have a health breakdown, to the point where people in old age start to inappropriately gift assets, like houses, to children. Here are the things you need to contemplate as you deal with your family in old age:

- Do your children know that they are your executors or backup executors in your Will? It is advisable to have a frank discussion about dying with your children, and to go through your Will with them to ensure there are no surprises.
- Did you make all of your children co-executors or did you choose only one or two, leaving the other children excluded? This is a disaster waiting to happen and can pit siblings against each other after you are gone.
- As in phase three, be cautious about giving away your assets and money in old age to your children. First, giving an asset like a cottage

or investment to a child triggers a sale for tax purposes and you may now have a large tax liability due next April. Second, putting the asset in their hands exposes the asset to the possibility of a divorce of the child. And third, you may need this money or assets to pay for your health care before you are gone—don't give it away because it will be hard to get back.

- Giving away your house to a child to avoid probate fees on death may not be wise: you can lose your tax-free status of the home if your child now owns their own house and yours.

- Consider a testamentary trust incorporated in your Will which is a more tax effective method to distribute your wealth to your family after you are gone.

- Consider a generational skipping life insurance policy for your grandchildren. Purchasing a universal life insurance policy where you pay the premiums, your child owns the policy, and your grandchild is the life insured can pass wealth in a controlled fashion to your heirs and avoid income tax and probate fees on your death. Since your child owns the policy the grandchild cannot just cash the policy in and spend the money. Over the life of the policy the earnings in the policy grow tax deferred, offering a desirable tax break. And finally, the child can cash the policy in at age eighteen and use the money for post-secondary education or leave the policy in place and never need to buy insurance again in their life. This is a nifty and often overlooked use of insurance.

- Any business interests that you own need proper shareholder planning to ensure that your shares pass to children or your surviving spouse. It is essential that a properly drafted shareholder agreement be put in place no matter how small the company, along with a process to fund the buy out of your shares on death. Typically life insurance is purchased among shareholders and their families to provide cash flow at death.

As you can see from the wealthbuilding process, financial considerations involving children and grandchildren exist at every phase of the wealthbuilding process, and touch many different areas of your finances including investing, tax, estate, and debt. While many financial advisors never even ask if you have children, you need to ensure that all planning aspects presently related to your family and in the future are addressed properly.

More Financial Strategies for the Children
RESP, In-trust Account, or Formal Trust: What is the Best Way to Save for Minor Children?

Today there are three different vehicles to use that allow you to save for children.

1. RESPs
2. In-trust accounts
3. Formal trusts created by lawyers and accountants

The right vehicle for you to use will depend on several factors:
1. Purpose for the savings
2. Desire to create the largest savings pool of money possible
3. Desire for control over the money

Many advisors would lead you to believe that the appropriate choice for a child's savings should be based on tax or investment reasons—neither of these is correct. You can achieve roughly equal tax results from all three types of savings plans; there are ways to income split and shift taxation of the income onto the children for tax savings. As well, under all three plans, you can defer taxation on the capital gains earned. You can also own similar types of investments in all three plans.

Let's examine the different criteria that will help you decide how to save for your children or grandchildren:

Purpose for the savings: The purpose of the savings is critical to deciding what method to use for a child's savings. An RESP can only be used to save for post-secondary education, so if the child decides not to go to university and instead open a small business, major penalties may be incurred if there are RESP savings in place based on the current rules. An in-trust account can be used as a savings vehicle for any purpose and is a very flexible savings tool due to its simplicity. A formal trust is equally as flexible and can be used for any purpose.

Creating the largest pool of money: I have already said that all plans can provide similar tax breaks and similar investment options. This means that they should provide equal results over time. This would be the case, except that RESPS now offer an additional tax-free refundable savings grant each year of up to $400 per child per year. This extra cash gives RESPs an advantage over the other two plans and should result in the most money over time.

Desire for control over the money: In my opinion, having control over the proceeds is the most important aspect of deciding how to save for children and grandchildren. With an RESP the children better go to university or there's hell to pay. Parents as contributors don't have a lot of control over the proceeds since the use of the funds are limited to the child going to school.

Although in-trust accounts are a great way to save money for a child, they do not offer a parent any control over money after a child turns eighteen. Because some in-trust accounts are set up with only a signature on a simple document, there is little guidance on what would happen with the money should one of the parents die, the child die, or the parents divorce. Worse, the account is so simple that when the child turns eighteen they are entitled to free and complete access to all of the money. Further, should the child marry and divorce in their teens or twenties, the money in the in-trust account may be subject to division upon divorce. In-trust accounts offer a tax-smart savings approach, but use of these accounts should be carefully planned.

Formal trusts may be more expensive to implement (due to legal and accounting fees), but they are the most ironclad—being able to withstand deaths, marriage breakdowns, and most other forms of life's issues. They can be used for any kind of spending that the contributing parents find acceptable. The principal is guarded and safe from the child's bad habits. There is nothing better for dictating how and when anyone can have access to money and assets in general. The tradeoff for this superb protection is the annual professional fees to set up and maintain the trust.

Overall, the most money will come from using an RESP, but the kids better go to school. The most flexible and best controlling vehicle is the formal trust. I would suggest that most parents or grandparents should start with an RESP for their kids, and if the savings will be very large (maybe due to an inheritance) to then consider a formal trust. As a rule of thumb, if the savings for a child will amount to $60,000 or more, the cost of the formal trust can become worthwhile for the extra protection.

File a Tax Return for Minor Children Even Though It Is Not Required

You are not required by law to file a tax return for a minor who has no income. But you may want to think about filing a tax return for your child for a completely different reason—RRSPs.

Any individual with less income than the basic tax credit (now approximately $7,000) will have no taxable income and therefore no tax to pay. This is why most minor children, who have little or no income, have no need to file a personal tax return each year. However, if they have any employment income at all, it qualifies for RRSP earned income and will start the accumulation of their RRSP contribution room. You just have to file a return with this income so that CRA can start tracking the child's RRSP room.

Still not convinced that you want to go through the hassle of preparing a return each year for small amounts of your child's income? Here are some numbers to do the final convincing that it is worth it:

Assume your ten-year-old child delivers newspapers for three years and earns $1,000 per year.

Then let's assume your child, now thirteen, gets a part-time job at McDonald's and earns $3,500 per year for the next three years. Now let's assume your child, sixteen, gets a job with greater part-time hours over the school year and full-time hours over the summer, earning $5,500 per year for two years, until age eighteen. How much RRSP contribution room would be created (based on current RRSP rules), assuming the parents had filed tax returns for the child each year?

RRSP Earned Income Total over years	$24,500
RRSP Contribution Room factor	x 18%
RRSP Contribution Room	$4,410

Let's go further now and assume that at age eighteen the parents or grandparents open an RRSP for the child, and contribute the full $4,410 on the child's behalf using money gifted to the child. This contribution could be invested and earn 8% per year until age sixty-nine (fifty-one year compounding period). The child would have an RRSP worth $223,000 at retirement. That's a lot of money to be overlooked.

Help Adult Children While Saving on Tax

There is a lot of tax planning possible with respect to your adult children. Here are two examples of how you can improve the entire family's net worth.

Contribute to your adult children's RRSPs by gifting them money. Children in their late twenties or early thirties are usually still buried under student debt, car loans, and maybe even a mortgage. At the same time they are working full time and accumulating significant RRSP contribution room—they just don't have the money to contribute to their plan!

If you as a parent or grandparent, use your excess cash to contribute or gift money to adult children to allow them to make RRSP contributions, you will improve your overall family wealth position. You can essentially defer tax on all of your investment earnings if you contribute the cash into children's RRSP if you are the parent and are paying tax at up to 46% on the investment earnings. This is a tax deferral of up to forty-six cents of every dollar earned every year as long as the money stays tax sheltered in their RRSP. Tax sheltering more of your investment income this way will help to maximize your family net wealth.

However, remember that once you give money to a child, you give up control over that money, and potentially expose it to the divorce of a child, bankruptcy, or uncontrolled spending. So remember to weigh these factors before you make any gifts, along with your own need for the money. Note, there are ways to structure gifts to family members to protect against the risk of future loss. Talk to a professional financial planner about these strategies.

Help Your Children with Debt and Cut Your Taxes at the Same Time

Consider paying down your adult children's debts. Once again think about maximizing family wealth, instead of just your own. The best way to show you the impact of paying down your children's or grandchildren's debt is to provide a numerical example:

Current situation: Child has a $30,000 loan paying 8% interest per year, or $2,400 interest per year. This interest expense is paid out of after-tax cash flow, meaning your child is paying this cost with their net paycheque.

Dad has a $30,000 GIC earning 8% per year or $2,400 interest per year. Dad is also paying 46% tax on this interest ($1,104 per year) to leave only a net return of $1,296 after tax. As a family, the total return per year is $2,400 cost of debt for the child offset by a $1,296 after tax return for a total loss of $1,104. The child is paying out more in interest expense than Dad is earning, after tax.

Here's the strategy: Move assets around within the family unit and improve family wealth significantly. Dad should cash in his GIC and pay off the child's debt. Once that is done, the situation changes to:

- Dad paying off the $30,000 debt for his child with his $30,000 GIC.
- no interest expense since debt no longer exists.
- no interest income since the GIC has been cashed out.

An annual zero family return is much better than an annual loss of $1,104. This saving would be repeated (to some extent) every year as long as the child's debt is paid by the parent.

As you can see, just by reorganizing your family wealth you can improve and grow your overall wealth. However, gifting money to children in any case may not be appropriate if you will need the money yourself, or if there is a concern about your children's marriages or credit situations. Take precautionary steps to structure any gift appropriately to guard against unexpected risks. Talk to a professional financial planner.

Don't Gift Them Too Much!

Gifting children large amounts of money for the mortgage on their family residences can be very dangerous to the best interests of your family net worth. In many provinces, money invested into the family home will be subject to division between spouses in a breakdown of a marriage.

So many people ask me about gifting assets to help out their kids and generally I try to discourage them from doing it, or at least have them talk to a lawyer to ensure it is done with as much protection as possible. People often say, "Kurt, I have good kids, I can trust my kids," or "My kids will always be there for me if I need the money back."

And I say, " I know you trust your kids, but..."

You can't control whom your children marry. No matter how much you trust your children you can never predict what will happen with their future lives. This potentially exposes your gifts to them to loss from marriage breakdowns, future bankruptcies, and reckless spending habits.

Secondly, I wouldn't even go so far as to expect children to be there for you. If you gift them money, they are likely going to spend it, apply it against debt, or put it in their RRSPs. None of these three options are very liquid in a way that they could easily return the money should you need it for an emergency.

Finally, how can you gift large amounts of your money before you are dead? You don't know if you will need it in the future! For example, no one knows what the future cost of health care will be in Canada. We are seeing more user fees already, so having more money in your grasp is a great safety net.

Still, if you truly want to help your children by giving them cash, try these ideas:

- Give them small amounts at a time that you can truly afford to lose.
- Thoroughly document all gifts and maintain these documents as an audit trail should one of your children's families ever break up; consider loaning the money instead of gifting.
- Give your children money and don't let them pay down their mortgage or use it as a deposit for the family home. There is a greater likelihood that your child can get this money back after a divorce if it is not used for the family home.
- Get advice from a lawyer with expertise in gifting and marriage breakdown issues.

HOW INVESTMENT INCOME IS TAXED WHEN AN ADULT GIFTS AN INCOME GENERATING ASSET TO A FAMILY MEMBER

	Gift to spouse	Gift to adult child	Gift to minor child
Interest income	✔	✘	✔
Dividend income	✔	✘	✔
Capital gains	✔	✘	✘
Foreign income	✔	✘	✔
Rental income	✔	✘	✔

✔ Continues to be taxed in the name of the giver
✘ New income is taxed in the name of the child

Be Cautious About How You Share Assets with Family

This is a discussion about joint ownership of assets between family members, and gifting of assets to family members. Few Canadians realize there are serious financial issues that need to be considered around basic strategies like joint ownership and making a financial gift. Tax rules come into play, as well as legal aspects. The best way to sensitize you to these issues is to tell a few stories.

Example One: Mom and Dad's Joint Bank Account

Often one spouse earns the lion's share of income. Unfortunately this same spouse often pays most of the income tax, while the other spouse may be in a lower tax bracket. Sometimes a spouse will think that by having his/her paycheque deposited into a joint account that he/she can now split income earned from this joint account with the lower taxed spouse. This is not possible. Even if two spouses legally share a bank account or an investment account or a rental property, that does not mean they can share the taxable income! Legal and tax aspects are different and should not be confused. From a tax point of view, the spouse that is earning the income must declare all investment earnings from that income each year. CRA examines who actually contributed the investment capital to determine who is taxable on it. The name on the account doesn't matter.

Example Two: The Family Cottage

Elderly parents decide that they will gift the family cottage to their only child now instead of leaving it to him in their Will. This way they can avoid probate fees on the cottage on their death. Wise strategy? Think again! Gifting the cottage to an adult child is a formal deemed disposition for tax purposes resulting in the realization of any capital gain that may have been earned on the cottage since the day it was purchased. That means that the tax on the appreciated value of the cottage is now due next April. Gifting an asset to someone in the family is effectively treated as a sale for tax purposes. I've seen heartbreaking situations where families didn't know they were triggering the tax bill, didn't have any cash to pay the tax, and were forced to sell the cottage to come up with the tax money.

Example Three: Help from Your Daughter

An elderly mom who is struggling with old age asks her daughter if she would mind taking over the responsibility for paying her bills and doing her banking. The daughter agrees. To make it easy for her daughter to pay the bills, the elderly mom makes the daughter joint on her bank accounts, savings, house, and other assets. Two months later the daughter has a car accident down the street and it is determined to be her fault. The other driver, who is injured, sues the daughter for damages. The daughter loses the case and is faced with a $2 million payment. She doesn't have the money and is forced to go bankrupt. In the bankruptcy proceedings, it is determined that her half interests in her elderly mom's properties and investments should also be taken.

Example Four: A Daughter's Wedding

It is your only daughter's wedding day. As a gift to her and your new son-in-law, you give them $50,000 cash as a deposit on the purchase of a new home. Two years later your daughter and son-in-law get divorced. When it comes time to divide up their assets, half of your wedding gift ends up in the hands of the now hated son-in-law.

Example Five: A Trust for a Grandchild

Grandma opened an in-trust savings account with her local bank a few years ago to put some money aside for her granddaughter Sara. By the time Sara reached eighteen, there was $30,000 in the account. Grandma was pleased that this money would likely pay for two years of university. But Sara had other plans. She withdrew the entire $30,000 the day after her eighteenth birthday and bought a used car with some of the money. She used the rest of the money for a month-long vacation. Since Grandma had used a poorly structured in-trust account for the savings plan, she had no recourse to get her money back to provide direction on its usage.

These are five simple examples that demonstrate how quickly someone can get into trouble with joint ownership and gifting strategies from a legal or tax perspective. Ensure that before you move large amounts of money or assets around within a family that you talk to a financial expert about the rules.

Conclusion on Wealthbuilding and Your Children

If you value your family and view your wealth as the wealth of your entire family, then complete your financial planning with all of them in mind. If your family includes ten people, that is ten tax brackets, ten legal situations, ten debt levels, ten net worths, and ten saving and spending levels. There may be a lot more wealthbuilding opportunities to create family wealth when you take this broader perspective. Make sure that all of the planning that you undertake (investing, tax, estate, insurance) considers the "big picture" of your broader family goals, resources, and complexities.

Chapter Eleven
Wealthbuilding and Retirement Planning

Between the ages of eighteen and sixty we are in a race—a race to accumulate enough wealth to provide a desirable lifestyle in retirement.

Many Canadians don't start planning for their retirement until they are age thirty-five or so, leaving them only twenty-five years to generate enough financial resources for retirement. Unfortunately many Canadians never make it. They choose to ignore retirement planning and end up with a savings shortage in retirement.

Let's look at how your retirement planning should evolve as you progress through the four phases of wealthbuilding:

RETIREMENT PLANNING AND THE WEALTHBUILDING PROCESS

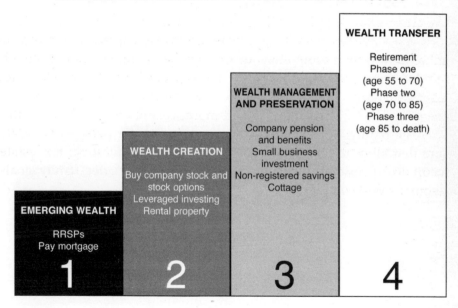

Phase One: Emerging Wealth

Here are the essential strategies to get a good start towards your retirement plan during the first phase of wealthbuilding:

- Start your RRSP and maximize the permitted contributions, even if you have to borrow money from family or a bank to do so. Use the RRSP refund to repay the loan or to get a head start on next year's contribution.

- Join your employer's pension plan or group savings plan if they contribute money on your behalf. If the employer does not contribute any money for you, skip their plan and open your own with a financial planner and enjoy wider product choices and the services of a financial expert.
- Don't buy a home until you are thirty or older. Use your earnings from your career in your twenties to start a retirement savings plan and to build a larger deposit for the home purchase. Be disciplined so as to avoid large expenditures on vehicles and vacations.
- Pay down expensive debt and consolidate your remaining debts into one debt payment to minimize borrowing costs.
- Stay away from car leases—they can be the highest cost form of borrowing. Drive your vehicles for five years or more and either purchase the vehicle or take a bank loan to purchase.
- Don't have children until you are thirty or older. The financial cost of a family can make it very hard to afford to save and even buy a home. Plan your life and start with the creation of a permanent savings base first, not last.
- Save 10% of your paycheque every month—this should be non-negotiable. Have it automatically taken off your paycheque and you will never miss it. Transfer the money directly into your RRSP if you have the contribution room.

Pay for a Mortgage or Pay for an RRSP—Which One?

To determine whether you should contribute to your RRSP versus paying down your mortgage, here are some of the variables that need to be considered in the analysis:

- Your mortgage interest rate (today and in the future), the size of your mortgage, and the mortgage amortization period.
- The size of your RRSP today, your planned RRSP savings per year, your expected rate of return to earn within the RRSP in the future, what you do with any tax refunds, your marginal tax bracket in the future, and the size of the RRSP you will need overall.

As you can see, the analysis of RRSP versus mortgage is not straightforward, as many of the variables to consider must be guessed at, with best estimates being utilized.

However, here are some general guidelines based on the dozens of analyses I have done for clients on this very topic.

Generally, the younger you are (under fifty) the more sense it makes to maximize your RRSP. The success of having a big RRSP depends on getting a lot of money inside the plan early in life and leaving it for a long time. If there is a pause in the process at any time, you will harm your chances of having a large RRSP for retirement purposes. Therefore, avoid interfering with RRSP contributions while in your twenties, thirties, and forties. Maximize your contributions each year, reinvest tax refunds, and even borrow to contribute if you must.

If you have a mortgage with a very high interest rate, or if you have an RRSP where the investments earn very little, the argument may sway to the other side and you may want to consider paying down your mortgage first.

However, by contributing to your RRSP each year you can take the tax refund resulting from the tax deduction and apply it against your mortgage as a lump sum payment each year. This approach allows you to work on both objectives at once, resulting in elimination of the mortgage years earlier.

Phase Two: Wealth Creation

As your wealth grows and you have more free cash flow you have the ability to make great strides in wealth creation while still at a relatively young age. Your challenge will be the ability to control your desire to spend money on lifestyle. With more free cash flow people tend to want bigger homes, fancier cars, and more vacations. I have seen many people with large incomes, often in their thirties and forties have a low net worth because they are spending every dollar they make. Balanced spending and saving is essential to proper wealthbuilding. Here are some important strategies to consider for retirement planning during the wealth creation phase of retirement planning:

- Maximize RESPs each year for children and use in-trust accounts for extra savings to accumulate enough money for your children's future schooling costs. Relying on an RESP will not be enough. The costs of education for a four-year university degree will likely be far more than your RESP balance.
- Strive to eliminate all non-tax deductible debt by the end of this phase. That means no mortgage on any real estate, no car debt or leases, and no credit card debt. If you have the cash flow, consider taking on offensive debt (discussed earlier in this book) as another tool to grow your long-term wealth. Leveraged investing can be a powerful

method to build wealth at an exponential speed.

- Continue to save at least 10% of your combined pre-tax family income each year. Most of this may come in the form of your RRSP contribution, but plan on saving in a regular investment account as well. Simply put, if you don't have a juicy pension plan with your employer, your RRSP will not be enough savings on its own to provide the retirement you want. Generally speaking, a Canadian family without a pension plan should shoot for $1 to $2 million in total savings for their retirement, excluding real estate. Real estate does not provide an income to live off.

RRSP Planning Essentials for Phase Two Wealthbuilders

Contribution versus Deduction

Many people are not aware that an RRSP contribution is not the same as an RRSP deduction. Your annual contribution room is calculated based on last year's earned income, generally your salary. Whatever your contribution room is, that's the amount you can contribute into an RRSP. The RRSP deduction is different however. The deduction relates to how much of the RRSP contribution you made you that will actually deduct on your tax return this year. Your RRSP contribution and tax deduction do not have to match. You can choose to take a smaller deduction and carry forward the extra deduction. You may want to do this if your income is rising. The important thing is to make the largest RRSP contribution you can each year to get the money in the plan earning more income on a tax-deferred basis. The tax deduction is important, but secondary. Just get the money in the plan first!

Large Unused RRSP Contribution Room

The Notice of Assessment that you get each year after filing your tax return shows your RRSP contribution carry forward, if any. This is the amount of money you can put into your RRSP in the future. This number can become quite large if you have not made the annual maximum contribution. The problem is, however, that you likely don't have the money to make the big catch-up contribution that would really give a boost to your retirement savings. I have a possible solution for you: get your parents or grandparents to gift you money for this contribution. You get the tax deduction from the RRSP contribution. They no longer pay tax on the investment income their money was generating—instead it will grow tax deferred in your RRSP. Overall, the family is ahead.

When to Draw Down Your RRSP

The beauty of an RRSP is the tax sheltering it provides on income earned over the life of the RRSP. Over forty years this can create a significant savings pool. When you take this view of your RRSP, any dipping into the plan earlier than age sixty-nine seems like blasphemy. At the same time you may want to think about dipping into your RRSP earlier if you have a much lower income today than you will in the future. Drawing down your RRSP while your total income is lower means you can make RRSP withdrawals and pay less tax on these withdrawals. This may be better than waiting until age seventy when your withdrawals will be larger so that you will pay more income tax. Note that withdrawals from an RRSP or RRIF may be subject to withholding tax by the institution. If you need $5,000 from your RRSP, you better find out what the withheld tax amount will be, so you can take out a bit more to account for it.

The right answer to when to withdraw depends on several variables. You want to maximize the deferred value of the RRSP but you also want to minimize tax on withdrawals. Generally I'd say you are better off leaving the money in the plan until retirement. Don't forget to examine the non-financial variables as well. If you retire at age sixty without a pension, you will need to draw your RRSP immediately to live off.

Spousal RRSP or Not

You should contribute to a spousal RRSP if you can safely say that your spouse will have a lower income in retirement than you will. The reason this matters is that your spouse will have to pay tax on RRSP withdrawals in retirement, so you want to put the RRSP in the name of the spouse who will pay the least tax in the future. Note too that contributing to a spousal RRSP affects your RRSP contribution room, not the spouse's. The spouse continues to have their own RRSP contribution room that is unaffected by what you do.

Suitable Investments for Your RRSP

There are two kinds of investments, in my opinion, that are suitable for an RRSP. Fixed-income investments are good since they generate highly taxed interest income. Putting all your fixed-income investments inside an RRSP shelters them from high taxation.

Second, put high return investments like stocks and global equity mutual funds into your RRSP. Because they can generate huge returns over the long term it is better to shelter these returns from tax by holding them inside your RRSP.

Fees in Your RRSP

It is generally undesirable to have any kind of fee charged against assets within your RRSP. This is because the fee is eating away at your tax sheltered savings, and you can only contribute a limited amount of new money each year. It would be far preferable to have all RRSP fees and expenses of products within your RRSP charged to you directly for payment.

Phase Three: Wealth Management

As you move closer to retirement, often around age forty-five to fifty, you start to think about whether you have enough money saved. Up to this point, many Canadians choose to ignore any formal planning, which can be disastrous. Sit down with a financial planner who can examine what you have saved, what you can save, and what you want your retirement to look like. Get a written plan with strategies that you can implement now to ensure the retirement that you want. As retirement gets closer, become more focused on the results of your written plan and modify your saving strategies as necessary. Make sure the annual savings levels address your goals!

Don't forget, you may want to retire at sixty or sixty-five, but your employer may have other plans. Many Canadians are surprised by offers of early retirement or being laid off when older because they are more costly to employ. Your retirement planning should have enough cushion built in to allow for these kinds of surprises.

Gone are the days of a comfortable retirement at fifty-five thanks to a company pension. First, we are living much longer than ever before. Second, the cost of retirement is more expensive. Third, most of us no longer get pensions. The reality is that most Canadians should expect to work full time until age sixty at a minimum. Even past age sixty, many Canadians are working part time for extra income and also because they enjoy it. While you can get CPP benefits at age sixty, if you wait until sixty-five you will get more money. Also at age sixty-five, you will receive OAS benefits, provided your income is not too high. CPP and OAS can add $15,000 of annual income to your bottom line and greatly help your retirement cash flow.

If you have company stock or stock options make sure you have an exercise-and-sell program in place ten years before retirement. Know the tax consequences and how the after-tax amount of stock wealth will factor into your retirement plan. Waiting too long to exercise could see the stock price drop right before you retire and seriously compromise your retirement plan.

Other than paying for your children's school costs, resist the desire to give them substantial amounts of money for other purposes (e.g. home purchase, weddings, vacations, cars) at this point in your life. You are too young and have too much life to live yet to know if you will need those funds in the future.

Phase Four: Wealth Transfer

With mature wealth and often your working career behind you, it is time for retirement. Post-retirement planning is complicated and should be taken seriously. Here are some considerations for structural planning strategies relevant to all Canadians in retirement:

The Three Parts of Retirement

View your retirement in three parts: part one is from age fifty-five to age seventy, part two is from age seventy to age eight-five, and part three is beyond age eighty-five. These three parts often mean completely different lifestyles for the retiree with major changes made to taxes, investments, cash flows, estate, spending levels, and goals.

Part One

In part one you are contemplating retirement and ultimately do retire. Figure out whether you can afford to retire, and then sort out how to spend your retirement savings. Retirement can be a shock after thirty years of working. You will also go through the shock of having a high income while employed to a much lower income when retired. And, your expenses in retirement may be higher than when you were working, as your leisure time in retirement is expensive. So your cash flows gets turned upside down, literally overnight. Are you ready?

You also need to sort out what your retirement income will consist of. During your sixties, you may earn a mix of pension income, CPP income, OAS, investment income from your savings, RRSP withdrawals, and part-time work income. Potentially, you have six different income sources in retirement that require planning, prioritization, and tax considerations to maximize after-tax cash flow. Most important, sit down with a financial planner who can organize your income sources and determine the best way to design your retirement income.

Part Two

There is a reason that age seventy is the cutoff between parts one and two of retirement. Sixty-nine is the latest age at which you can convert your RRSP to an RRIF (Registered Retirement Income Fund). After forty years of building an RRSP it is now time to spend it. Most Canadians will wait until this point so they can defer the taxation of the RRSP as long as possible. Further, many Canadians take as little out of their RRIF as possible after sixty-nine to continue to defer the income taxation. How much you withdraw and pay tax on is really a function of your spending needs. There should be an annual review of your spending levels against the amount of savings that you have to ensure that you don't run out of money, pay as little tax as possible, and have the money you need to live your life.

During this part of retirement one spouse may die, you may have health issues, and you will likely start spending less and staying closer to home. You are also drawing increasing amounts out of your RRIF as set out by the government's RRIF withdrawal schedule. Compared to part one of retirement, you have more income and are spending less. Also, your Will, insurance, taxes, and cash flow may need updating for the new realities of your retirement.

RRIF WITHDRAWL REQUIREMENTS

Age	RRIFs established after 1992	Age	RRIFs established after 1992	Age	RRIFs established after 1992
71	.0738	79	.0853	87	.1133
72	.0748	80	.0875	88	.1196
73	.0759	81	.0899	89	.1271
74	.0771	82	.0927	90	.1362
75	.0785	83	.0958	91	.1473
76	.0799	84	.0993	92	.1612
77	.0815	85	.1033	93	.1792
78	.0833	86	.1079	94	.2000

Part three of your retirement is your eldercare years. During this time you are likely alone (no spouse), face advanced health care issues, and are living in a nursing home. All aspects of your finances need to be revisited as it is possible that your goals, attitude towards money, costs and estate, retirement and investing preferences, are all different now. All the financial strategies that you set when you started retirement likely need to be reworked. Many Canadians overlook this and their finances suffer. It is important to recognize the evolution that you are going through and that your financial solutions and even your advisors need to evolve with you.

Real Estate and Retirement

Decide what you are going to do with your real estate during the course of your retirement. Where will you live twenty years into retirement? Or, how will your real estate needs change if you have a stroke or after the first spouse dies? If a cottage is going to be passed down to your children, will you do that while you are alive or through your estate, and what are the differences in these two options from a financial and legal point of view? Real estate has a lot of issues attached to it as well as a lot of money involved, so get proper planning. For example, it may make sense to put the cottage in a family trust on your death to ensure fair access to all of your children. And it may make sense to keep your home in your name (not make it jointly owned with children while you are alive) to preserve the tax-free status of your house and also protect it against the possible divorces of your children.

Structuring Part-Time Work for Maximum Tax Write-offs

If you work part time in retirement, try to structure the work as a self-employment relationship so you can write off a wide variety of costs. Find work that really is a hobby and that you would like to do. Consider starting your own business—you may be able to write off a host of business related costs like a home office, business use of your car, computer and internet usage related to the business, cell phone costs, and much more. By deducting these costs against your revenue, your average tax rate can be much lower compared to that of an employee.

Moving Closer to the Kids

There are lots of things to think about before you sell and move away from the homestead your family grew up in. These types of decisions are about more than just money. While the rest of this answer will focus on the financial aspect of this decision, I feel it is important to mention that I rarely recommend people move away from their communities, their backyards, and their lifelong friends. These non-financial factors are often more important than a few more bucks in your pocket. Living in a condo where you won't know your neighbors and where you can't walk on the grass in your backyard in your bare feet is hardly an improvement. Also, don't follow your children around the country in order to live closer to them. Chances are you won't see them more often, and you'll just end up babysitting the grandchildren. Is that the way you wanted to spend your retirement?

However, if you have a cash flow crunch, downsizing your home may be a good idea. People with a lot of money tied up in assets, like a home or land, but who have little cash flow to live off are called "asset rich, cash poor." All of their wealth is tied up in assets that don't generate any income.

Let's look at an example of how much cash flow can be freed up:

Grandpa and Grandma have a home in Toronto, which they have owned for thirty-five years, and is now worth $460,000. This is their only home and they are thinking about selling it and moving into a smaller home in the suburbs that costs only $160,000.

If they sold and repurchased, how much money would that add to their cash flow?

Since this is their only home, the capital gain would be tax free. Grandpa and Grandma would be able to invest $300,000 ($460,000 less $160,000). Investing $300,000 at 6% annually would add $18,000 per year to the couple's pre-tax income. That would likely amount to more than $12,000 per year of after-tax cash flow to the couple's income. That's an extra $1,000 to spend each month as long as they live!

With such a big boost to cash flow, I'm not sure how seniors can really ignore the impact. Adding substantial cash flow to their lives gives them the freedom to do so much more. This can be a significant improvement in quality of life that supports the sale of an expensive, empty house.

Taking Money Out of Your RRSP or RRIF in Retirement

Oftentimes, seniors are in a high tax bracket at sixty-nine and therefore pay the top marginal rate on their RRIF withdrawals. Yet they had been promised that they would be able to withdraw the money and pass less tax. What happened?

Nothing happened. Your RRSP savings and other savings worked as good or better than expected resulting in you having a lot of income in retirement. So much so, that you remain in the top tax bracket beyond your working years and well into retirement. Is that so bad? You are paying tax because you have more money.

Here are a few ideas on how to get more money out of your RRIF:

- Emigrate. If you do this and leave your RRIF in place after you leave, you can likely get your money out of your RRIF slowly each year with minimum withholding taxes—likely no more than 25%.
- Withdraw the minimum amount from your RRIF each year, and don't make the withdrawals until the last possible moment. This will contin-

ue to maximize the deferral of money inside your plan. Although RRSPs must be converted to RRIFs by age sixty-nine, the first withdrawal does not have to be made until December of the year you turn seventy.

- Base your RRIF withdrawals on the age of your younger spouse, if you have one. RRIF withdrawals are calculated according to age and by using a younger age you can continue to minimize withdrawals out of the plan. This continues to defer tax.

- Make early withdrawals from your RRSP or RRIF in years where your total income is less, even before you retire. Anytime after age sixty, if your total taxable income drops, consider withdrawing money from your RRSP or RRIF for the lower tax rate. This approach is not always the best, and it really depends on what tax amount you pay, what you do with the money after you withdraw it, and future investment returns you earn. Have a financial planner examine your total financial picture to see if you can truly benefit from reducing your RRSP or RRIF early.

- Claim tax deductions on your tax return that will offset your income inclusions from RRIF withdrawals you make. For example, interest expense from investment loans that you take out can be tax deductible in many cases. If you borrow to invest in a taxable account, the tax deductible interest cost can offset an RRIF income inclusion resulting in a net zero tax position.

More RRIF Rules
Converting Early to an RRIF

Don't do it. I can't imagine why anyone would convert their RRSP to an RRIF before the mandatory age of sixty-nine. If you need money to live off out of your RRSP, just make a withdrawal! At least this way you can take the withdrawals when you need them. Once you convert to a RRIF, you are forced to regularly take a fixed withdrawal amount, and you can't stop them.

Taking More Than the Minimum Out of the RRIF

The government dictates how much money you can withdraw from your RRIF each year. They set a minimum and there is no maximum. Whether you should take out more than the minimum required depends on your need for the cash, your current and future marginal tax bracket, and whether you have any other savings outside of your RRIF. Generally, if you have no other savings and you need the cash to survive, you will likely need to make greater RRIF withdrawals if you can't get a part-time job. Note that larger RRIF withdrawals will be subject to with-holding tax on each payment. If you have a pool of money outside of your RRIF in an open taxable account, the decision of which pool of money to spend becomes trickier. The RRIF withdrawals clearly draw more tax than the non-RRIF spending. However, the income generated within the RRIF is tax deferred and this is desirable as well. There really is no right or wrong answer as no one can accurately forecast all the variables involved. Given this, your RRIF withdrawals and your overall cash flow needs should be based on a well-defined investment program that examines all your personal traits to determine what the best way to produce cash flow is in your scenario. I'm a fan of taking the minimum out of your RRIF and living off the open taxable money. This preserves the tax deferral of your RRIF. If later in life your income drops and you fall into a lower tax bracket, consider increasing the RRIF withdrawals to take advantage of the lower taxation.

RRIF Liquidity

Since you are required to make annual withdrawals from your RRIF according to a government defined schedule, it is important to have the cash free within your RRIF each year for this payment. Don't make the mistake of putting all of your RRIF balance into a five-year bond, leaving you with no cash for the withdrawals. And don't put all the money into equities or equity mutual funds either, again leaving you in the potential-ly negative situation of having to sell stock or an equity mutual fund in a down market just to generate the cash you need for the RRIF payment.

RRIF Investments

Within a year of the mandated conversion, your old RRSP, which maybe focused only on growth, must be converted into a new income-generating plan. This is a big change for your savings, and the question is: have you actually changed your portfolio to reflect this new direction? An income-generating portfolio looks much different than a growth-ori-ented portfolio. Make sure you make the necessary changes to deal with this new stage of your life.

RRIF Withholding Taxes

There may be withholding taxes on any extra withdrawals you make out of your RRIF. In fact, extra withdrawals up to $5,000 are subject to 10% withholding tax, withdrawals from $5,000 to $15,000 are subject to 20% tax, and withdrawals greater than $15,000 are subject to 30% tax. In order to minimize this withholding tax, make all extra withdrawals in less than $5,000 increments. That means if you need $16,000, make four separate withdrawals of $4,000 over four separate days. The withholding tax is not an extra cost, by the way, it is simply a prepayment of the tax you will otherwise pay on the income on next year's tax return. Think of the withholding tax in the same way you think of your paycheque tax withholdings.

To RRIF or Not

When you turn sixty-nine, and are required to collapse your RRSP, you actually have three options for the money in your RRSP at that time:

1. Convert the RRSP to an RRIF and start taking minimum required withdrawals from the plan every year according to the government's formula. This is by far the most popular option among Canadians as it provides the most flexibility over your money.
2. Buy an annuity with all of your RRSP proceeds and receive a form of pension for the remainder of your life. While this is the easiest choice to manage over the long term, an annuity may be a poor investment compared to other choices. This can limit how much you will receive.
3. Collapse the RRSP and receive all cash at once. Withdrawing all of the money from the RRSP at once is fully taxable, subjecting the money to perhaps the highest rates of tax all at once.

Evaluate Your Need for a Systematic Withdrawal Plan

A systematic withdrawal plan, or SWP, is a popular planning tool to provide an income stream to an investor, usually elderly investors in retirement.

An SWP operates as follows: on a regular basis (monthly, quarterly, or other) an investor can obtain an income stream from their investment portfolio through an automated sale of investments and a distribution of accumulated income. An SWP is used to provide this income stream, by providing the investor with a mix of income and capital from their portfolio to meet their need. The investor can select the level of cash flow they want to receive and the SWP can be established within the dealer's or fund company's computer system to provide this amount directly into your bank account. A financial advisor can set up an SWP for you, and it can be turned on or off with only a few days notice. Many seniors use SWPs as part of their regular income in retirement.

The SWP generates the necessary cash flow by selling some of your portfolio investments as needed and mixing this capital amount with whatever earnings have also been generated by the portfolio (interest, dividends, etc.). The payment an investor typically gets is a little bit of investment income and a little bit of return capital. That's right, you get a bit of your own investment back as part of the cash flow payment. Together this mixture of income and return of capital is yours to spend.

SWP Tax Efficiency Claim

Often an SWP payment is sold as a tax effective income stream for an investor. There are three inaccuracies in this statement. First, it is not an income steam. It is a cash flow stream. Only part of the cash flow is actually income or return earned from the investment. The rest of the cash flow stream is a return of your original investment. This is not a return. Do not compare an SWP cash flow yield with the rate of return on an investment—this is not a fair comparison because of the return of capital component on the SWP. In effect, an SWP is giving you some of your own money back if the SWP is set up on a taxable investment account.

The second inaccuracy is that an SWP is a tax efficient cash flow stream. It is considered tax efficient because the cash flow yield consists of the non-taxable return of capital as part of the payment you receive regularly. This makes the effective tax rate on the cash flow payment artificially low since you won't be taxed on your own capital—you only pay tax on the income generated by the investments. The SWP cash flow is not tax efficient in my opinion for this reason. Sure there is less tax paid overall on the cash flow because only some of the cash flow is actually taxable income. But to call this tax efficient is misleading.

The third inaccuracy relating to SWPs relates to the forced sale of securities each payment period in order to generate the proceeds for payment. Generally, depending on the investments owned, a small amount of your funds are sold each payment period to generate the cash needed to make the payment to your bank account. This may see equity funds being sold at down market times which is generally not desirable. This may also see equity funds being sold at high market times, which triggers taxation and harms after-tax returns. On the bright side, at least it will be capital gains return, which is tax preferred. Either way, this forced sale of securities to meet the payment needs is not desirable for your equity mutual funds. Further, someone should be tracking all these forced sales of funds for tax purposes, because calculating the capital gains you will need to declare each year will be a headache if the SWP is operating on your taxable savings account.

Cash Flow Options

Another approach to obtaining cash flow from your portfolio other than an SWP is to structure your portfolio to contain enough fixed-income investments to provide several years of income in advance. For example, if you need an income of $50,000 (after-tax) every year, you may take $150,000 ($50,000 x 3) of your savings and invest it in short-term bonds to mature the year you need it. Then invest the rest of your money into a longer term portfolio that reflects your investor profile. As the years progress, re-supply your short-term money pool using income earned off the long-term portfolio and through timely sales of the long-term portfolio to supplement the short-term cash flow needs. By controlling the sale of your long-term holdings (stocks and equity mutual funds) in this way, you can control your tax liabilities and incur them in years when your tax rate is lower. Also, less selling of equities promotes greater deferred taxation and enhances wealth accumulation. Finally, controlled selling of equities may give you better control to sell high (a good goal) instead of selling every month whether markets are high or low the way an SWP does.

Owning a Rental Property Can Boost Retirement Income

Canada is filled with rental properties. This strategy will discuss the merits and pitfalls of owning a rental property to enhance your retirement income.

Real estate can be considered another asset class to invest in, just like stocks and bonds. Given that, it should be evaluated against those asset classes as an investment.

Here are some of the pros and cons of real estate as an investment:

Pros
- Rental properties can generate two types of investment income. First there is annual rental income from renters (minus expenses). Rental income is taxed as regular income on your personal tax return, assuming you own the rental property personally (versus in a holding company). The second kind of investment income is capital gains that come from appreciation in the fair market value of the property. This accrued gain is only taxable when the property is disposed of and can be a very lucrative aspect of property ownership. Landlords in Toronto, for example, have seen their property values turn them into millionaires in many cases.
- Rental income qualifies as earned income for purposes of determin-

ing RRSP contribution room. This means you can build RRSP contribution room from your rental profit that ends up on your personal income tax return each year.

- A rental property is a business, and all businesses can deduct business expenses before arriving at taxable income. Owning your own business may allow you to write off a variety of business expenses and to also pay salaries to your spouse and children if they are involved in running the business of your rental property. These income-splitting opportunities can result in less family taxes overall.
- A rental property is a good inflation fighter. Every year our cost of living rises—one only has to look at how the price of stamps has risen over the years. In many provinces a landlord can regularly raise rents each year. That means the landlord can increase their income equal to or ahead of inflation. This is not something that is possible with an interest-generating investment.

Cons
- To buy one property, the cost is often hundreds of thousands of dollars. For most Canadians, their total savings pool cannot afford the risk of buying only one investment. Should the real estate value ever plummet, this could devastate your savings. Most investors may prefer a diversified stock and bond portfolio where the risk of significant loss is mitigated through ownership of several securities together. This can be a double-edged sword of course, look at what happened five years ago: as the stock market crashed due to the tech bubble, the price of real estate continued to rise in many parts of Canada. The message is that proper diversification in any kind of asset is important.
- Minimum investment amounts depend on the property, but can be considered to be more than $50,000. This compares to your ability to buy a mutual fund or a stock for as little as $25.
- Your ability to liquidate the real estate holding may take years. But, if you need cash from your publicly traded stock or bond portfolio, you can usually sell the same business day and get your cash the next. Selling real estate can be a tedious process, enlisting an agent, advertising the sale, and so on. With real estate it is very hard to get at your cash should you need to. And if the market turns down when you need to sell, you may have to put off that open-heart surgery in the U.S. you were needing.
- If you own one rental property in one region of the country, you are

susceptible to wider market swings in value. For example, if you owned a condo in Toronto in the late 1980s you were devastated by a prolonged downturn in the condo market. Compare this to a stock portfolio where you are able to own securities in companies of many types, in many industries, in many countries, etc. This diversification reduces the likelihood you will be exposed to a significant loss in any one investment. Not so with real estate.

- Many rental properties may not offer the total rate of return that a stock of equity mutual fund may offer over the long term. Total return for a rental property consists of the rental income plus the capital gain that exists due to appreciation in the value of the property. In regions of the country where property values don't rise very often, it may be more profitable to own a stock portfolio than a rental property.

- The hassle factor: the burden of fixing someone's toilet in the middle of the night is a reality of being a landlord. Sure you can hire a property management company to do all this, but say goodbye to a lot of your profits.

- If one of your tenants slips on the front steps because the steps are icy, what happens if they sue you? Landlords must ensure they are insured against such perils.

- If you rent out a room in your home for revenue, you should be aware that you may be compromising the tax-free status of your home, or at least part of your home. Technically you are using part of your home for business purposes and it is not your principal residence. This negates the tax-free status normally associated with your main place of residence. Most people don't want to lose this tax-free status, so make sure you talk to a tax accountant about the issues of renting out part of your home.

- The very purchase of a rental property further complicates the tax exemption on principal residences. All Canadian families are allowed to have one tax-free residence. If you buy a second property, it will be taxable on sale assuming that you claim your main residence as your principal residence. Whenever you own more than one piece of real estate, ensure that your principal residence exemption is carefully evaluated.

When you look at all the variables, rental property as an investment may not make sense due to the cost. But as a separate asset class for those who can afford it, and in the right part of a city, it can be a long-term wealth enhancer for many Canadians.

Reverse Mortgages

Reverse mortgages can be useful where seniors living in mortgage-free homes are looking for more cash flow to live off, yet are not ready to sell their home and move elsewhere. A lending company offers to loan them money based on their home value (as collateral) and the money can be used to supplement their existing cash flow. The company will keep track of the loan and charge interest on it, but not force repayment of the loan until the elderly couple dies. At that time, the company will have first claim on the couple's home: it will be sold and the proceeds from the sale would be applied against the outstanding loan and accrued interest.

The advantage of reverse mortgages is the additional cash flow without having to move. The disadvantage of reverse mortgages is that you may outlive the money that will be paid by the company that now has a mortgage on your home. Also, you may not like the fact that you no longer really own your home since you have a growing amount of debt being applied against it. Finally, investigate what happens to the plan if you get sick and must sell your home before you die.

Borrowing Money from Your Life Insurance

There are instances with some insurance policies whereby you can remove money from the policy by effectively taking out a loan against the cash value. Since this is a loan and not income, these amounts received would not be taxable. Insurance companies that permit this lending will charge you an interest rate on the loan and compound the interest as long as the loan is outstanding.

One strategy is to take out the loan to supplement retirement income. Since the loan is not taxable, an investor's cash flow can be greatly enhanced. Often, the insurance company will simply demand repayment of the loan and interest on the death of the life insured, and take what they are owed out of the insurance payout proceeds.

There are several variables to consider before embarking on this strategy:

- If the insurance proceeds on your death are designated for a specific purpose, any loan you take today that will be repaid out of the death proceeds could harm your original goal for the insurance.
- Do you really need the additional retirement cash flow? If not, why take on a loan with non-tax deductible interest expense to generate a cash flow that isn't necessary?
- Have you explored other strategies to enhance your retirement income before resorting to borrowing money?

- If you really need to borrow to generate retirement cash flow, have you explored a regular mortgage on your house or other debt to be compared with the cost of debt against the insurance policy loan?
- Shop around among insurance companies that offer the ability to borrow against an insurance policy before you buy.
- Find out what happens if you live so long that the insurance company cuts off your regular cash flow loans because the loan and accrued interest now exceeds the face value of your insurance policy on death.

Most Canadians, in my opinion, have no need to borrow against a life insurance policy in their retirement years. They may not even need an insurance policy. Your needs for both of these products is contingent on your own unique financial circumstances. Evaluate your needs with a professional financial planner.

Are Income Trusts Just Glass Houses Waiting to Break?

Income trusts are all the rage today. As yields on bonds have dropped, many investors have aggressively moved en masse into a variety of income trusts to chase higher yield. While a handful of income trusts are reasonable investments, many of them may not be suitable for most investors. I sat down with a retired investor last month who owned fifteen different income trusts. When I asked him why he bought them all, he said he liked that they earned 10% per year. That's his first misconception. An income trust generating 10% cash flow may not be a rate of return. That 10% may be a cash flow yield that consists of some real return and some return of your own capital. This is not a pure return. So to compare 10% cash flow yield to a 4% GIC interest real return is not a fair comparison. A GIC at 4% may, in fact, be generating more real return than an income trust at 10%. This gentleman skimmed the surface in trying to understand this investment and really didn't know what he had bought.

Next I asked him where he got the cash to buy these fifteen income trusts. He stated that he cashed in several bonds and GICs to buy the income trusts. Dangerous move. Many income trusts are very risky "small cap" stocks. These are companies that most of us would never otherwise buy. None of them are listed in the S&P 500 or TSX 60 Index of Canada's largest stocks. If you must buy income trusts, at least swap money already in equities, but you may not want to use your bonds.

Many of the income trusts are balancing acts where stock prices are propped up by the promise of regular large distributions to investors. At the same time, distributions are made possible by the maintenance of a lofty share price. Should a distribution be skipped or reduced for any little reason all of this could come tumbling down. It has already happened to at least two income trusts in Canada in the last few years.

REITs Are One Form of Income Trusts

One form of income trusts are real estate investment trusts or REITs. REITs are portfolios of real estate investments, including shopping malls, office buildings, apartment blocks, or residential homes. The rental income generated from the tenants of these properties, minus the expenses of operating these properties, often form much of the distributions you receive as a shareholder. Some REITs pay out 10% or more as a regular distribution.

While I consider REITs to be more conservative than most income trusts, they too are not without troubles. Recently I reviewed an REIT and noted that it was distributing payments to investors that exceeded the money that the REIT was earning in the month. The cash distributions were actually being financed! If the REIT is making promises beyond which the business can sustain, it may not be a wise investment in the first place.

Artificial Poverty

In some provinces if you move into a provincially funded nursing home, the province will charge you a fee to live there according to your income level based on your tax return. The higher your income, the higher your cost, since the province feels higher income people are in a better position to pay their fair share. Each province has their own system.

Because the system is set up on an income-tested format, it has proven easy for many Canadians to "beat the system." By reducing their elderly parents' total income in the years before and during entry into the nursing home, families can make their parents look "poor" and thereby make it possible to pay less to the government for keeping their elderly parents in the nursing home. The elderly parents can be made to look poor by stripping away their net worth and income sources by transferring this wealth to their children before death.

While this is a money saving technique, I have a problem with this approach to net worth maximization. Transferring wealth to the next generation before death will expose the elderly person's net worth to their children's potentially wasteful spending. Not to mention that if children get divorced or go bankrupt, the parents' net worth (that they now own) may just disappear.

If you are set on maximizing government benefits, consider transferring parents' assets into a trust instead of having them gifted to children. Using a properly set up trust can minimize the parents' net worth and total income in the desired way. It can also allow the parents to keep control of their assets since a trust is a separate legal entity.

Minimizing nursing home costs are one example where your taxable income levels can affect other fees. Another example is clawbacks of pension income like OAS if your taxable income is too high. Family trusts and investment holding companies are two tools that can help you to protect your wealth and keep more money in your hands longer.

Wintering in the States in Retirement

If you are spending substantial amounts of time in the U.S., I hope you are counting the number of days you spend there each year. If your days add up to 183 or more each year (talk to a tax professional about the exact formula to calculate days), you may qualify as a U.S. resident and have to file a U.S. tax return.

Canadian and U.S. cross-border tax issues are some of the most complicated forms of tax planning, so if you are spending large amounts of time in the U.S., talk to a cross-border tax expert (not any CA will due) about your issues.

Your case is even more complicated if you have purchased U.S. real estate because of the U.S. tax consequences. For example, when you sell the real estate your American lawyer should withhold income tax of 15% of the proceeds on the sale. You also will have to file a U.S. tax return to report the sale and pay tax in the U.S. You'll also have to report any gain on your Canadian tax return in Canadian currency as well. If you die with the real estate, and if it is an expensive property, you may have to pay some U.S. estate taxes at rates of up to 55%. And if you legally rent out the U.S. property you will now have to file a U.S. tax return to report the rent and claim tax deductions.

Unless you want to permanently emigrate to the U.S. or another country, I would suggest you follow these basic guidelines to avoid having to pay any kind of U.S. income or estate taxes at all:

- Don't buy a U.S. real estate property. Just rent instead.
- Don't ever rent out your U.S. property.
- Make sure you don't spend more than six months in the U.S. in any given year.
- Don't own significant amounts of U.S. stock. If you do, hold them

inside a Canadian trust, a Canadian holding company, or a Canadian mutual fund. These vehicles can make you exempt from U.S. estate taxes.
- Get rid of large amounts of U.S. assets before you die.
- Get an opinion from a qualified U.S. and/or Canadian tax expert that everything you are doing follows the latest tax rules in both countries.

Annuities

An annuity is an investment product whereby you give an insurance company a lump sum and the company agrees to pay you a rate of return on your money over a multi-year period and also return a regular cash flow that is composed of an investment return and a return of some of your own capital. Annuities are attractive for seniors who want a very simple investment solution (all money is managed on your behalf and you just get a cheque in the mail each month) and for seniors who want to ensure they never run out of money (you can buy annuities that will guarantee payments until death). They are also attractive because the taxes you pay are lower since the cash flow you get from the annuity is a mix of earnings and a return of original investment.

The reason you never hear about annuities anymore is that they are more popular when long-term interest rates in Canada are much higher than they have been lately. This is because the rate of return and the payments you will receive over the life of the annuity are based on the interest rates that exist when you buy them.

I wouldn't recommend that anyone consider annuities unless they match the scenarios below:

- You are incapable of taking care of your money due to illness, incapacity, old age, or other unusual circumstances. In these cases, annuities can provide a guaranteed cash flow stream.
- You want to take advantage of the $1,000 pension tax credit that is available for all Canadians who have qualifying pension or annuity income.
- Anyone who wants to make their investments very simple because they would prefer to enjoy life not worrying about their finances.

If you do look into annuities, there are some factors you will need to consider in deciding the type of annuity you want to buy:

- How long the annuity should run (e.g. your entire life or less)

- If you want the cash flow to be adjusted over time for inflation
- When you want the annuity payments to start
- If you want your estate on your death to get any remaining annuity money

Overall, if you want the largest payments to result from your annuity purchase, keep it simple. Generally, the fancier the annuity the less money you will get. Most Canadians should explore all other investment management options before considering annuities. Despite their simplicity, annuities lack the flexibility that most investors demand today.

Beware of Offshore Tax Havens

For most of us, the idea of placing money offshore, out of the hands of CRA, is a pleasant dream. In reality, there are few opportunities for the average Canadian to defer or eliminate tax using a legitimate offshore trust strategy.

Canadian residents are taxed on their worldwide income. As long as you live in Canada, you are generally required to report all income earned anywhere in the world, regardless of how or where, on your Canadian tax return. This generally includes income in an offshore trust where Canadian residents have an interest in that trust. There are some exceptions, however, to this general rule in the context of offshore trusts. If the trust is established by a non-resident settlor—the contributor of the property in the trust—and has a non-resident trustee, the undistributed income will not be subject to Canadian tax if the settlor is a resident of Canada for less than sixty months. Income distributed to a Canadian beneficiary will be taxable. This exception is particularly useful in the context of a multinational family where different family members are residents in different jurisdictions and there is a genuine intention by the non-residents to benefit the Canadian residents.

Without getting into a lot of detail, this is what to remember about offshore tax havens: if you are a conservative Canadian with average wealth, plan to always live in Canada, and your relatives are Canadian and will likely always live in Canada, there are generally no opportunities to save tax on investments using a legitimate offshore strategy. However, if you are ever planning to leave Canada permanently, if you have relatives who are not Canadian and want to become Canadian, or if these non-Canadian relatives want to leave you family assets from their estate, then you should consider consulting a qualified tax advisor about offshore tax strategies.

For individuals in Canada who believe that placing money in an off-shore bank account and not reporting income on your Canadian tax return is an acceptable offshore strategy, be warned that your strategy is against the law. Since you are taxed on your worldwide income as a Canadian resident, you are obliged to report all of your income. If you choose not to report any offshore income, you are committing tax evasion and may face fines and imprisonment for these actions.

Where it is possible, planning the use of offshore trusts should be very carefully structured and paperwork should be precisely prepared. Properly done, this is legitimate tax planning and is not a form of tax evasion. Due to the complexity of this type of planning, ensure that you use a global tax advisory service that can deal with the cross-border international issues.

The Real Uses of Offshore Planning

As mentioned above, while there are opportunities for offshore tax planning to avoid or minimize Canadian taxation, these opportunities are the exception rather than the rule.

There are many other reasons to deal offshore than just tax. Here are some of the more popular reasons:

- Investment diversification: Canada is a small country in the global economy and there are thousands of global money managers that an investor cannot access in Canada. Investing offshore can allow you to diversify your investment portfolio beyond what you can typically buy in Canada.
- Creditor-proofing: If you are sued in Canada and lose the battle, or if you go bankrupt, it may be difficult for your creditors to take your assets held in a foreign jurisdiction. Many doctors in the U.S. for example, have set up their net worth in offshore accounts to protect them against malpractice lawsuits.
- Confidentiality: many foreign jurisdictions are renowned for their secrecy and refusal to tell foreign governments and police about their client accounts. High profile people often find this confidentiality comforting.
- Convenience: If you are world traveller, holding some of your wealth in countries you visit can ease your traveling and avoid having to deal with foreign currency conversions.

Overall, the world is becoming a smaller place where it far more common to have some element of global finances leading to greater amounts of cross-border issues. If you have non-Canadian assets or income of any kind, and you are a Canadian resident, it is very likely you should be declaring these assets to CRA and annually paying tax on any income. Whether it is a bank account in Hong Kong or a rental property in Florida, it is taxable in Canada annually! If you are not claiming this income, you are breaking the law. And, at the rate that Canada is sharing information with foreign governments, it may only be a matter of time until the taxman catches up with you.

Can You Have Too Much Money in Your RRSP?

There is no simple answer to this question. In order to determine what is appropriate for you to have in your RRSP, you have to do a mathematical calculation and forecast under both scenarios: contributing to an RRSP for your entire life or not contributing to an RRSP but, instead, saving in a non-tax sheltered plan. This will involve making a lot of assumptions that may or may not happen, such as: future tax rates, future investment returns, future re-investment amounts, future savings amounts, future spending needs, and so on. With all these assumptions all you can do is make an educated guess as to which approach will be better.

Let's look at an example below.

Scenario One: Let's assume that a Canadian investor will deposit $5,000 into an RRSP for thirty consecutive years. This will mean a tax deduction and tax refund of one half of the contribution or $2,500 per year. Then assume that the refund is reinvested in a taxable savings account and both this money and the RRSP money will earn an annual compounded return of 8% per year, consisting of 6% interest and 2% deferred capital gains. At the end of the thirty years assume that liquidation of the portfolio will trigger any built-up taxes all at once at 50% tax and 23% capital gains taxation. Under this scenario, an investor would have $497,490 at the end of thirty years after tax.

Scenario Two: Assume that the same $5,000 savings amount is invested in a taxable account, earning 8% a year in the same proportion as above. The annual return on these investments will be taxed at the top marginal rates of 0% for deferred capital gains (assume buy-and-hold whereby capital gains are only taxable when sold) and 50% on interest. The last assumption is that the capital gains return (2% per year) wouldn't be taxed until the end of the thirty years. Under this scenario, an investor will have $428,565 at the end of thirty years.

Conclusion: The RRSP option resulted in more money.

The Canadian RRSP system is one of the greatest tax shelters remaining in the western world. It will usually result in greater net worth than if you don't use it. There are exceptions however. I would encourage you to contribute to your RRSP and also create a taxable savings pool if possible. That way you have a combined investment portfolio that can offer the benefits of both. Clearly from the above example, you can see that the number of variables that must be examined make your RRSP or non-RRSP investment strategy very personal, warranting an examination of variables that you are comfortable with.

Beyond GICs

The alternatives to owning GICs are to own Canadian Treasury Bills or Government of Canada Bonds, to name a few. These bonds are market-traded bonds, the ones that the government issues to pay down our debt. These are not Canada Savings Bonds, term deposits, or anything similar. Market-traded bonds can be bought and sold daily (like stocks) but offer the safety (and more) of GICs. Anyone can buy Government of Canada Bonds at any time, so there is no excuse to say you can't find them. Talk to your financial advisor.

Here's a summary of the advantages of bonds over GICs:

GICs	Desirable Characteristics	Bonds
GICs will pay you a fixed rate of interest for a specific time period.	Highest possible returns	Bonds do the same and can regularly offer higher returns than GICs.
There are no fees to buy GICs. But, if your GIC interest rate is less than the rate of a bond, that is a form of fee.	Fees	A fee in the form of a commission when you buy or sell the bond.
GICs offer little range: typically thirty-day to five-year maturities to pick from.	Range of maturities	Bonds offer one-day to thirty-year maturities to pick from. Much better choice for planning purposes.
GICs can rarely be cashed in early. If they are, you typically lose your interest.	Ability to sell without penalty	Bonds can be sold at any time without loss of interest. A bond may be sold at a capital loss, however, if bond markets are depressed at the time.
GICs generate interest income that is the highest taxed kind of investment income in Canada today.	Tax treatment	Bonds generate interest and also may offer capital gains or losses. Gains are taxed at a lower tax rate than interest.
GICs are very simple to buy.	Simplicity	Bonds are easy to buy, but not as easy as GICs.
Only one basic kind of GIC.	Varieties	There are Government of Canada Bonds, provincial bonds, municipal bonds, U.S. bonds, international bonds, and more.
CDIC guarantees your GICs up to $60,000. This is a restrictive penalty.	Guarantees	The Government of Canada guarantees their bonds without limits.

Government of Canada Bonds are less risky because the CDIC guarantee on GICs that we all relish is actually a limitation. The government has gone out of its way to protect you even though you have decided to invest through a company (typically a bank) instead of buying a government bond directly. In other words, if you had bought a bond directly from the Government of Canada, for any amount, it is fully guaranteed. But because you decided to risk buying your GIC through a bank or other institution, the government will only protect you for up to $60,000. That CDIC guarantee puts a limit on your protection—why would you want that? Get out of GICs forever, and get into Government of Canada Bonds and other bond investments.

Managing Inflation and a Rising Cost of Living

A lot of people don't think about inflation when it comes to their retirement and that can be disastrous. For example, no doubt all of us know someone who retired years ago on a fixed pension—pension benefits that are not indexed for inflation over the years. If this person retired twenty years ago on a pension of $20,000 per year, today they are trying to survive on exactly the same pension amount. In the last twenty years inflation has destroyed their purchasing power and taken them from a comfortable retirement to one of near poverty. Their pension stayed flat, while the prices of stamps, milk, cars, and everything else continued to rise. They lost ground because they forgot about inflation.

Someone who has bought a lot of GICs in the last twenty years may have been pushing themselves into poverty without realizing it. Look at this example:

If you bought a GIC paying an interest rate of:	4%
Then paid tax on the interest income,	
losing up to half of the return to tax (assume 50% tax rate):	(2%)
Leaving you with a net return of:	**2%**
Now let's subtract the impact of inflation the same year:	(3%)
What you actually made:	(1%)

After inflation you may have been taking economic steps backwards with each GIC purchase!

There are several different ways to counter the impact of inflation with your finances that will lessen the impact of inflation on your money and lifestyle:

- Get some high dividend yielding stocks or equity mutual funds inside your investment portfolio, since dividends have a tendency to be raised over time and this will counter the impact of inflation.
- Get some real estate investments (rental property, REITs, or other) since rents paid to landlords (you) tend to rise over the years with inflation and these raised rents can be passed on to you in the form of higher returns.
- Be on the lookout for investments that offer an inflation-adjusted return. Some bonds, called real return bonds, offer a rate of return that gives some consideration to the impact of inflation each year.
- Get at least a small amount of well-diversified stocks or equity mutual funds in your investment portfolio to offer you the potential for a total rate of return that will far exceed inflation for the year. Ensure, however, that any equities you purchase fit in with your overall investment plan. This last approach is likely the easiest to implement and advisable for all long-term investors.

Managing Retirement Cash Flow

I'm often contacted by retirees who are surprised at the amount of tax they continue to pay in retirement and are looking to maximize their after-tax retirement cash flow by reducing taxation. Let's look at a solution for this concern by looking at a sample scenario.

Retired senior, age seventy

Annual pension income	$50,000
Annual CPP income	$9,300
Annual OAS income	$5,000
RRIF income	$8,000 this year and more each year as per RRIF mandatory withdrawal requirements (approximated)
Interest income	$20,000 this year (5% times taxable savings below)
Total income	$92,300
RRIF savings balance	$200,000
Taxable savings	$400,000

Retired spouse, age sixty-seven

CPP income	$2,000
OAS income	$5,000
Savings	$0

Based on the basic scenario above, let's now examine several different retirement issues:

1. How can you reduce your income taxes?
2. How can you enhance your after-tax income?
3. What happens when the first spouse dies?

The following strategies are not a comprehensive list of options but are merely some specific thoughts on these issues.

How can you reduce your income taxes?

- Apply to the government to have your CPP payments split between the two spouses. This is as simple as filling out a government form once. But recognize that it is forever. Equalizing the CPP payments will shift some income from the higher-earning spouse to the lower earning spouse.
- Decide how much income you need to live on versus how much income you are earning. If you are earning more than you need for day-to-day cash flow, restructure your income streams to produce more tax efficient dividends and capital gains returns.
- RRIF withdrawals must be made according to a pre-set schedule that is based on your income or your spouse's income. Therefore, you can minimize all RRIF withdrawals by basing them on the age of the younger spouse. This will maximize a continued tax deferral within the tax-sheltered plan. Also, consider making larger RRIF withdrawals in years when your taxable income is lower. This would allow you to remove more from the RRIF at a lower tax cost.
- Replace the investment generating the interest income with another type of investment that will generate a more tax-smart investment income. For example, purchasing a low turnover Canadian equity mutual fund will generate an annual return that is largely deferred capital appreciation. This form of return is only taxable when disposed of, thereby deferring taxation into the future. This maximizes after-tax wealth far better than a fixed-income investment.
- Consider whether there are any assets that the lower income spouse can sell to the higher-income spouse in order to legitimately transfer taxable wealth into the hands of the lower-taxed spouse. For example, if the lower income spouse has jewelry that can be sold to the other spouse for cash, this will allow the lower income spouse to invest the money received and earn a return at a lower tax rate. This strategy

can also work for cottages, vehicles, and other assets of value that the lower income person brought into the relationship.

- Get a professional tax-planning review by a qualified tax professional to ensure that both spouses are annually maximizing their tax deductions and tax credits.
- Use the income of the higher-earning spouse to live on. The lower income spouse can save their income for investment. That way any investment income generated by the lower earning spouse will be less taxable.
- Move to Alberta where taxes are lower on personal income.
- Move out of the country to a lower taxed jurisdiction where Canadian income sources can be preserved in Canada but will face less taxation when paid to a foreign country. Ensure that you talk to a tax specialist who can help you to evaluate all the pros and cons of emigration.

How can you enhance your after-tax income?

This can be accomplished in two ways in this case: increase total income and decrease taxation. Above we have dealt with reducing taxation. Here are some ways to increase total income:

- Arrange your taxable savings portfolio and RRIF to own investments with the potential of generating higher long-term portfolio returns. Generally, equity investments outperform fixed-income investments over the long term. However, any portfolio change should be examined in the context of your entire investment program.
- Preserve your government benefits. In the above example, your high income is causing a partial clawback of OAS benefits. This can be avoided by transferring the taxable savings portfolio into a new holding company owned by the taxpayer. All the income generated on this money will now be held inside the holding company (and taxed there) until it is decided to release this income from the company and put into your hands. Because this income is moved off of your personal tax return, it is legitimately "hidden" for purposes of calculating taxable income leading to a clawback of benefits. Evaluate all of the pros and cons of putting a holding company in place before doing so.
- Get a part-time job in retirement. Something that you enjoy.

What happens when the first spouse dies?

On the death of the first spouse, generally no tax implications arise if the spouse inherits the net worth of the deceased. Under the Income Tax

Act, assets can transfer to another spouse "at cost," deferring taxation on any taxable assets until the death of the last surviving spouse. This will not be the case, however, if assets are left to children or other heirs. Here is a brief summary of the taxation of some common assets on death:

- Principal residence. CRA allows your main home to be tax free no matter how much it is worth. If you have more than one piece of real estate, talk to a tax specialist about how to plan for this appropriately.
- Cash. Any form of cash investments such as GICs or Canada Savings Bonds are not taxable on death. Any interest income they generate is taxable, but pure cash simply passes to the heir untaxed from an income tax point of view.
- RRSPS and RRIFS. These accounts are tax sheltered, so on death of the last surviving spouse they become fully taxable. This can result in a significant tax liability if you have a large RRSP or RRIF.
- Appreciated stocks or equity mutual funds in a taxable portfolio. These investments are fully taxable on the appreciated capital gain in the year of death of the last surviving spouse.
- Family cottage or business. These assets are taxable on the appreciated capital gain in the year of death.

Understanding Fixed-Income Investments for Retirement

Seniors often search for the highest return possible with the least risk on their investments. More specifically, they relate these criteria to their fixed-income investments.

This section will review a variety of investments that older Canadians may consider for their investment portfolio income. We will discuss fixed-income investments according to the following criteria: return potential, volatility risk, fees, flexibility, and taxes. It is important to note that this is not a complete list of possible fixed-income investments that seniors could consider, nor are the criteria above all the factors that need to be considered before purchase.

RRIF versus Open/Taxable Accounts

The analysis of the fixed-income products listed above will ignore whether they are best suited for ownership within your RRIF/RRSP or within a taxable account. Clearly, income earned from these products situated within a tax-sheltered plan is deferred until withdrawal from the plan. In an open account, taxation of investment income is annual, based on a calendar year.

For purposes of the analysis below, the tax consequences will be reviewed for products that are owned in an open, taxable account only. It is important to consider whether owning fixed-income products within an RRSP or within an open account is better for your financial situation.

Canada Savings Bonds (CSBs)

Debt issued by the federal government, providing a fixed interest rate in exchange for your bond purchase. Available in a variety of denominations but with a fixed maturity. Cashable on the first day of any month. Available through many institutions. Generates interest income.

The Good: Cashable whenever you want. Easily available.

The Bad: Better returns available from other products. Some interest may be lost if cashed in at the wrong time. Generates highly taxed interest income. Provides interest income annually.

Recommendation: Not worth purchasing.

Government of Canada Bonds (bonds traded on the bond markets daily)

Debt issued by the federal government providing a fixed interest rate in exchange for your money. Available in a variety of denominations and a variety of maturities. Cashable every business day. Generates interest income if held to maturity and interest and capital gain/losses if sold actively, since market value fluctuates daily, depending on market interest rate movements.

The Good: Maturities of one day to thirty years available. Fully government guaranteed. Cashable at any time. Better returns possible compared to other fixed-income investments. Potential to generate capital gains return in addition to interest. Provides interest income quarterly, semi-annually, or annually.

The Bad: Minimum investment of $5,000. Available for purchase only through financial advisor with full securities licensing. Can result in a capital loss if sold after market interest rates rise.

Recommendation: Every investor would be well served owning Government of Canada Bonds and holding them to maturity.

Government of Canada Stripped Bonds

Regular Government of Canada Bonds in which the interest-paying component has been separated from the bond principal, and each sells separately as an investment. Stripped bonds sell at a discount from their future maturity, within an implicit interest rate that will be earned annually. No interest payments are ever received. The value of the investment simply rises until it reaches the face value at maturity. Taxation occurs annually, based on the calculated implicit rate of return.

The Good: Similar returns to Government of Canada Bonds. Cashable at any time. A variety of maturities available. Possibility to earn capital gains on top of the interest return, if they are sold prior to maturity after interest rates decline. Fully guaranteed investments.

The Bad: They provide no income stream, yet they are taxed annually on the return they earn. Possible to generate a capital loss if sold prior to maturity, after interest rates go up.

Recommendation: Fantastic fixed-income investment for a RRIF or RRSP.

Government of Canada Treasury Bills (T-bills)

These are short-term debt obligations of the federal government that are fully guaranteed. Maturities range from thirty days to one year. Cashable at any time. Generate interest income but can add capital gains or losses if sold prior to maturity. Minimum investment of $5,000. T-bills are sold at a discount of their face value and mature at their face value. This means that no interest is paid until maturity.

The Good: Cashable at any time. Reasonable interest rates.

The Bad: Only available up to one year maturity. For sale only through fully licensed advisors. Not good for a regular income stream.

Recommendation: May be a good short-term investment versus a GIC. Shop the rates to see which is better. Not useful for a retirement income stream.

Money Market Funds

A mutual fund consisting of a pool of short-term, very liquid investments that are actively managed by a professional money manager for an annual fee. Access to your money is usually within twenty-four hours. Some mutual funds charge fees to buy and sell. The investments usually owned by money market funds consist of T-bills and short-term bonds of governments and corporations. Fund generates interest income monthly, quarterly, or at other intervals.

The Good: Mutual funds are widely available. Minimum investment is as low as $25, which buys a share of the entire pool of investments. The professional money manager takes care of the buying and selling of investments on your behalf. You can buy and sell the fund any business day.

The Bad: Some money market funds may own investments you would never own personally. Some money market funds charge high annual fees and high fees to buy and sell.

Recommendation: Great investments for a variety of purposes but buyers should become comfortable with the kinds of investments that the fund owns and should shop around for lower fees.

Bond Funds

A mutual fund consisting of a pool of short-term, medium-term, or long-term market traded bonds that are actively managed by a professional money manager for an annual fee. You can access your money within a few days. Some mutual funds charge fees to buy and sell. Fund generates interest income monthly, quarterly, or at other intervals. Managers actively trade the bonds based on interest rates changes to try to generate additional capital gains returns on top of the interest earnings.

The Good: Over the long term, actively traded funds have generated rates of return on an after-tax basis that are superior to other fixed-income investments. They are a flexible investments that can provide a regular retirement income stream. Choice for varieties of bond funds is broad, and they are easily available at many institutions.

The Bad: In the short term (over only a few years) it is possible to lose money with a bond fund, as a result of the active trading by the money manager. Annual bond fees and the commissions for buying and selling can be high.

Recommendation: Bond funds can play an important role in the longer-term portion of your fixed-income portfolio. Shop around on fees. Verify that the holdings of the fund are to your liking.

High Yield Funds

A mutual fund consisting of a pool of more aggressive cash-flow generating investments, such as preferred shares, royalty trusts, convertible securities, lower quality corporate bonds, and debentures. These are riskier investments that will offer greater return in exchange for taking on greater risk. High-yield funds are actively managed by a professional money manager for an annual fee. Access to your money is usually within a few days. Some mutual funds charge fees to buy and sell. Fund generates interest, dividends, and capital gains monthly, quarterly, or at other intervals. Managers actively trade the investments based on interest rates and stock market changes to try to generate additional capital gains returns on top of the interest earnings.

The Good: Higher returns are possible. Potential to earn tax-friendly capital-gains returns on top of interest income. Can be purchased with small amounts of money. Cashable at any time.

The Bad: These are not blue chip investments and may have very high risk levels. May have high annual fees and commissions to buy and sell.

Recommendation: Suitable for only the aggressive fixed-income portion of your portfolio, or not at all.

Conclusions on Wealthbuilding and Retirement

This has been a long chapter, highlighting the complication of retirement finances and how much there is to evaluate. Let's sum it up with a test to see if you have got all of your retirement issues sorted out. Take this quiz and evaluate yourself:

Pre-Retirement
- Should you contribute any spare money you have to pay down your mortgage or to top up your RRSP?
- Should you borrow to invest? Should you borrow to make an RRSP contribution?
- Should you bother to contribute to an RRSP anymore?
- Should you save for your child's future using an RESP or just pay as you go out of your cash flow?
- What is the best age to buy a house? Is a home a good investment at all?
- Should you buy a car, lease a car, or take a loan to buy a car?
- Are you saving enough to provide for the retirement you desire? How do you know?
- Do you have the right investment portfolio mix for this stage of your life?
- Do you own the right kind of investments for your personal situation?
- Do you have the right kind of insurance? Do you have too little or too much life and disability insurance?

- How much money are you saving each year, and what is the logic behind the amount you are saving?
- Are you doing all you can to minimize your taxes each year? Have you had a tax-planning opportunity review in the last two years?
- Are you doing all you can to minimize your family tax bill?
- Is your employment situation structured tax effectively?

Post-Retirement

- Should you start receiving CPP payments as early as age sixty or as late as age seventy? What factors are relevant in the decision? Should you split CPP payments with your spouse?
- At what age should you convert your RRSP to an RRIF and start drawing from it? Everyone hears that you must do this by age sixty-nine, but maybe you should start as early as sixty or fifty-five? What is the right answer for your situation and what are the relevant decision factors?
- How should your investment portfolio composition change once you retire? Should it change again once you start drawing on the money?
- If you need an income from your investments in retirement, how should that income be structured? What kinds of investments should you own to generate the income you need? Have you examined the various choices you have for income sources? Should you take income from your RRSP or RRIF, or should you take income from your taxable savings?
- Have you done all you can to minimize income taxes in retirement? Is your retirement cash flow structured tax effectively? Do you own tax-smart investments? Have you taken advantage of income splitting opportunities between you and your spouse?
- If you have a company pension plan, group RRSP, or Deferred Profit Sharing Plan (DPSP), have you reviewed the various benefits and income options within these plans and selected the options most suitable for your situation?
- Have you taken steps to maximize government benefits as a senior?
- Are all of your assets set up to minimize fees and taxes on the death of the first spouse? Are your financial affairs set up so that the surviving spouse will be able to manage the family finances after you are gone? Does he or she even want to?
- Do you know what you can spend each year out of your savings in order to have enough money to last the rest of your life? Do you know if you have enough income to last your lifetime?

- Have you examined the tax and legal implications of giving assets and investments to your children in old age? Do you know if you can afford to give them anything at all?
- Have you reviewed the merits of using life insurance for various net worth enhancement strategies in old age?
- Has your Will been updated since you retired?
- Have you explored ways to financially assist your children or grandchildren without exposing your money to undesirable loss? Can you lower the family tax bill by implementing these strategies?

Chapter Twelve
Wealthbuilding and Your Estate on Death

No matter how uncomfortable the discussion, sit down with your family and a qualified professional advisor to take steps to properly plan your estate. The planning starts when you are young, as you will see in this chapter, and must be updated throughout your life. It is important to set an estate plan and to review and update it every few years. Your lifestyle may change, and legal and tax rules will definitely change, so you will need to keep up to date.

EVOLUTION OF ESTATE PLANNING AND THE WEALTHBUILDING PROCESS

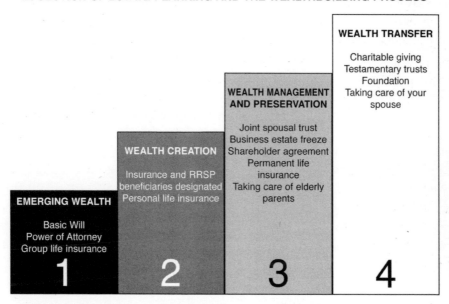

WEALTH TRANSFER
Charitable giving
Testamentary trusts
Foundation
Taking care of your spouse

WEALTH MANAGEMENT AND PRESERVATION
Joint spousal trust
Business estate freeze
Shareholder agreement
Permanent life insurance
Taking care of elderly parents

WEALTH CREATION
Insurance and RRSP beneficiaries designated
Personal life insurance

EMERGING WEALTH
Basic Will
Power of Attorney
Group life insurance

1   2   3   4

Phase One: Emerging Wealth

At the beginning of your wealthbuilding process you may be a young single person. Estate planning couldn't be farther from your mind. As you progress through phase one, get married, and perhaps have children, preparing a Will becomes essential. Failing to name guardians for your children could mean that the province will take your children if something happened to both parents. Also, a Will ensures that your wishes are followed when you die. A basic Will can be completed by a lawyer for approximately $300, which is better than preparing your own

Will. Even at a basic level, a lawyer's expertise on such an important matter is worth paying for.

You will likely also start your RRSP during this phase of life and will have to name an RRSP beneficiary. If you don't do this the default is typically set to your estate. You can save time and money if you designate the beneficiary to be a person in your family. Make sure you do the same thing with your group life insurance coverage through your employer and any personal life insurance that you buy.

The most important aspect of estate planning in phase one of the wealthbuilding process is having the right attitude. Very few Canadians take time to plan their estate when they are younger, thinking they will live forever.

Phase Two: Wealth Creation

Many people building wealth in phase two have finished having children and may even be on a second marriage. Their net worth is more complicated with more assets and liabilities. These changes warrant updating a Will every few years, and the introduction of more sophisticated planning. For example, you may have a million dollars or more of life insurance. If you and your spouse died, would you really want your children to get control of this money at age eighteen? Or do you want your brother to be named guardian of your children and trustee of your estate after your death, to spend all of that money on a new house for himself? Consider having your life insurance pay into a testamentary trust created through your Will that will hold your millions (including the sale proceeds of your home) if you and your spouse die. The trust legally protects the money against risks like excess spending and the possible divorces of your children. The trust may also pay lower tax on the income earned in the trust than many beneficiaries would.

Another estate issue often found at this phase is the death of elderly parents. You may find yourself the executor of your deceased parents' estate. Do you know what is involved? In some cases it can take over a year to wind up an estate, while also having to keep brothers and sisters in the loop as to what is happening. Do you have the time and are you located near your parents? Take the time to ask your parents if you are the executor and assess if you really are the best choice.

Phase Three: Wealth Management

At the peak of your wealth creation, you may be in need of the most sophisticated estate planning needs of your entire life. I once ran into a wealthy fifty-five-year-old Canadian who was a passionate art collector. Rather than leave his children the headache of selling off all of his art when he died, he had enlisted professional art experts to step in if something happened to him and help his family turn his art into money. Put the experts in place now and save your family the grief and cost.

Here are some of the important considerations that need to cross your mind in your final years:

Surviving Spouse

What will happen to your surviving spouse? If you have been the financial guru in your household and your spouse doesn't even know where the bank statements are, dying and leaving them with a formidable financial net worth can be terrifying. No matter how much they resist, get them involved in understanding the family finances during retirement. They may hate you for it now, but they will thank you later. Even if they continue to resist, then work with a younger, qualified financial planner who can step in and assist your widow/widower to manage after you are gone. Forget the kids, they are too busy to get involved despite what they may say.

Long-Term Care Planning

Take steps to arrange long-term care while you are healthy. Investigate home care solutions, nursing homes, and other facilities that someday you may need to rely on. Many of these institutions and services have waiting lines, and without advanced planning you could be in big trouble. I recently spoke to a family where proper planning was not completed for elderly parents and the couple ended up in separate nursing homes.

Don't Plan Your Own Estate

No matter how simple your estate is, complications can arise. Further, you may not be a lawyer or a tax specialist who knows about and can take advantage of legal and tax-planning opportunities related to your estate. Preparing your Will or planning your estate is a good time to pay the big fees to bring in professionals and obtain some worthwhile planning. Dying is the culmination of your life—don't underestimate the complications it can create for your family. If you have any doubts, talk to someone who has had to deal with winding up an estate.

Don't Prepare Your Own Will

Will planning is not just about deciding what to do with your current assets and liabilities. Get your lawyer and tax specialist to team up to prepare your Will so that it will be legally accurate and tax wise. Stay away from do-it-yourself Will kits; they are oversimplified, and one omission of a planning strategy can lead to an entirely different estate result.

Involve Your Family

When it comes to picking an estate executor, think very carefully. It is a huge responsibility that you may want to share among all your children or none of them. If you are thinking about using your neighbour or your brother-in-law as the executor, make sure they are aware of the legal liability associated with such a role. Ensure they are paid fairly for their role. Get your heirs together and try to get them involved in your estate planning.

Shop Around For Assistance in Dealing With Your Estate Matters

In the last ten years just about every financial institution has started offering estate planning to their list of services. Just look at the banks: most of them now call themselves "Bank and Trust." With so many providers now going after your business, it is easier for you to find help with estate planning—but at what cost?

In dealing with estate matters, you will need a team of advisors: a lawyer, an accountant, an executor, a real estate agent, and an insurance agent. These professional advisors will require clear directions and roles. Ensure your estate plan is set up to deal with them all appropriately.

Phase Four: Wealth Transfer

In my experience, most Canadians don't get serious about estate planning until age sixty or later. At this final stage of the wealthbuilding process, much of your life is now behind you and future inter-generational wealth planning becomes a priority.

For the rest of this section, we will cover a variety of important concepts relevant to having a mature life at the highest wealth level.

What is estate planning?

Estate planning is the act of taking steps to properly plan for the financial implications of your death. This can involve several issues: legal, tax, cash flow, and others, such as appointing guardians for children. There are all kinds of rules that need to be followed—rules from the Income Tax Act and provincial and federal laws, for example. Estate planning involves the implementation of planning strategies that take advantage of all the rules in order to save estate taxes, legal fees, accounting fees, probate fees, and time and hassle.

On a more specific basis, estate planning involves, for example, preparing a Will and powers of attorney; establishing the use of trusts in your estate; appointing executors and trustees for any trusts you create; appointing guardians for your survivors, if needed; setting up charitable donation plans; and selecting other professional advisors for your estate.

Many people think that estate planning is about minimizing income taxes and probate fees. It's not. Sure, income tax and probate fee minimization are important, but they are not the most important aspects of estate planning. The most important aspect is simplicity.

If estate issues are not kept simple, the heirs will have to deal with complex financial and legal affairs, sometimes when they are still in mourning. These matters might include dealing with testamentary trusts, life insurance proceeds, joint accounts, income tax returns, or trying to find all the bank accounts the deceased owned, and so on. If they are estate executors, they may not have the financial sophistication to do the job, or they may not have the time or the interest for such work. If the estate planning is not simple and clear, it may also cause animosity among the heirs and result in high legal and accounting fees to sort out the issues. So, keeping your estate simple may result in a bit more cost up front, but it may save piles of aggravation and professional fees later.

Here are some examples of complications in your estate plan that can cause grief to your survivors when your estate is being wound up after your death:

- Leaving assets jointly owned among family members can add a level of complexity to your estate. Making assets jointly owned permits these assets to flow around an estate upon death, going directly to the surviving joint owner. If you had intended to treat all of your heirs equally in your estate, joint ownership of assets may wreck those plans unless the jointly owned assets are properly planned for.
- Leaving your heirs as beneficiaries on your RRSP, RRIF, or life insurance can also result in estate complications if you had planned to equalize the value of your estate among all your heirs. These assets pass directly to beneficiaries; you need to give special consideration to these assets when dividing up the remainder of the estate.

- Preparing your own Will using a do-it-yourself kit can be disastrous. There are so many legal and tax rules to factor into your estate planning that no Canadian is well served by preparing their own Will. If there is ever a time to spend some money on professional help, Will planning is that time. Making a mistake due to poor planning can destroy your family or cause them grief for the rest of their lives, possibly another seventy years or more after your death. To ensure that all of your estate planning wishes are carried out appropriately, consult a tax lawyer or a lawyer and a tax accountant to have a proper Will prepared.
- Have your Will prepared on a tax-effective basis. It may not be appropriate to divide up your estate based on the market value of assets alone if some of your assets have large tax liabilities attached to them. Specifically, stock portfolios, real estate, equity mutual funds, and RRSPs/RRIFs deserve special consideration. Failure to examine these types of assets on an after-tax basis can have disastrous consequences. Generally, before heirs get their share of your estate, all outstanding taxes previously deferred during your life will now be due. Failure to plan for the tax bill on death can leave heirs with unequal inheritances.

Proper estate planning is critical to preserving the value of a lifetime of wealth accumulation. Ensure that you take the time to talk to your family and enlist qualified professionals to help you plan all aspects of your estate needs and wishes.

The Facts on Taxation of Assets on Death

Here are a list of common assets owned by Canadians and their tax implications on death. It is important to understand these basic rules as the tax consequences of dying can be significant.

Principal residence: Every Canadian who owns a home of any kind (house or condo) that is their primary residence can own this asset free of taxation for their entire lifetime. So if you own a home that you bought forty years ago for $20,000 and today it is worth $300,000, the difference of $280,000 is not taxable when you die. It is also not taxable when your spouse dies.

Cottage (or any second piece of real estate): A married couple is only allowed to have one tax-free principal residence between them. Before 1982 they could each have one, permitting a family to own two properties tax free. Further, before 1972 there was no taxation at all on the sale of assets. Given all these rules, it can get quite complicated to determine how much of the capital gain on your cottage is taxable. On death of the first spouse, no tax is paid on the cottage capital gain. But, on the death of the last surviving spouse, the capital gain on the cottage is fully taxable (due to a deemed disposition that results on death), leading to a potential whopper of a tax bill on the old family cottage. Make sure that you take steps to deal with this huge tax bill long before death or risk losing the family cottage altogether through a sale to pay the taxman.

RRSP or RRIF: RRSPs and RRIFs are tax-deferred savings plans. Since none of these assets have ever been taxable, every dollar of money removed from these tax-sheltered plans is taxable upon removal. On the death of the first spouse there is generally no taxation that results, but on the death of the last surviving spouse the full balance of the RRSP or RRIF is taxable. Take steps to explore the strategies that exist to deal with this devastating tax result. By designating a beneficiary of the RRSP, the RRSP proceeds are paid directly to that person on your death, bypassing your estate and avoiding probate fees. However, at the same time, the tax liability on the RRSP must be paid by the estate regardless of whether the cash goes directly to the beneficiary. I have seen many a family hurt when one child gets the RRSP proceeds on death of a parent, while the other child is left paying the tax bill for the RRSP through the estate, eating up their half of the inheritance. Make sure your will is properly planned to consider tax consequences of assets.

Stock or equity mutual fund portfolio: Any accrued capital gains that have built-up on your stock or equity investments held in a taxable account are taxable on the death of the last surviving spouse. Only the capital gains are taxable, not the entire asset. No tax is due on the death of the first spouse, rather the assets simply transfer to the remaining spouse without triggering any tax.

Fixed-income investments: GICs, cash, and Canada Savings Bonds are not taxable on death. Rather, their interest income is taxable. For some fixed-income investments, like bond mutual funds, it is possible to incur capital gains and losses upon death. Again, however, only the gain or loss would be taxable, not the entire asset.

In Closing

When a person dies in Canada they face taxation on income or capital gains that exist on any assets they own. There is no taxation of the entire asset since the asset or investment capital, not income. Only in the case of RRSPs or RRIFs are the entire assets taxable, and this is due to the special circumstances of the assets being tax deferred. As well, taxation is generally deferred until the death of the last surviving spouse.

If you own substantial assets of any kind, ensure that the tax liabilities that may be created on death are planned for to avoid unpleasant tax suprises.

U.S. Estate Taxes and Your Canadian Estate

Even if you don't vacation in the U.S. or haven't ever visited the U.S., your estate may still have to pay U.S. estate taxes on your death.

U.S. estate taxes are a tax on certain U.S. assets, they are not a tax on people. This means if you own certain U.S. assets over a particular U.S. dollar threshold, your estate may be required to pay U.S. estate taxes. This tax has nothing to do with whether you spend there, as U.S. income tax does. And although U.S. income taxation is much lower than it is in Canada, U.S. estate taxes don't follow this pattern. They can be as high as 55% of the value of your qualifying estate!

Who qualifies?

At this time, Canadians who own U.S. assets that amount to more than US$1 million will get caught by the U.S. estate tax regime and may have to pay estate tax to the IRS on death.

What qualifies?

There are several different kinds of assets that qualify, but the two key assets are U.S. stocks and U.S. real estate. For example, if you own a rental condo in Florida that is worth US$300,000 and you have a U.S. stock portfolio worth US$1.5 million held in three different accounts here in Canada, you may have a U.S. estate tax problem.

What doesn't qualify?

Conveniently enough, if you own your U.S. investments through Canadian mutual funds, these assets are exempt from U.S. estate taxes— U.S. estate tax applies to assets and not to people, and mutual funds are typically set up as trusts.

Are there ways to avoid this tax?

First, the threshold to qualify is rising, so fewer Canadians will have to pay this tax. Second, there is a U.S. tax credit system that your estate may benefit from that reduces the U.S. estate tax payable. Third, even if you pay some U.S. estate tax, this tax will generally qualify as a credit on your Canadian tax return, offsetting your Canadian tax liability on death. Fourth, there are planning strategies that can be implemented to avoid U.S. estate taxes. For example, sell enough of your U.S. stock portfolio to move below the threshold. Or purchase ownership of the condo through a holding company you own, since U.S. estate laws apply to people, not companies or trusts (effective prior to 2004).

Note that your estate will need to file a U.S. estate tax return if you own qualifying U.S. assets on death. The return will need to be filed regardless of tax due. Don't ignore your liability for qualifying investments—the IRS may go after your U.S. assets to collect what you owe.

The important thing is to be aware of U.S. estate taxes, and if your U.S. assets start to become significant, talk to a qualified tax accountant or lawyer to learn how to lessen the taxes or eliminate them altogether.

Choosing an Estate Executor

An executor is the person (or persons) that you appoint in your Will to be responsible for winding up your estate after you die. They will have responsibility over several things, including, paying bills; collecting income; selling assets; paying for funeral costs; finding the Will and having it probated; taking care of assets within the estate until they are distributed to heirs; having the final tax returns prepared on a timely basis; and completing any other tasks necessary to deal with your estate. Most people don't want to be an executor because it can be very time consuming, often with little or no compensation from the estate. But more important than this is that the executor is financially liable should they make any errors in the estate. For example, if the executor distributes all the cash to heirs and then finds out that the estate owes CRA $50,000, the executor is personally responsible for that money. Think hard before agreeing to be an executor—it is a huge responsibility that should not be agreed to lightly.

If you are going to appoint a child as executor, I recommend that you either appoint all of your children equally or don't appoint any of them. It is important that all the children are put in the same position of control, even if one doesn't want to do it, or lives too far away, or isn't financially savvy. Each of the children should be required to sign cheques for distributions of money from the estate. If only one child is appointed as executor, the others may come back and blame that sibling for unfair treatment. Even if you trust your children to be fair after you are gone, if there is a lot of money on the table, anything can happen. And you won't be there to mediate.

If it is impossible to appoint all of your children as co-executors, consider having an outside party (friend, accountant, trust company) as co-executor with one or more of the children that you do appoint as executor. The outside professional can assure the other children that the estate will be dealt with fairly, because of the outsider's objectivity. Often the other children will be more comfortable knowing that a sibling cannot sign an estate cheque without a second signature.

Whomever you select as executor you need to ask if they want the role. Many will be scared off by the legal liability and the amount of time necessary to commit to the estate proceedings, which, in some cases, can amount to years of part-time work. Make sure you also give consideration to the age of the executors—a family friend may die before you do.

Next, give consideration to proximity. If you select an executor who lives on the other side of the country or even across town, this may not be practical. If, for example, your home is listed for sale after your death, the executor may need to cut the grass, show the home, pay the bills, etc. Is there money available to pay for the airplane tickets to fly the executor to your area every time something needs to be done? Is this how you want to spend the money?

Finally, remember to set out instructions in your Will to have the estate pay the executor for all their time and effort. The amount of payment can be determined in several different ways, but a general rule is to pay an hourly rate or a percentage of the assets within the estate every year. A rate of 2% to 5% of the estate value is reasonable based on the work involved and the legal liability.

Did Your Accountant Review Your Will?

I recommend that someone with tax-planning expertise be involved with the preparation of your Will. If your lawyer is not a tax lawyer, then a tax accountant should assist in Will preparation.

If the lawyer alone prepares the Will, they may not give consideration to the tax due on certain assets on your death. This can result in a wildly different result than intended, as you will see in the example below. You need to have your Will prepared on an after-tax basis, so that distributions to your heirs are tax adjusted. A lawyer who simply makes plans to add up all your assets and divide by the number of your heirs could be setting your heirs up for trouble.

An Example Of Poor Will Planning

Mom and Dad, before they died, had only three assets that made up their net worth. They had $500,000 cash in an investment account, their house in the city worth $250,000, and a cottage worth $500,000. The city home was their principal residence.

The cottage was owned jointly with Child 1 for the last ten years, before the real estate boom that saw the price of the cottage rise from its original cost of $100,000. They had made the cottage jointly owned with Child 1 because their other child was living in another province and no longer used the cottage. Child 1, who lived locally, wanted to inherit the cottage, so they transferred the cottage to joint ownership in order to avoid probate fees on death. Mom and Dad intended to have Child 2 get the other half of the estate—$500,000 cash—to keep everything fair. The city house would be sold on their death and the tax-free proceeds divided equally between the two children. For the rest of this example, we will ignore the money from the city house. The parents had their Wills written to reflect the above.

When the first parent died, no tax was due since all assets were transferred to the surviving spouse at cost. When the second parent died, taxes became due on the assets.

Let's look first at the situation of the cottage. Since it was jointly held, it passed outside of the estate and was immediately turned over to the other surviving joint owner (Child 1). There were no holdups in the release of this asset. Child 1 received the keys upon presentation of the death certificate and was finished dealing with the estate.

Now let's deal with the free cash in the estate. The cash that was meant for Child 2 could not be released immediately, no matter how badly the child wanted or needed it. This cash ended up in the estate, which meant that it couldn't be distributed until all aspects of the estate had been considered. Bills needed to be paid, the executor needed to be paid, probate fees had to be paid, and, most important, the CRA needed to be paid for outstanding tax liabilities.

Tax liability

On the death of the last surviving spouse, all assets owned by the spouse are "deemed disposed of." This means that any income or gains that had been accumulating on assets owned are now fully taxable on the final tax return. This would include RRSP and RRIF values as taxable income in the last deceased parent's final tax return. Several different tax returns may need to be filed in the year of someone's death.

In the example above, the final tax return of the last surviving parent had to account for the unrealized capital gain on the half of the cottage that was owned by the parents. The deceased's share of the gain on the cottage was ($500,000 minus $100,000) multiplied by 50%, which equals $200,000. Tax on the final return for this gain would be approximately $50,000. So $50,000 had to be paid to the CRA from the estate proceeds. Once that was done and a Clearance Certificate on the deceased's tax situation was received, then the remaining estate proceeds could be distributed to Child 2.

But Child 1 received $500,000 and Child 2 only received $450,000. Child 2 sued Child 1 to sell the cottage and pay the rest of the money to equalize the estate the way that the parents had intended. From then on, the siblings talked to each other only through lawyers.

In the above example, the parents had good intentions, but because the Will wasn't set up tax effectively, the family was destroyed forever. On the death of the parents, the assets should have been divided up based on their after-tax values, not market values. Don't let this happen to you and your family. Get your will prepared tax effectively.

Using Banks for Your Executor

As mentioned earlier, over the last ten years, many financial institutions have moved into estate and trust services. These new services include almost every aspect of planning and services dealing with death. For example, you can engage these institutions to be your executor, advise your executor, probate your Wills, file your last tax returns, set up trusts, maintain your trusts after death, distribute proceeds to your heirs, and so on.

The following are advantages of using these institutions to take care of your estate plans:

- The company is an ongoing entity that will never die; you can never outlive your executor if it is a company.
- Many of these companies are large enough that they have all kinds of professional resources to assist you with a variety of needs: lawyers, bankers, accountants, and investment managers.
- Using one of these companies as your executor is a completely objective way to seek advice.
- These companies are national, and in some cases international, so they can deal with the complexities of a spread out estate.
- Hiring these service providers means you don't have to burden a

family member or friend with the responsibility and legal liability of being an executor.

There are also some disadvantages of using a trust company for estate planning:

- Employees in these companies will come and go, and you or your heirs may not see the same person twice.
- Employees in these companies may lack the expertise and training to handle advanced aspects of your estate.
- The biggest disadvantage of using these trust services is the cost. It is such an issue that the institutions offering theses services rarely give you a fee schedule up front, and even getting a fee schedule at all is difficult. Some companies charge you every time they lift a finger on your account. Also, some items, such as the final tax return or selling the family home, cost extra on top of the high initial fees.

Using a trust company for your estate needs is a personal choice. Get an opinion on whether your estate will have sufficient complexities to warrant such a service. If you decide to hire one of these companies, shop around to compare services and ask a lot of questions—particularly about fees.

A Testamentary Trust Is a Must

Testamentary trusts are one of the most overlooked estate planning opportunities for Canadians. A testamentary trust is created on the death of an individual to take advantage of lower tax rates applicable to trust income than may be available to the beneficiaries of your estate. The advantage is that the trust is taxed as a person, benefitting from the graduated tax system that we all benefit from as individuals. But since the trust has no income except for estate investment income, the effective tax rate can be low.

If your estate is immediately distributed to your heirs, typically your children, and they all are already in the top tax bracket, they will pay a high tax rate on the income they earn if they invest their inheritance. On the other hand, if the money remains in the estate within a testamentary trust, then the tax is paid within the trust on investment income earned, and the after-tax proceeds are then parceled out to the beneficiaries, often resulting in less tax paid.

Let's say a person had a net worth of $600,000 cash upon death. This person had a simple Will, everything was clear and correct, and within days the entire value of the estate was evenly divided between the two children, who were adults. Each child received $300,000 and invested it in their own name. They earned 10% return—$30,000 interest—in the first year after the death of their parent, which was added to their regular income. Since they were already in the top tax bracket, all of the interest in both cases was taxed at approximately 50%. They each lost $15,000 to tax and kept $15,000 of their total return. Each year combined they paid $30,000 of income tax on earnings and kept $30,000.

In the next scenario, the parent revised the Will to have all estate proceeds flow into a testamentary trust that was created on death from the estate. Both children were beneficiaries of the trust and would ultimately receive all the assets. Before that time, the estate assets stayed within the trust, were invested there and were taxed there. After-tax proceeds were paid out annually to the beneficiaries. There was a big difference in the tax impact: Using the same amounts as in the example above, all the investments were in the trust after death and the full $60,000 of annual income was taxed in the trust. The trust had no other income so the average tax rate for the trust was less than 25%. The trust paid less than $15,000 of tax on the full $60,000 of income earned in the first year. And this was repeated every year! So the beneficiaries each received half of the $45,000 ($60,000 minus $15,000) of after-tax proceeds and were not taxed further.

In summary, the second option provides after-tax cash flow to each beneficiary that is $7,500 more than the cash flow from the first scenario. The same would be repeated every year until the trust is wound up. Talk to a qualified professional about the uses of a testamentary trust for your estate.

Leaving Money to Young Children

Whether it is an inheritance or a gift, you may not want younger children to get their hands on inherited money too soon. And as the children get older, future events in their lives may affect the money you give them now. Even if you trust your children completely, you cannot control what happens in their lives, so you should take precautions to prevent the money from being reduced or lost.

For significant savings I encourage you to have a family trust put in place. Your family lawyer or accountant can assist you with the creation, planning, and paperwork. Once it is set up, you'll also need to file an annual tax return. The accountant can take care of this on your behalf.

The cost of setting up the structure and maintaining the trust may be as much as a couple of thousand dollars a year. That's why you need a reasonably large amount of money in the trust to really make it worthwhile. Here's how it works:

There are three different parties involved in a trust arrangement. The beneficiaries are the people who will receive distributions from the trust in the form of income and/or capital receipts on a predetermined or discretionary basis. The trustee is the manager of the trust and is responsible for maintaining the trust, following the rules of the trust agreement, managing the investment within the trust, and paying the distributions from the trust. The trustees interact with the lawyers and accountants who help create and maintain the trust. The third party is the settlor, who is the party or person responsible for setting up the trust and making the initial deposit of cash or assets to the trust.

Here is an example of how an intervivos (living) trust would be established: The grandparent would be the settlor of the trust and would work with a lawyer to draft a trust document that outlines the operations of the trust in the future. The trust document can be ironclad, able to survive any future marriage breakdowns, deaths, or bankruptcies. In the trust document, the grandparent would specify how the assets will be managed, who the trustees and beneficiaries are, how and when the assets and income would be distributed to the beneficiaries, and, ultimately, when the trust will be wound up and the capital distributed to the beneficiaries. The trust can be set up to follow any kind of wishes the settlor wants. Almost anything is possible.

Once the trust is set up and the money is deposited to an investment account in the name of the trust, the settlor's role is over. The trustees will now follow the rules that the grandparent established when the trust was set up. Perhaps in this example, the grandparent could dictate that the money deposited into the trust will be invested conservatively by the trustees, and the investment income will be paid out to the granddaughter each year until she is twenty-five; at that time all the capital assets inside the trust will be flowed out to the granddaughter and the trust collapsed.

There are a couple of important things to note about this trust:

- Any income earned and retained inside the intervivos (living) trust (discussed above) will be taxed at the top marginal tax rate for individuals in Canada (this differs from a testamentary trust created after death, which is taxed at the regular graduated marginal rates for individuals); income flowed out to beneficiaries each year will be taxed in the hands of the beneficiaries at their graduated tax rates and it is generally advantageous to do this with an intervivos trust.

- Once the money is put inside this trust, the settlor permanently loses control over this money, although the settlor could be one of the beneficiaries as well. This type of living trust is not created as a tax minimization trust—it is generally created for non-tax-planning purposes such as asset protection against an irresponsible child. There are many different trust uses possible, so it is important to explore whether a trust could be used in your personal finance situation.

Joint Ownership to Avoid Estate Taxes and Fees

There are many issues to examine (legal issues and tax issues, to name two) before making assets jointly owned with anyone.

Many Canadians don't realize that there are tax and legal implications, and often just see one or, worse, none. Let me examine specific tax and legal issues of making assets jointly owned. (I will assume that there is a transfer of legal and beneficial ownership of the asset in making it jointly owned.) The table below contains just a few examples of the complicated rules around simple joint ownership.

The Breadth of Joint Asset Ownership Rules You Need to Consider

SITUATION	LEGAL ISSUES	TAXATION ISSUES
Dad makes a bank account of cash jointly owned with Mom.	Each parent would now have a legal entitlement to the proceeds of the account; if Mom goes bankrupt after getting in a car accident and being sued, half the proceeds are exposed to loss to creditors.	If Dad contributed all of the funds in the account, he must continue to pay tax on all interest earnings from the account, regardless of whose name is on the account.
Mom makes a bank account of cash jointly owned with a sixteen-year-old son.	If the son gets married in the future, and then divorced, the son's half interest in Mom's account is exposed to loss on divorce.	Since Mom contributed the cash for all of the investments, she will continue to pay taxes on any dividends and interest on the entire account. Half of any capital gains will be taxable in the minor child's hands.
Dad makes a bank account of cash jointly owned with an adult daughter (adult children are aged eighteen or older).	Half of the money is now exposed to possible excess spending, bankruptcy, and divorce of the child.	If Dad is gifting half of the account to the daughter, then the daughter will now have to claim half of investment income on the account. Generally, gifts to adult children result in no attribution of taxable income back to a parent.
Mom makes an investment account holding equity funds with large unrealized gains jointly owned with the adult daughter. Mom also makes the family cottage jointly owned with the adult daughter.	Half of the money is now exposed to possible excess spending, bankruptcy, and divorce of the child.	If Mom is gifting half of the asset to the daughter, the daughter will now have to claim half of any investment income on account in the future. Also, there is a deemed disposition on half of the existing capital gain on the assets immediately that Mom must pay tax on in the current year.

Here are the key points to remember about making assets jointly owned:

- Taxation of investment income in Canada is guided by attribution rules in the Income Tax Act. Attribution means that taxation of income and capital gains is based on who created the pool of investments. If the person who purchased the investments changes the name on the investments to another family member, the original purchaser may still pay tax on the investments.
- Making assets legally jointly owned with your children can expose your life savings to loss from marriage breakdowns and other costly events that happen to your children. No matter how much you trust your children, and no matter what age they are, you cannot determine what will happen in their lives. Take steps to protect your assets.
- If you want to give your children control over your accounts to assist you with managing your finances in old age, consider giving them a power of attorney over the money instead of joint ownership. This way the money remains completely legally yours (and safe from loss from a child's divorce, for example), but they can have some control over the funds to be able to help you out.
- Making assets jointly owned with your children may or may not allow you to avoid probate fees. It depends on whether you transfer beneficial ownership of the assets. Transferring beneficial ownership means you are really giving some of the assets to your children for their ownership and use. This differs from just putting their name on the account to help you complete transactions while it is still all your money. If you transfer beneficial ownership by making an asset jointly owned, then you will avoid probate fees on death on this asset. But, at the same time, changing beneficial ownership will result in a partial deemed disposition on any existing capital gains on the assets you are making jointly owned. This may result in taxes due at the time of the joint assignment and may not be desirable if the gain is large (say if you make a cottage property jointly owned). But if you make an asset jointly owned and don't intend to transfer beneficial ownership, not only do you not trigger a deemed disposition and tax on a portion of a built-up gain, but you also don't avoid probate fees. Simply, you can't have your cake and eat it too.
- Even more important is the cost and benefit analysis that should be done before making an asset jointly owned to avoid future probate fees. If you make the family cottage jointly owned (or gifted com-

pletely) to your children, this could immediately trigger the realization of the tax bill that has been accumulating on your cottage gain since you purchased it. It does not make sense to trigger a $100,000 tax bill today to save $2,500 of probate fees in twenty years. Don't rush to rearrange your affairs without evaluating the common sense of the strategy.

The tax and legal issues around joint ownership and gifting of assets to your children are significant. With tax alone, there are different tax rules depending on the type of asset made jointly owned, the type of income generated by the asset, and the person you make an asset jointly owned with. For example, tax issues around making a cottage jointly owned are different than rules for making a bank account jointly owned. Interest income can cause different tax results than capital gains. And joint ownership with your spouse has different tax implications that joint ownership with your adult child or your minor child. Before you make any significant assets jointly owned or gift them away, talk to a qualified professional about all the tax and legal issues that need to be planned for to accommodate your wishes.

Power of Attorney

Rather than making assets jointly owned to permit your family to assist you in managing your life in old age, consider giving your family power of attorney over some of your assets. A power of attorney (POA) is a document that authorizes another person or persons (your family or your lawyer or someone else) to act on your behalf. The POA can be very general in nature, authorizing the stated persons to do almost anything you can do. Or the POA can be restricted, limiting the stated person's authority in a number of ways.

Below are some of the ways that POAs can be limited:

- You can give someone POA to close the sale of your new home on your behalf while you take an extended vacation out of the country.
- You can give someone POA on your behalf for a specific time frame.
- You can give someone POA on your behalf if something happens to you, such as if you become incapable of managing your own affairs after having a stroke.

It is important to consider using a continuing POA, otherwise a POA will be automatically revoked if you become mentally incapacitated. This would leave you with no POA at all. Also, consider appointing all of your children together ("joint and several") on your POA to ensure that they communicate with each other and agree on all aspects of managing your affairs.

If you already signed a continuing POA at your bank, be aware that it may be limited to business that you have at that bank and will not relate to your assets and wishes beyond that institution. You may need another POA to cover all the affairs intended.

Have your lawyer review and update your POA forms if you haven't had them examined in several years. Legal forms change, new legal precedence is established, and your goals can shift, requiring an update to your POA forms.

If you own property or assets outside of the province you live in, you should talk to your lawyer about the need for a separate POA (and a separate Will) to cover your wishes for those assets. They may not be covered by the POA (or Will) for your province.

A continuing POA deals with matters related to your property, but not your health and physical well-being. To have someone make decisions on proposed medical treatments on your behalf, you need a separate document called a POA for personal care. Personal care includes your safety, health care, clothing, nutrition, hygiene, and shelter.

When you die, all of your POAs cease to apply. At that time, the executor of your estate takes responsibility for managing the affairs of your estate until they are finalized.

Every Canadian would be well served by having some form of POA in place. Work with a professional financial advisor to review your POA preferences.

Preventing Huge Tax Bills on Death

There are many financial issues surrounding cottage ownership and passing it on to the next generation of family. Consider the following example: Mom and Dad bought a cottage in 1975 for $20,000. In 1981, the market value was still only $20,000. In 1985, an additional bedroom was added for $20,000. In 1994, the fair market value of the cottage was $175,000. In 1998, the value of the cottage was appraised at $210,000. Also in 1998, Dad made the cottage jointly owned with their adult daughter to avoid probate fees on death and to gift the child half the interest in the property. Mom died in 1999. Dad died in late 2000. After both parents died, the child inherited the cottage. The estimated value at that time was $340,000.

Now let's examine all the financial issues surrounding the cottage and the family through the years.

- It is important to keep track of the cost base of the cottage from the beginning because it will be used to calculate the taxable capital gain on sale or on death. In this case, the cost base, or ACB, is $40,000, consisting of the original cost plus the cost of additions throughout time. It is a good idea to keep receipts to back this up.

- Since the cottage was purchased before 1981, there may be an opportunity to shelter the gain up to this point with something called the principal residence exemption. Before 1981, each Canadian was entitled to own one property on a permanently tax-free basis. In 1981, the rules were changed to permit only one tax-free residence per family. On capital gains earned before 1981, it would be possible to still apply two exemptions so that a couple can shelter accrued gains on a house and on a cottage. In this case, there was no gain in this early period, but for many Canadians this would be an extra tax-saving opportunity.

- Also on the cost base, before 1994, there was the opportunity to use a capital gains exemption on the cottage and other assets to shelter another $100,000 of gain that existed at that time. In our example, this would have permitted the cost base on the family cottage to be increased from $40,000 to $140,000, avoiding tax of more than $20,000 for someone in the top tax bracket in Canada. If you missed taking advantage of this step up a few years ago, you lost out on avoiding some tax.

- When Dad made the cottage jointly owned with the daughter 1998, he transferred beneficial ownership in half the cottage property and, with that, triggered half of the accrued capital gain that existed on the cottage. This capital gain amounted to $70,000 ($210,000 minus $140,000) multiplied by 0.5 equals $35,000. For a top-tax-bracketed individual, that amounts to an immediate tax bill in 1998 of roughly $13,000! Making assets jointly owned with your children is not always a smart move. In addition to owing tax, Dad also gave the son some control over the cottage, and may expose the property to the son's credit and divorce risks.

- When Mom died there was no tax to pay on the cottage because she did not legally own the cottage nor did she own the cottage for tax purposes, since she didn't contribute any of her own money at any time to buy the cottage. Even if she had, on the death of the first spouse it is possible to transfer assets to the second spouse without triggering any tax on accrued gains that existed to that point. This is the case for all Canadians. A family typically only faces a tax bill on family assets with accrued capital gains on the death of the last surviving spouse.

- On Dad's death, all family assets that remained were taxable all at once: all of Dad's (and Mom's former) RRIFs or RRSPs and all assets with accrued gains. Cash is not taxable on death, by the way. In this case, there was more tax to pay on the cottage since the value had increased again after it was made jointly owned. The final tax on Dad's share of the cottage gain amounted to $200,000 ($340,000 minus $140,000) multiplied by half of the ownership ($100,000). This resulted in a tax liability of approximately $25,000.

So now we get to the question at hand: if Dad's estate doesn't have the $25,000 to pay CRA, or if Dad doesn't like the idea of losing so much to taxes, can anything be done to eliminate or reduce the payment? You can't eliminate this payment. This is tax due—no way around it. But you can make plans to offset the impact of this result. Here are some options:

- The child can negotiate with CRA to set up a repayment schedule (like a loan) to pay the taxes due. CRA will be fair with the child in this regard. Interest will also be due, of course.
- The child could get a loan from a financial institution to pay CRA.
- The child could sell the cottage and use some of the cash proceeds to pay the tax bill. But this may not be a desirable result.
- Mom, Dad, and daughter could have purchased a life insurance policy before the parents' deaths that would have paid out a tax-free death benefit that could have been used by the estate to pay the tax bill. The daughter could have paid the life insurance premiums when the parents were alive so that Mom and Dad wouldn't be burdened with the cash flow requirements.

Legacy Planning

Many Canadians are leaving more and more of their estates to charity. In this section, we'll examine methods to structure charitable gifts both while you are alive and after you are gone. The options today are much broader than simply leaving money to a charity in your Will.

To the extent that if your total donations exceed $200 per year, you receive a tax credit of about 45% of the value of the donation, in most cases. You are limited in claiming donations each year up to 75% of your net income plus 25% of the taxable capital gains arising from donations of capital property. Charitable donations made in the year of death are limited to 100% of your net income and unused credits can be carried back and claimed in the year before death by filing a tax return adjustment form.

Gifts in Kind

You can always donate property to a charity instead of money. The gift is normally valued at its fair market value and worth about 45% of its fair market value as a tax credit. At the time of the donation you are deemed to dispose of the asset, requiring you to recognize any capital gain on your tax return in the same year.

Individuals and corporations who donate securities listed on a pre-scribed stock exchange and mutual funds to charities need only include 25% of the capital gain (instead of the usual 50%) in their taxable income.

Cash versus Shares: What Should You Donate?

If it is your goal to make a donation to a charity, it will cost you less after tax if you donate a security (e.g. stock or a mutual fund) than if you sell the security and donate cash.

Gifts of Life Insurance

You are able to donate a permanent life insurance policy by transfer-ring ownership of the policy to the charity and also making the charity the policy beneficiary. The value of your donation will be the policy's cash surrender value. However, to the extent that the cash value exceeds the cost of the policy, you must claim a capital gain on your tax return for the year you make the gift.

Once you have donated the policy to the charity, and if you continue to make premium payments, each payment will be considered to be a charitable contribution entitling you to additional tax credits.

It is important to note that if you make the charity a beneficiary of your insurance policy and do not transfer ownership of that policy to that charity, then you will get a tax credit for a donation only when the policy pays out on your death. And there will be no tax credits for the ongoing premiums that you pay for. To maximize the tax breaks you need to have the charity own the policy as well.

Purchasing an Annuity for a Charity

In this strategy, you give a charity a lump sum of money up front and receive an annual fixed payment for the rest of your life. This is how an annuity works:

If the amount that you give to the charity is greater than the market price that you would otherwise pay for an annuity that you could buy from an insurance company, then you will receive a charitable donation tax credit for the excess. Also, a portion of the annual payments that you receive from the charity's annuity may be taxable to you. If the total annuity payments that you receive over your life are greater than the market price of the annuity, then the excess must be claimed as income during your life.

Charitable Remainder Trusts

If you have an asset that you would like to donate to a charity on your death, but you need the asset during your lifetime, you may want to leave a "residual" interest in the asset to the charity. You could set up a charitable remainder trust to do this. This is a trust where you get the income and usage of the asset during your lifetime, but after you are gone the charity gets it. The value of the residual interest is calculated at its discounted present value and this becomes the value of your tax credit. This approach is attractive for several reasons: first, you control the asset while you are alive; second, you get an immediate charitable tax credit; and third, it sometimes simplifies your estate planning.

Note that depending on the type of asset you will place in the trust, there may be some tax to pay when the strategy is set up.

Chapter Thirteen
Wealthbuilding and Your Real Estate

For many Canadians, the largest purchase they will make in their entire life is their home. A book about wealthbuilding would not be complete without an analysis of how your real estate should evolve as your wealth grows.

Phase One: Emerging Wealth

Most young people dream of buying a home someday. While it will become a reality at some point, many young people purchase a home too soon. I've crunched the numbers with some reasonable assumptions and have concluded that it would be better to start investing in RRSPs in your twenties, get them caught up, and then save money towards a down payment.

When you want to purchase a home, do not use the Canadian government Home Buyer's Plan that permits you to dip into your RRSP to add to your down payment. The fifteen years that most people will take to repay the RRSP, will leave the RRSP too far behind by the time they reach middle age. There just won't be enough time to save enough money for the best retirement possible.

When purchasing a home it is far better to put down 25% as a deposit in order to avoid the need for insurance and to minimize mortgage interest costs.

Overall, resist the temptation to buy too early in your life. If you are currently renting at a reasonable cost or living at home, it is likely less expensive to continue what you are doing and hoard cash for a larger down payment in the future.

If you need to finance your home with a mortgage, engage a mortgage broker to shop for the best deal for you. They can shop for rates at all the banks, offering you more choice.

In times of low interest rates, keep your mortgage term short and variable. If rates start to rise, prepare to lock in a variable mortgage by converting to a closed mortgage. Again, shop around for the best rates. On a debt as large as a mortgage saving even one-tenth of a percent on your mortgage interest rate matters.

Pay your mortgage weekly, not monthly or bi-weekly. The more frequently you make payments, the faster you will pay it off.

In most cases, it is wiser to use spare money to pay down your mortgage than to leave it in the bank in a savings account or mutual fund. There is one exception: contribute as much as you can to your RRSP every year and use the tax refund you get to pay down the mortgage. By doing both, you wealthbuild even faster.

Avoid the desire to buy a condominium. I call them pockets of air in the sky and anyone who lived through the condo crash in Toronto in the late eighties remembers how much they can drop in value in a short period of time. With a city able to build thousands and thousands more, a supply glut could leave you with a depressed price when you need to sell. And then there are monthly maintenance fees. In my opinion, monthly fees for condos are out of control, and make the original affordability of condos almost unaffordable. If you simply must buy a condo, it is often far better to buy a suite in an old building where monthly fees are lower than to buy in a new, flashy building. You really don't need the swimming pool or gym in your building. It may cost you a lot less in total if you don't buy it as part of your condo package.

Phase Two: Wealth Creation

So now you have some money and maybe a couple of kids and a dog. Your thoughts turn to buying a bigger home. Wait a minute. Before you put the home up for sale consider whether some home renovations to the existing home can accomplish your goals. By avoiding the real estate commission from selling your home, it may leave you financially ahead.

If you do decide to change homes, try to wait a few years during which you continue to pay down your mortgage. The worst thing you can do is to have a large mortgage and end up with a larger mortgage. During your thirties and forties and even your fifties, your goal should be to eliminate all of your debt. If you are not going to be able to accomplish this then don't upscale your home or move to a bigger home that will cost you less (perhaps due to a farther location).

Phase Three: Wealth Management

Many Canadians with money will consider the purchase of a cottage or a beach condo in the U.S. as a second property for vacation purposes. This is a wonderful strategy available to those who can afford it, but one word of caution: temper the amount of real estate that you own with the amount of investment wealth that you have. You may end up "asset rich and cash poor." You may need to sell some of this real estate and invest the money to produce an income from which you can live off.

At this phase of the wealthbuilding process, many Canadians will also consider the purchase of a rental property of one type or another. I'm a fan of rental real estate for several reasons: it offers you regular income as well as the potential for a capital gain if the real estate value rises over time. It is a business, allowing you to write off business expenses to reduce the taxes you pay. And because you can raise rents over time, this acts as an inflation fighter to allow you to keep pace with the cost of living. You don't get that with a GIC or bond! And, if you don't want the hassle of collecting rent or fixing toilets, hire a management company to do it. If you purchase a rental property, make sure it is a great location.

If your elderly parents approach you about taking partial or complete ownership of their home, you should likely resist this request. They may be trying to avoid probate fees on their death or just simplify their estate. But if you own your own home already as your principal residence, owning your parents' home means it will be taxed as an investment property in your name. Chances are your parents will save more in income tax by keeping the home as their principal residence than they will save in probate fees.

If you work in a high-risk profession, it is generally a good idea to have your spouse own your home. Consider using a trust if you are not married. If you are ever sued and lose, you can protect your home by keeping all major assets out of your name for legal ownership. However, investigate the tax complications of this creditor-proofing strategy before you implement it.

Phase Four: Wealth Transfer

Only contemplate a change in your real estate after your financial planner reviews your retirement finances. If you would benefit from having some of your money in the house turned into retirement income, the financial planner can help you to determine the appropriate amount to reinvest in a new home, while investing the rest to live off.

The decision to rent or own during your late retirement depends on your income and how much rent you would have to pay. Once again, a financial planner can work with you to examine your wealth and make suggestions as to what you can afford. Speak to a planner far in advance of making a real estate change.

For estate planning purposes, hold your home in joint ownership with your spouse so that on your death the home ownership passes to your spouse with no probate fees. When there is only one spouse left, a home should be in the last surviving spouse's name alone. The home should be disposed of through the estate when the last surviving spouse dies.

If you own rental real estate or vacant land, a cottage, or other real estate, take steps before death to plan for the sale or transition of these assets. Don't leave it up to your family to deal with an asset that you know best. Plus, you may be able to take advantage of tax-planning maneuvers that can help deal with the estate planning costs of these real estate assets (e.g. perhaps you should own the real estate through a holding company).

Chapter Fourteen
Wealthbuilding and Risk Management

In Canada, there are different kinds of advisors that want to help you grow your wealth. But long before you should be focusing on growth, take steps to preserve what you have first. There are many dangers to being wealthy that need to be guarded against. Wealth preservation through risk management is important through all of the phases of wealthbuilding. However, the nature of your risk management techniques will evolve as your wealth grows and broadens, and as your family changes over time.

EVOLUTION OF RISK MANAGEMENT AND THE WEALTHBUILDING PROCESS

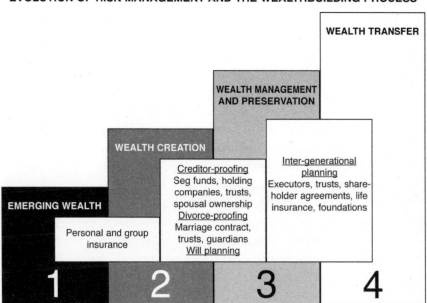

It is important to recognize the various types of risk that you are protecting yourself against, as each type of risk may require its own strategies. Below are some risks to consider—this is not a comprehensive list, but one that shows many of the most important risks to plan for:

- Not being able to pay your bills due to inability to work because of illness.
- A dependant family member being left without money if the key or only income earner dies prematurely.
- Your assets being stolen.

- Your assets being taken away after a lawsuit forces you to declare bankruptcy and your assets are stripped to pay creditors.
- Loss from divorce.
- Loss from the divorce of a child.
- Loss from excessive spending by a family member.
- Disabled family members or family members who are not financially savvy being taken advantage of where their money is used inappropriately.
- Investing your savings too aggressively, or in investments that go bankrupt, where your savings are depleted.
- Excess loss due to income tax or probate fees.
- Running out of money in old age.
- What you don't know. For example, if you buy a mutual fund and overpay on fees and don't know about it, that is money taken out of your net worth that will leave you with less in your future.

Phase One: Emerging Wealth

As you start to build wealth, cover the basics of risk protection:
- Understand your group insurance benefits provided through your employer. Chances are that group insurance does not offer enough coverage for disability, so purchase separate disability insurance as a core policy or as a top up to your existing coverage. Your chances of disability and being kept out of the work force are actually greater than the likelihood of dying.
- If you get married in this phase, and you have a reasonable amount of wealth (home, savings, etc.) that you are bringing into the marriage, consider a marriage contract (pre-nuptial agreement) to preserve your ownership of these assets should your marriage dissolve.
- If you have a career with a higher-than-average likelihood of being sued (e.g. doctor, dentist, accountant, etc.) take steps to credit-proof your net worth by holding as many assets as possible in your spouse's name alone or in a trust that can shield your assets against loss.
- At the time of purchasing a new home, the lender may demand that you also purchase mortgage insurance. This is insurance that will pay off the mortgage if you die by paying the life insurance proceeds directly to the lender. Mortgage insurance can be inflexible and expensive. Rather than purchasing their mortgage insurance, purchase a basic life insurance policy on your own. This way you completely control the coverage and may end up paying less cost for the coverage also.

Phase Two: Wealth Creation

As you start to build wealth at a more rapid pace, risk management increases in significance and different risk protection measures become important:

- At a higher salary and total income level you have a need for better and more life and disability insurance. Don't forget to increase and enhance your coverage as your income increases and your standard of living improves. Your need for more coverage will peak later in phase three of wealthbuilding, where your assets will be large enough to self-insure you against death or disability. But, right now, when insurance is a safety net between you and financial instability, don't take short cuts—get good coverage.
- Have a Will prepared by a lawyer.
- Explore the pros and cons of seg funds for creditor-proofing of your RRSP. Seg funds appear similar to mutual funds, but, for a higher cost, these insurance company products offer protection against loss from bankruptcy, guarantees of your original investment capital over ten years, and avoidance of probate fees on death.
- As you generate more money in this phase of wealthbuilding, the temptation is to invest aggressively. Aggressive brokers would have you buy oil and gas limited partnerships, commercial real estate, tech stocks, bio-science stocks, precious metal investments, labour-sponsored venture funds, hedge funds, and other specialty products. At this phase of your wealth creation you need little or none of these. Focus on building a solid base of blue chip investments as a foundation to all of your future savings. Limit your "crazy money" to a tiny amount of your investment wealth. By working with a professional financial planner, not a salesperson compensated by commission, you can build a proper investment plan.

Phase Three: Wealth Management

When you reach phase three of wealthbuilding, you are at a mature level of wealth. It is no longer about accumulation, it is about protecting what you have.

- With adequate savings to protect against loss of income from illness or death, the need for life and disability insurance for risk protection wanes. Instead, Canadians motivated to maximize their estate value for their heirs may purchase permanent insurance at this stage as a form of tax minimization and wealth enhancement at death.

- If you are a senior executive at this phase, your career may be winding down. If you are forced out of your company into early retirement or let go, engage a financial planner to review the status of your retirement savings to ensure you have enough money to live on for the rest of your life. Staying on top of the development of your retirement savings is essential during your entire working life. Do not fully retire until you know that your quality of life will be preserved.

- Using an in-trust account to save for a child or grandchild offers weak legal protection of your money. When the child turns eighteen the money can be drawn out at any time. If you will be putting substantial amounts of money in the hands of young people (under thirty), or if they will receive an inheritance from grandparents during this time, explore the use of a formal trust to hold this wealth and preserve it against loss from excess spending, bankruptcy, or divorce.

- If you own a successful business, you should consider incorporating the business instead of running it as an unincorporated sole proprietorship. A corporate structure offers the legal protection to shield your personal net worth against the legal risks of the company. Take this one step further and also incorporate a holding company to hold the shares of your operating company. Move all excess cash from the operating company to the holding company every year to keep this money out of the hands of creditors should someone sue your operating company. Money in the holding company can be shielded against the risks of the operating company.

- If you enter into a second marriage, and you have children from the first marriage, complete two important planning steps. First, have your Will ensure that some of your wealth is left to the children from your first marriage. If you die first, it would not be pleasant if your new spouse excluded those children from getting any of your estate. And second, consider a marriage contract for your second marriage.

- With established savings in place, update your investment plan to reflect your needs. Ensure your portfolio is properly diversified, resist the desire to purchase aggressive products, and consider a more conservative asset mix that offers more income-based investments to fund your retirement cash flows. Bonds, preferred shares, bond funds, and conservative stocks become more appropriate than income trusts and aggressive equities if you need this money to provide an income. Many income trusts in Canada are small cap stocks and can be considered aggressive. Review your investment portfolio from the ground up, determining your annual after-tax income needs, gross it up by your tax rate, and look to purchase investments that can provide this income.

Phase Four: Wealth Transfer

During your final phase of life, you shouldn't focus on preservation only (a good example is people who only buy GICs with their savings). Maintaining even a small amount of growth investments is important for your entire life. Besides offering an above average return potential, the lower tax status of equity investments can keep more wealth in your pocket instead of the taxman's!

- If you are finalizing your Will at this phase, explore the tax and legal benefits of a testamentary trust to hold your family's inheritances. This trust may save your family thousands of dollars of income tax while legally protecting your wealth from the risks in your child's life after you are gone.
- If you have been the financial expert in your family, don't die and leave a spouse in the dark about how to manage money. Even if he or she is kicking and screaming, educate them about the basics of your personal finances today and introduce them to your key financial advisors.
- Get your Will updated if you haven't in several years. You may have more grandchildren now that you wish to include, or the legal, tax, and estate rules may have changed presenting more opportunities for planning.
- Make sure your Will is designed tax effectively, even if that means your accountant reviews the Will that your lawyer prepares. It is human nature to divide wealth pre-tax (son, John, gets the house and daughter, Mary, gets the investments), but estate planning works on an after-tax basis. Failure to factor in the tax consequences can lead to inequity among your children.
- Protect your estate by making several or all of your children co-executors in your Will. Also consider a co-executor who is not a family member to bring an objective and independent voice to sorting out your estate.
- For all assets that you own that have large accrued capital gains, the tax bill on death can be shocking and many families often have to sell the asset to pay the taxes. If the asset is a family business or a cottage, you would hate to give it up. Consider the purchase of life insurance

(you can still get coverage after seventy) to provide a tax-free pay out on death that creates cash flow to pay taxes.

- Take steps to research the costs and locations of eldercare, nursing homes, and doctors that you may need to engage in old age. Too many Canadians fail to plan and then get sick, only to find long waiting lists for health care facilities or they find the cost of desirable nursing homes beyond what they can afford. This can stress families who may have delayed their own planning to allocate money to a sick parent. All of this can be avoided with proper financial and health care planning long before old age.

It is very important to hire professionals to help you with risk management over the course of your life. While many Canadians think nothing of hiring investment advisor after investment advisor, or insurance agent after insurance agent, few Canadians during their entire life may engage tax and legal specialists to discuss how to protect wealth. Spending a few thousand dollars in fees is money well spent. Every few years, and definitely as you evolve through the wealthbuilding process, continue to engage legal and tax experts regularly to update them on your situations and to learn about how the rules have changed.

Chapter Fifteen
Wealthbuilding and Fees

Fees are a reality of the financial services industry. You cannot avoid paying various fees for your financial services needs, but you can control how much and what kind of fees you pay.

Most Canadians pay investment commissions to buy a stock, bond, or mutual fund. But did you know there are actually five different ways to pay fees for financial services? Or that the commission-based approach that you are using now may not be the best way?

EVOLUTION OF FEES DURING THE WEALTHBUILDING PROCESS

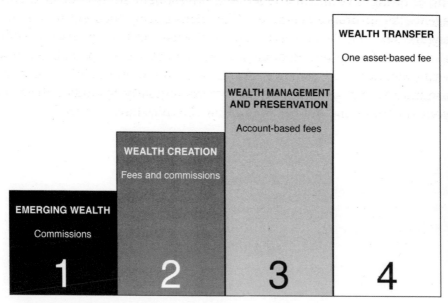

Here are the five different ways to pay for financial services in Canada:

1. Commissions to buy products like stocks, bonds. and mutual funds. These are one time fees to buy and sell. This is the method traditionally used by many stockbrokers.
2. Account-based investment fees, where buying and selling products is free or has a reduced cost and, instead, you pay a fee that is calculated as a percentage of the value of the entire investment account or group of accounts each year. This is the method traditionally used by

most high net worth money managers.

3. Hourly rate fees, where you pay a total cost based on the number of hours a professional advisor assists you. This approach is used by some investment advisors, but mostly by accountants and lawyers.

4. Flat rate fees, where you agree to pay a set cost for a specific amount of work. This approach is often used when you engage a financial planner to prepare a financial plan, an estate plan, or a retirement plan. The specific fee should be based on a description of the work provided by the financial planner.

5. A blend of two or more of the first four options where, for example, you may pay mutual fund commissions to your financial planner, but you may also pay $200 to have him prepare your tax return.

In many instances, all five of these fee choices are available from one advisor. For example, some advisors will prepare a financial plan and prepare your tax return at no extra cost if you are already paying fees under #2 above. Some advisors will charge you hourly rate fees for investment advice. The key point is to understand the differences between the choices and select an approach that you are most comfortable with. There are two main characteristics of the fee approaches that you should understand:

1. Objectivity
2. Tax deductibility

Tax Impact on Fees

When you can directly write off the professional fees that you pay on your tax return as a tax deduction, this can cut your after-tax cost almost in half and leave a lot more money in your pocket. Trying to make the fees that you pay as tax deductible as possible should be a priority to all Canadians, yet it surprises me how few people understand the tax impact of the fees that they pay. It is costing you a lot of money unnecessarily.

- Most legal fees are not tax deductible. There are a few exceptions, so review any legal costs that you incur with the tax accountant who prepares your tax return.
- Fees paid to an accountant to prepare a basic tax return are not tax deductible. You cannot write them off on next year's return. Fees incurred related to accounting work summarizing investment income

and calculating capital gains is tax deductible.

- Real estate commissions for selling your home are not tax deductible unless they are incurred as part of the moving expense tax deduction available under the Income Tax Act. Basically, if you are moving a great distance for a new career, you can write off your moving costs, including real estate commissions that you pay.

- A flat fee that you pay for a general financial plan (e.g. $1,200 once) is not tax deductible.

- RRSP administration fees charged annually by many investment dealers cannot be written off as a tax deduction. However, you should not pay these fees out of your RRSP money either. It is tax smart to pay this cost by cheque using money outside of your RRSP. At all times, paying fees using tax-sheltered RRSP money depletes the very savings you are trying to build. And because this is tax-sheltered money, your goal should be to preserve your RRSP and not use it to pay fees.

- Account-based fees, hourly rate fees, and flat fees paid for advice on how to invest your RRSP, are not tax deductible.

- Account-based fees, hourly rate fees, and flat fees paid for advice on how to invest your non-RRSP investments, are tax deductible.

- Account-based fees, hourly rate fees, and flat fees paid for advice on earning income such as running a business, are tax deductible.

Taxes, Fees, and Your Mutual Funds

Most Canadians are not aware that if they change all of their mutual funds to the "F" class version of the same fund, they can make more of the fees that they pay tax deductible. Most of Canada's major fund companies offer them, and they offer improved tax deductibility and control over investment taxation compared to their brother, the traditional "A" or "I" class funds that you likely own today.

Mutual funds come in two varieties: "A" class or "F" class. The "A" class mutual fund is the traditional version that most Canadians own. Whether you have bought it front load, rear load, or no load, it is likely the retail "A" class type. The only difference between "A" class and "F" class is fees—same managers, same companies, and same stocks and bonds inside the fund. The "F" class version has costs that are up to 1.5% per year less expensive than the "A" class version. That can mean significant savings for you. One catch: "F" class versions can only be purchased through financial planners at this time, not through discount brokers.

Here is a numerical example:

$100,000 in BCD Fund "A" class version, with an MER of 2.5% per year equals $2,500 per year cost. Or you could buy an "F" class version of BCD Fund and save money:

$100,000 in BCD Fund "F" class version, with an MER of 1.25% per year equals a $1,250 per year cost. If you also pay your financial planner 0.5% per year, your total cost is 1.75% per year or $1,750. Your total cost is far less than if you buy the "A" class version of the same fund.

The 0.5% fee that you pay your financial planner is tax deductible on your tax return as well, since the $100,000 is invested outside of your RRSP. At a top tax rate of 46%, the financial planner fee creates an annual tax deduction of $500, leading to a tax refund of $230. This tax refund reduces your financial planner cost for the year to $270 after tax and your total cost to $1,520.

So, are you going to continue to buy "A" class version of your favourite funds and pay $2,500 per year in fees, or will you switch to the "F" class version of the same fund and pay only $1,520 per year? I hope the choice is obvious. Check out "F" class versions and, while you are at it, ask the question, "Why didn't my financial planner tell me about this before?"

Objective Financial Advice and Perceived Fee Biases

Everyone wants to feel comforted by knowing that they are getting the best financial advice and best financial products possible to help them reach their goals.

So, in this vein, it is important to understand how fee structure can hinder or help you achieve this comfort.

Commissions paid for investment products or insurance policies are product specific—the compensation earned by the advisor is based on which product he or she sells to you. If commissions are not fully disclosed, discussed, and explained, investors may feel that the advisor is selling them products that pay the biggest compensation to the advisor. There are two ways to deal with this perceived bias. First, get properly educated about all fee choices (remember there are five!) and what the advisor will earn. With full knowledge of fees and differences in fees among products, an educated investor can make educated decisions. Second, don't pay commissions on products as your method of compensating your advisor. If you pay for advice based on an hourly rate, a flat fee, or, most popularly, using account based fees, the advisor compensation is clear, negotiated, and objective, since it is separated from the products.

Pay for Value

The right approach to fees depends on the type of investor you are. But, generally, everyone should be fee sensitive and care about value. There are two different kinds of investors, and you need to decide which you are:

1. Do-it-yourself investors. These are people who are prepared to do their own investment research on what to buy and sell; they may chat on the Internet with other investors for opinions on stocks and funds; they may attend evening seminars, where they hear the perspectives of analysts and fund managers. Do-it-yourself investors rely on themselves for their investing needs and deserve fee breaks to reflect the do-it-yourself approach. A do-it-yourself approach may or may not also include doing your own tax planning, estate planning, insurance needs analysis, retirement forecasting, etc.

2. Investors who use financial advisors. If you don't want to be completely responsible for your investments and your personal finances, then you are going to need to develop a relationship with a financial advisor of one kind or another. The type and extent of the relationship will depend on your needs, and the greater your needs, the higher the cost. Here are some questions you will need to ask yourself when searching for a suitable financial advisor:
   - How often do I want to talk to/see my financial advisor? Do I want to meet my financial advisor at my home or at their office?
   - Do I want them to provide investment research and buy/sell advice, and build a portfolio for me, or only some of this?
   - Do I want my financial advisor to provide financial planning advice on my retirement, estate, insurance, and other areas of my personal finances?
   - Do I want my financial advisor to consult me on tax planning and do my tax return?
   - Do I want to give them all of my investment money or only a portion?

Your answers to these questions will lead you to the type of advisory relationship you want and need. There are hundreds of advisory services available in Canada today, each offering a slight variation on service, at varying prices.

More than once I have heard clients say, "I'm not paying $500 for that advice when I can download it off the Internet for free." This very much exemplifies the state of the investment industry in Canada today, where more and more services are being offered for free or at low prices, making it harder for full-service advisors to get paid fairly. Good financial advisors can add a lot of value to the average investor/consumer and deserve proper compensation for this role.

It all comes back to my opening statement that clients need to define what kind of person they are, what financial services they need, and then price it accordingly. If you need a financial advisor for advice or simply to calm your nerves during ups and downs, then you should be willing to pay something for this financial advisor's time and expertise.

Are Low Fees the Best Way?

Focus on value—value is based on knowing your costs and judging the services and performance that you get based on this cost. Follow this simple formula and you end up with a value-based relationship that makes sense for you.

Paying high fees for personal advice is okay, provided you receive strong value for your money. Is value being provided for the cost? The average Canadian does not fully explore what value they get for whatever fees they pay.

Seeking the lowest cost provider can be very dangerous. Would you purchase the cheapest prescription drug if it doesn't heal you, or would you prefer to purchase the drug that will be the most effective? The same thing goes for your financial advisor. Put the time in to define what you want from a financial advisor and comparison shop to determine whom to hire.

The new fee-based culture

The trend in Canadian financial services today is to replace transactional mutual fund load fees and stock commissions with one all-inclusive fee that is charged annually as a percentage of the assets invested. The fee is calculated on the total market value of the assets in your investment account. This fee-based account billing approach can be more objective because there is no incentive for a financial advisor to trade your portfolio more frequently than necessary to generate commissions. Now the fee a financial advisor collects is based on the growth of your assets overall so that you and your financial advisor make money together. This fee approach aligns your goals effectively with financial advisor motivation and compensation.

Another trend happening in Canada is a general fee reduction due to the commoditization of advice. Not so many years ago, full-service advisors charged 3% of the market value of a trade to buy stocks for clients. Today, you can buy stocks yourself on the Internet for as low as $9.99, a fraction of the previous cost. This reduction in fees has benefitted the investor, but, in some cases, has made it difficult for the full-service advisor to survive. Fee-sensitive investors are taking their low fee expectations to full-service providers demanding fee reductions. Full-service providers are dropping their fees just to keep their clients. This is unfair if the full-service advisor is providing good value.

Much has been made in the last few years about the high costs of investing and investment products. While in some cases there are abuses and fees are simply too high, I believe the focus should be on value, not just cost. If tremendous value is being provided for a high fee, and you are pleased with this, I think this is acceptable.

Phase One: Emerging Wealth

At this first stage of wealthbuilding, your total fees may be low, but as a percentage of your wealth they may be the highest percentage of your entire life. Basic tax returns can be prepared by a local bookkeeper for $75. A lawyer will prepare a Will for you for approximately $300. Investment fees may include mutual fund loads and your total annual cost of investing may be 3% of your investment savings per year or greater. Your RRSP may be charged a trustee fee of $100 per year. Because your savings are smaller, but the work an advisor puts in is the same as for a larger account, you will pay higher percentage fees until your wealth grows bigger. Consider this a necessary cost of engaging an expert to help you build a financial plan at this important early stage. Life insurance premiums and the commissions that the agent earns are based on age, type of policy, and size of policy. Because you often need little or no personal insurance at this early stage of wealth development, your costs on it may be less than in the future.

Phase Two: Wealth Creation

As your finances become more sophisticated and your wealth grows, have a Chartered Accountant prepare your personal tax returns. This may cost $500 or more depending on the complexity of the returns. As your investment savings grow, move from a commission-based approach on fees to an account-based approach. Your savings are large enough at this point (a few hundred thousand or more) to negotiate a superior account-based fee approach with a lower cost and improved tax deductibility. Purchasing large personal insurance policies will cost you more and the commission that your agent will earn can be sizeable. Ask the agent to provide a written service summary of what they will do for you in terms of services for the commission they will earn.

Phase Three: Wealth Management and Preservation

At a mature level of wealth often defined as one million dollars of savings or more, all investment fees should now be account-based. The fee level that you pay will likely range from 0.5% per year to 2% per year on the first million. As a larger account you no longer pay RRSP trustee fees and many financial advisors will prepare tax returns and Wills at no additional cost. Simply put, as a large investment account, you have clout and can receive more service at a lower fee.

With a more complicated financial picture, you may also start to engage specialist advisors in the legal, tax, and investing realm who specialize in high net worth only. These specialists can assist with advanced Will planning, trusts, holding companies, proper investing for high net worth, international tax planning, and much more. They often charge up to $500 per hour but prove their worth. You don't need to engage them every year, but rather only as issues present themselves.

Phase Four: Wealth Transfer

Most fees between phase three and four will not change. But as you approach the end of your life, it is wise to incur legal and tax consulting fees to ensure your estate planning is current and effective. You should also plan to have your estate pay executor fees to manage and wind up your estate after you are gone. Many trust companies charge very high estate fees. Instead, engage friends, family, and trusted professionals and pay them fair market fees for the work they do.

Other Fees

Throughout this book I have spoken about several advanced planning strategies that you should consider. Here are the approximate costs associated with those strategies:

- Preparation of basic financial statements without an audit or review will cost $750 or more each year.
- Preparation of a basic corporate tax return or an estate tax return will cost $750 to $1,500 each year.
- Preparation of a Will that includes a trust will cost $2,000 or more.

- Initial legal costs to set up a holding company will cost $500 to $2,500.

While these costs may seem high, consider that your tax savings can be in the tens of thousands each year, easily justifying professional fees to set up and maintain the structure. Judge the cost in the context of the value you will get from the strategy.

Chapter Sixteen
Wealthbuilding and Selection of Proper Advisors

The types and numbers of advisors you employ should evolve through the different stages of wealthbuilding. The insurance agent, broker, and accountant that you used ten years ago may no longer be appropriate for you as you may have outgrown or evolved beyond their abilities.

EVOLUTION OF WEALTHBUILDING AND YOUR APPROACH TO ADVISORS

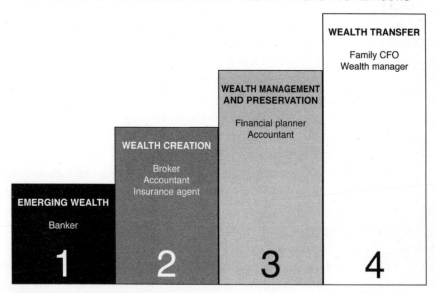

Phase One: Emerging Wealth

When you start your career and your family, I recommend that you consider hiring the following advisors:

- Certified Financial Planner
- Insurance Agent
- Personal Banker or Mortgage Broker

If you do your own tax return throughout the entire wealthbuilding process, I applaud you. Completing most personal tax returns is not rocket science, and it teaches you some tax basics. But, know your limits. If you are self-employed, have a Chartered Accountant complete your tax return. However, if you choose to continue preparing your own return, hire a tax expert to review your finances for tax-planning opportunities every few years. For a few hundred dollars of fees, the tax breaks he or she may find could be well worth it.

When your savings are small, mutual funds will be the way to go, and you can purchase these as part of a comprehensive financial plan built for you by a Certified Financial Planner. It is okay if they charge you investment commissions at this entry level to generate enough revenue for their work, just as long as they explain how the fees work and that you have the option to purchase mutual funds with a front load, rear load, or no load option. It never hurts to get a second opinion. Steer clear of financial advisors representing just one or a few mutual fund companies as they offer too little choice.

Take the same approach with your insurance agent. Stick to agents who can shop across at least eight insurance companies to provide a broader choice of products. Don't engage your dad's advisors—go out and find your own using proper research. Ask how they are compensated and how that compensation varies by product. You need to understand the rules of the game before you start to play!

Phase Two: Wealth Creation

As you now develop a higher net worth, have less debt, have more investable wealth, need more life insurance, have a higher income, and more, your need for more sophisticated advice grows. At phase two of the wealthbuilding process you may face your first need for a specialist—for example, a specialist to help you build a stock option strategy for your company stock or a specialist to implement a buy-and-sell insurance strategy for your private company shareholder agreement. Also, your investment wealth is growing and it is time to leave retail commissioned mutual funds for the next level of "F" class funds and investment accounts with fees based on account size, not the products bought.

It is also important to understand what kind of money management firm you are investing with—no one wants to be a victim of a firm that goes out of business. Your safest bet is with investment dealers that are members of the Investment Dealers Association and where your investment accounts are insured by the Canadian Investor Protection Fund (CIPF). Ask if your investment dealer is a member of both—the CIPF logo for a member firm is shown on their monthly investment statements. Smaller firms, often family owned, may have a weaker internal control system compared to a national firm that is highly regulated, can afford more compliance staff, and is audited each year for your protection. If you face losses, a larger firm likely has deeper pockets to help you get what you are entitled to. Small firms may also face a limited product choice hindering your selection for the best products and advisors may be less stringently trained and supervised. By the time you have reached a sizeable net worth, you are ready for larger, more established firms that can offer you the tools and expertise designed specifically for the high net worth advisory world that you are entering.

For your taxes, you can now afford to have a Chartered Accountant complete your tax return and provide tax-planning ideas each year. Also, have them review your Will and your investments for additional tax-planning strategies. While you could likely still prepare your own tax return, spend your free time with your family and pay the accountant to do a task that you would prefer not to do. You should always review the return, however, to understand what is being filed.

At this more complicated phase of your finances, you will start to feel the squeeze of being in the middle of a lot of financial issues: investing, tax, estate, career, debt, retirement, family, and more. You may not identify it yourself, but you really are in need of an integrated plan and a financial planner who can integrate plans from different areas of your finances and help you to make the right strategic decisions about your money. Many financial advisors choose not to offer this overall planning approach and choose to simply sell products. With a more complicated life, you need a dedicated and helpful financial planner, not a product salesperson.

Phase Three: Wealth Management and Preservation

Retired or not, your wealth at the start of phase three may consist of an RRSP worth $700,000, company stock worth $300,000, investment savings of $350,000, a paid-off home and cottage, and perhaps investments in a small business besides your primary career. You may have three or four sources of income including investment income, business income, salary, bonus, stock option allocations, pension plans, supplemental pension plans, and company benefits. Your debt consists of an investment loan for $500,000 invested in a business partnership. A private corporation holds the money you inherited from your parents along with your U.S. condo property in Arizona. Sounds complicated, huh? Time to call in the expert advisors. It may be difficult to do, but long-standing friendly relationships with old advisors may have to end if it is apparent you have outgrown their abilities. You have big league issues and opportunities now, and you should seek the second opinions of big league advisors specializing in advanced planning for high net worth Canadians. Here are some examples that you may want to consider:

- Consult an international tax expert for proper planning for foreign-owned real estate and business interests. You may find yourself paying U.S. income and/or estate taxes and this requires specialized advice to help you.
- Utilize tax-smart institutional and private wealth money management firms to invest and manage your investment wealth for a fee of 1% or less per year. Never engage or place all of your savings with only one money manager. Engage a high net worth financial planner to help with the selection and monitoring of these money managers, as well as overall family office services. Family office services may include cash flow management, bill payment, tax planning and coordination of tax return preparation, regular reporting on your net worth, and management of annual financial planning needs. A family financial planner oversees your finances, integrates the different areas, reports to you regularly on progress and results, and generally provides overall peace of mind.
- When you need a lawyer, recognize that many lawyers specialize their practices in certain areas. Some lawyers deal with real estate, some with family law, some with corporate law, and so on. For international planning of your net worth, consult a lawyer specializing in this area. For estate planning of your more complicated net worth, consider a lawyer working primarily or exclusively in estate planning.
- Even insurance agents will specialize to some extent. Some will work mostly in disability insurance. Others may focus on corporate life insurance planning. Don't just assume your life insurance agent down the street will do for your more complicated needs. By all means interview them, but speak to more than one agent to comparison shop. At your age, any insurance you purchase will be quite costly, warranting a cautious approach and second or third opinions before you buy.

Phase Four: Wealth Transfer

At this time of your life, most or all of the advisors you may need should already be in place from phase three. However, there is one more consideration: are they the right age? If your advisors are your age or older, is that really a good idea? You may outlive them or they may die the day after you do, leaving your estate in limbo. The typical example of this is a Will where brothers, sisters, or friends are named executors of an estate. But often siblings and friends are the same age, making their involvement subject to them being alive and healthy at the time. Engage advisors who are at least ten years younger than you to increase the likelihood that they will be in position to help your family after you are gone. And make sure you introduce your spouse to them so he or she knows who to contact if something happens.

Chapter Seventeen
Wealthbuilding, Accountability, and Control

This book has been about accumulating and protecting wealth. It has applicability to every Canadian. While the book is full of advanced planning strategies to help you get further ahead, the irony is this: many of the techniques are just common sense.

EVOLUTION OF ATTITUDE DURING THE WEALTHBUILDING PROCESS

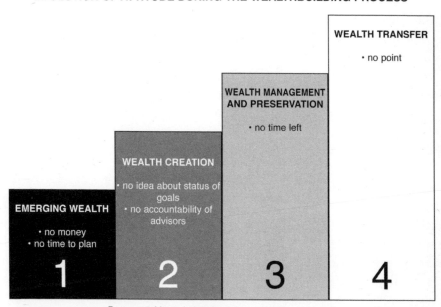

Proper goal-based planning is essential from the start.

Several common trends emerged during my interviews with more than one thousand people in the last five years to discover the state of their finances and uncover their concerns, issues, mistakes, fears, plans, and attitudes:

- Few had written down their financial goals or conducted regular checkups to assess whether they were getting closer to their goals; worse, their financial advisor rarely asked them about their goals and never measured progress.
- Few evaluated their financial advisor or their insurance agent according to the standards I have described in this book.
- Few evaluated their financial advisor against any benchmarks to

judge the value of the advisor. Worse, no one knew the total fees that they had paid the previous year to their different advisors (insurance agent, broker, accountant, banker).

- Approximately half knew what a financial plan is and only a few knew all the different areas it covers. None felt they had a financial plan.
- Most admitted to relying on the advice of their advisors and not spending enough time dealing with their finances each year.
- All welcomed a better approach to managing their finances if there was such an approach.

This entire book presents a logical framework for proper decision-making on your personal finances. The framework is based on your goals, which are always your starting point and your end point. The framework applies to taxes, investments, insurance, retirement, and all other areas of your finances. The framework allows you to integrate the pieces to create a unique plan. This framework teaches you a logical approach to getting value from your advisors and selecting the best advisors. And lastly, this framework helps you to evolve your approach to your finances, as you grow through the four phases of wealthbuilding.

Creating a Financial Plan

In Canada today, most financial advisors will use the term financial plan when they describe the services they can offer you. The problem is that many financial advisors define financial planning differently. Let's examine exactly how financial planning should be defined, so that you will finally have a standard to compare against.

Here are some key characteristics that help to define financial planning:

- A financial plan is a written document summarizing your personal information, objectives, financial issues, alternatives, recommendations made by the financial advisor, implementation action plan, and follow-up results. A financial plan is usually prepared as a summary at the end of an engagement on your financial issues and then updated annually for new events and results.
- Briefly, if a financial advisor is offering to prepare a comprehensive financial plan for you, you should be offered financial advice on all aspects of your personal finances together (investing, taxes, estate, retirement, debt, career, cash flow, etc.). Alternatives and decisions are integrated with other financial decisions that must be made at the same time.

- A financial advisor who provides advice on investing only is not providing a financial plan, but only providing an investment plan. Make sure your investment plan gives consideration to your broader financial objectives within the context of your overall financial plan. In other words, an investment plan alone is rarely enough.

- Financial planning is best defined by Advocis (also known as the Canadian Association of Financial Advisors): In order for a financial advisor to be a practitioner member of Advocis, the financial advisor must follow the six steps of financial planning as outlined in their bylaws. These six steps involve collecting a client's financial information, prioritizing client goals and issues, analyzing the alternatives the client has for meeting goals, providing recommendations on what the client should do, assisting with implementation once the goals have been decided, and following up with the client to ensure progress towards his or her goals. This practice of due diligence over clients' finances is applicable to their investments, cash flows, retirement, estate, insurance, pre-retirement, children's finances, and all other areas of personal finances.

- A financial planner is a guardian and an advice provider over their clients' entire financial picture. In some areas, the financial planner will provide expert advice, and in other areas he or she will work with experts on your behalf.

- Financial planning is conducted annually. The financial advisor will regularly check on your progress towards goals and seek to provide additional advice and strategies relevant to your finances.

- There are two different types of financial planning engagements: segmented and comprehensive. A segmented plan is a financial plan for a specific topic (e.g., a financial planning assignment to explore the possibility of early retirement). A comprehensive financial plan covers several areas of your finances together (investing, insurance, retirement, cash flow, etc.).

- It is important for you and your advisor to have an engagement letter as a contract. An engagement letter outlines parameters of your advisory relationship, fees to be charged, services to be provided, key dates to be met, legal liability, and other variables. The engagement letter is signed by you and updated annually. The engagement letter can provide comfort to clients and advisors in clarifying the advisory relationship. Engagement letters should be carefully crafted by financial advisors and carefully reviewed by clients.

- A true practising financial planner should be governed by a code of ethics and a set of practise standards, should follow a professional financial planning process, and should belong to an association like Advocis, which holds practising financial planners to a high standard.

Dangers of Financial Planning

There are many financial advisors in Canada who are providing documents called financial plans to clients. Here are some things you should know as you search for a financial advisor.

- Be cautious about a financial plan created for you by a fancy software program. Financial planning software has become quite sophisticated today, often providing overwhelming reports that few clients need or understand. Most people can be well served with only a basic, but thorough, analysis, completed with as little as a pen, paper, and calculator. Further, many financial advisors believe that their financial planning software is the value that they are providing to you, but they are wrong: the software is no more than a tool, and technical abilities are the value that your financial advisor should provide. Beware a financial advisor who hides behind software!
- Ask to see a financial advisor's financial planning practise standards. These are the behind-the-scenes controls to ensure the quality of what you are given. Here are some examples of what you may wish to see:

  - The engagement letter governing your relationship
  - Membership in a financial planning association. If they belong to Advocis, is the advisor a practitioner member?
  - Names of those who supervise and review the financial plan provided to you.
  - Confirmation that the financial advisor is subject to practise audits each year. A practise audit involves a peer reviewing an advisor's work to ensure it continues to be high quality.
  - The code of ethics that your advisor follows.

Getting Control Over Your Finances—Frequencies

Everyone should spend time each year focusing on personal finances. Some issues, like tax planning and investing, must be dealt with more frequently, while other issues, like estate planning and analysis of insurance needs, require less attention.

The following is a general schedule that outlines the frequency with which you should turn your attention to your finances:

Investing: Review investment performance three times a year at most. Note that this is a monitoring review only, not necessarily a need to change your investments.

Taxes: Focus specifically on tax planning annually to examine new opportunities. Note that this tax-planning review is not the same as preparing your tax return.

Insurance: Life and disability insurance are generally an issue at specific times during your life, rather than during a calendar year. For example, having a baby may warrant new life insurance. Review your insurance levels every few years and whenever a life event occurs.

Cash flow maintenance: Your need for an income can warrant a weekly review of the structure of your cash flows, their tax effect, and their timing.

Estate: Update your Will every few years, or when life events change your personal circumstances.

Retirement: In your pre-retirement years, annually gauge your progress towards your retirement financial goals and the need to tweak your strategies.

Your financial big picture: Once a year, get above it all. Look down on your entire financial gameplan and assess its effectiveness in an integrated and comprehensive fashion. This may be the most important, yet often overlooked, aspect of planning. Note that having regular checkups is a good start, but that urgent matters should not wait for scheduled reviews. If you have a sudden life event that affects your finances, or if an investment falls apart, make time immediately to deal with the issues.

Communicate effectively: Regular, proactive communication with your financial advisors is essential in order for you to know what is going on and what new opportunities lie ahead.

Understand options and recommendations: If you take the time to financially educate yourself, ask why you are buying a product, and encourage your family to get financially "with it." You will become more comfortable with—and knowledgeable about—financial strategies that you implement. When markets fall, you will be more tolerant if you are more informed.

Trust cautiously: Financial advisors should earn your trust and respect. Not every bank teller is an experienced financial expert who can advise you on your affairs. Practice due diligence, establish expectations, measure them, shop around, and re-evaluate your advisors regularly.

Learn about finances on your own: The Internet, financial magazines, seminars, and other mediums, offer ample opportunities to learn about money. It doesn't take long to learn enough basic personal finance to be a more informed consumer.

Understand financial strategies: Many financial advisors are more than happy to embrace your desire to learn. If they are not prepared to explain strategies and products thoroughly, question why you hired them.

The financial world is very complicated. It is easy to tune out and leave the issues to your financial advisor or to ignore them completely, but you cannot afford to do that. Money is the centre of your financial future, and your stewardship of it matters. Become informed. Ask questions. You are the best guardian of your finances.

Benchmarking for Greater Accountability

If you have ever worked in a company or owned your own business, you know that good companies are full of structure, goals, and accountability. Companies set targets, implement strategies to try to meet these targets, and measure results. Ultimately, people are fired if specific results are not met.

Corporate financial standards can be effectively implemented in an individual's personal finances as well. Most of the financial accountability standards of a corporation can be applied to your personal finances. Here are company standards that you can apply to your own life:

Prepare a budget: Know how much you spend. If your cash flow is tight, you should look at how you spend every dollar. But if your income is higher, simply be fiscally responsible on your spending habits. Lifestyle spending should be balanced with the wealthbuilding techniques described in this book.

Set annual targets: Set the targets you want to accomplish financially in a given year and write them down. For example, a goal may be to save $5,000 this year. Evaluate your progress towards this goal during the year to ensure you stay on track.

Set clearly defined long-term goals: Goals such as a financially comfortable retirement or providing for a child's future education require long-term planning and should include annual progress evaluations.

Expect regular, written reports from your financial advisor: Just like a manager reports to a vice president of a company on the results of a division, your financial advisor is hired by you to produce results.

Demand a regular written summary of accomplishments, costs, and comments on progress or the reasons for a lack of progress.

Conduct variance analysis on poor results: For example, ask for a line-by-line written analysis of why your investment portfolio missed targets for this year.

Lay out written action plans across your financial strategies: Use these plans to measure progress next year.

Maintain strong cost control: First, know what you pay. Second, compare your cost to the value of the services that you get. If you don't feel you've received good value, renegotiate the cost, increase the services you get (e.g. prepare your tax return at no extra cost), or change the advisor.

Conduct regular meetings on progress: Management in a company may look at quarterly results to judge progress and make adjustments. Different areas of your finances require different timelines for review. Have your investment advisor prepare a results report on your investments two or more times a year. Have your accountant prepare a tax-planning opportunity report once a year. Have your insurance agent summarize your insurance levels and results every few years.

Build individual plans and an overall plan: Build plans for your estate, your retirement, your taxes, and other areas of your finances. Then, build a consolidated plan that integrates the different areas and addresses your goals. This is the same way a company develops departmental plans and combines them into one overall company plan that the president of the company oversees. You are the president of your finances and should have your own integrated financial plan.

Coordinate your hired advisors to work together: Put your accountant, your financial planner, your lawyer, your banker, and your insurance agent in a room together to build an integrated financial plan for you. Dealing with each one separately creates a poorly fragmented approach to your finances.

Be prepared to fire and hire advisors: Exercise your right to hire and fire based on advisors' lack of success in meeting your goals. A corporate executive will fire employees if they don't perform. You should do the same for financial advisors who don't produce the value and results that you need. You should not be developing a personal relationship with a financial advisor. This impairs your objectivity and ability to act rationally if results are not met. Financial advisors are often trained to get to you emotionally. Remain impartial.

The following chart can be used to help you develop an accountability checklist for your personal finances.

ACCOUNTABILITY

As an employee, your company has effective accountability measures. Do you have these same accountability measures in your personal finances? If not, why not?

Corporate finances		Personal finances
✔	Budgets prepared	
✔	Annual targets established and revisited	
✔	Well defined long-term goals	
✔	Regular, written reports on results	
✔	Variance analysis of results	
✔	Management discussions and analysis of results	
✔	Specific action plans with follow up	
✔	Strong cost control	
✔	Regular meetings on progress	
✔	Integrated segmented planning within an overall master plan	
✔	Advisors working in concert within a master plan	
✔	Hiring and firing of key team advisors based on success or failure against goals	
✔	Emotion and relationship don't interfere with decision making	

Epilogue

There are a lot of financial books in Canada on personal finance. But I hope that my explanation of the wealthbuilding process shows you that the management of your finances should change and be updated continually to reflect your evolving circumstances. Don't be scared to evaluate new financial solutions. And don't get so emotionally tied to your financial advisors such that you lose your ability to objectively evaluate them and end the advisory relationship if needed.

In *Tax-Smart Investing*, my first book, I introduced Canadians to the concept of after-tax investing, offering fifty unique strategies on how to pay less income tax on investments. Even seven years later this book continues to be an important read of foundational investment planning for Canadians wishing to pay less income tax and build more tax-smart investment portfolios. It is still surprising, however, that more Canadian money managers still don't "get it" that tax matters, and how some of Canada's most reputable money managers still fail to properly consider income tax in their investment portfolio construction.

In my second book, *Rosentreter's Rules: 100 Financial Strategies to Reach High Net Worth*, I wrote about the importance of managing your financial big picture and building an integrated overall financial plan instead of just buying products. This included 100 different strategies on how to better manage your finances. *Rosentreter's Rules* taught that managing your finances has a process, and that following this process leads to better results.

In this book, *Wealthbuilding*, I have shared my experiences in dealing with Canadians of all ages and wealth levels to demonstrate that your approach to your finances is evolutionary. It is evolutionary because as your financial situation changes over time, so should your approach to financial strategies, products, and advisors. In order to get the best results it is important to recognize changes in your life and adapt your approach accordingly. By doing this, you have a greater likelihood of building wealth faster and preserving wealth more effectively.

Thank you to all my readers of the previous two books and your wonderful comments about my writing. I enjoy teaching and helping people to better manage their finances. It is an intimidating world of personal finance in Canada today, and I am glad to share my experiences in order to help even one person. I hope you have enjoyed reading this book and I hope it leads to greater peace of mind over your finances—today and always.

Index

Kurt Rosentreter, CA, CFP, CIMA, TEP, FMA, B. Commerce
(Honours)

Chartered Accountant

Certified Financial Planner

Senior Financial Advisor & Branch Manager, Berkshire Securities Inc. in Toronto

Past co-founder of the billion dollar national wealth management practice at one of Canada's elite "Big 4" Accounting firms

Best selling author on wealth management with six popular books published and more than 500 articles carried in national magazines and newspapers in Canada in the last ten years

Public speaker and educator on personal finance across Canada

Past National Board Member, Canadian Association of Financial Planners, Canadian Association of Financial Advisors, and the Financial Planner Standards Council

Course Instructor on Personal Finance, Ontario Institute of Chartered Accountants

Past or present financial commentator to *The Globe & Mail*, *The National Post*, Canada AM, CBC, *Canadian Business Magazine*, *Profit Magazine*, *Maclean's Magazine* and more than twenty-five regional newspapers and radio stations.

Previously nominated for Canada's Top 40 Under 40.

www.kurtismycfo.com   1-877-275-5878   krosentreter@berkshire.ca

Interested in having Kurt speak at your corporate event, church group, or social club? Contact him directly for availability. Copies of this book will be given away at all speaking events, free of charge!